3/99

D0734288

WITHDRAWN

www.zaxby.com

Emily Brontë

Twayne's English Authors Series

Herbert Sussman, Editor

TEAS 550

EMILY BRONTË'S DIARY PAPER, 31 JULY 1845 (DETAIL).
Reprinted from Clement Shorter, *Charlotte Brontë and Her Circle* (1896).

VILLA JULIE COLLEGE LIBRARY
STEVENSON, MD 21153

Emily Brontë

Steve Vine

University of Wales, Swansea

Twayne Publishers
An Imprint of Simon & Schuster Macmillan
New York

Prentice Hall International
London • Mexico City • New Delhi • Singapore • Sydney • Toronto

Twayne's English Authors Series No. 550

Emily Brontë
Steve Vine

Copyright © 1998 by Twayne Publishers

All rights reserved. No part of this book may be reproduced or transmitted in any form or by any means, electronic or mechanical, including photocopying, recording, or by any information storage and retrieval system, without permission in writing from the Publisher.

Twayne Publishers
An Imprint of Simon & Schuster Macmillan
1633 Broadway
New York, NY 10019

Library of Congress Cataloging-in-Publication Data

Vine, Steven, 1961–
    Emily Brontë / Steve Vine.
        p.   cm. — (Twayne's English authors series ; TEAS 550)
    Includes bibliographical references and index.
    ISBN 0-8057-1659-9 (alk. paper)
    1. Brontë, Emily, 1818–1848—Criticism and interpretation.
    2. Women and literature—England—History—19th century.   I. Title.
    II. Series.
    PR4173.V48   1998
        823'.8—dc21   98-11025
                                                                            CIP

This paper meets the requirements of ANSI/NISO Z3948-1992 (Permanence of Paper).

10 9 8 7 6 5 4 3 2 1

Printed in the United States of America

For Jackie,
Tom, and Sam

"more myself than I am"

Contents

Preface

"Emily Brontë is the sphinx of our modern literature," wrote Clement Shorter famously in 1896, and many nineteenth- and twentieth-century readers and critics have continued to stress the enigmatic or elusive power of Emily Brontë's writing and persona. This tradition was begun by Brontë's sister Charlotte in 1850, two years after Emily's death, when she introduced the second edition of *Wuthering Heights* and argued that a "secret power and fire" resided in Brontë that animated her writing with an original and oracular force. "An interpreter ought always to have stood between her and the world," wrote Charlotte.

Charlotte's image of Emily Brontë as an abstruse genius or native sibyl has proved remarkably durable. Until well into the twentieth century, critics were more inclined to discuss Brontë's literary production as an inexplicable natural phenomenon rather than as self-consciously fashioned art. Work done by formalist, Marxist, feminist, and poststructuralist critics in the twentieth century, however, has developed an increasingly complex sense of Brontë as a writer who engaged energetically and critically in her writing with questions of genre, ideology, gender, and language. The present study takes stock of these twentieth-century revolutions in Brontë criticism and revisits Brontë not to reaffirm the image of Brontë-as-enigma but to examine the strategies by which she searchingly questioned the categories of nineteenth-century culture — and contested the restrictions imposed on her as a Victorian woman writer. Emily Brontë emerges from this study not as a "sphinx" enclosing a mystery or secret but as a writer who developed plural strategies to refuse and resist the patriarchal categories of her world; her sphinxlike reputation, therefore, is read not as a strategy of secretion but of evasion.

Remarkably, Emily Brontë's critical reputation rests almost entirely on the stature of her single novel, *Wuthering Heights* (1847). Although she penned a substantial body of poetry, only 21 of her poems were published in her lifetime—in the joint volume *Poems by Currer, Ellis, and Acton Bell* (1846), written together with her sisters, Charlotte and Anne. Charlotte published more of Emily's poems (significantly revised by her) in 1850, and further incomplete collections appeared in the early years of the twentieth century; but it was not until C. W. Hatfield's edition of

The Complete Poems of Emily Jane Brontë (1941) that the entirety of
Brontë's poetic output became available. Although Hatfield's edition
established the canon of Brontë's poetry, the attention of literary critics
remained firmly fixed on *Wuthering Heights*. It is a remarkable and
regrettable feature of Brontë criticism that her poetry has been the
object of a sustained critical neglect. Too often, the poems, if considered
at all, are used merely in a supporting role to the novel; it is one object
of this work to overturn this occlusion of the poetry. The poetry and the
novel are thus the object of equal attention throughout this study.

As well as the poetry, the present study brings into view other
neglected aspects of Brontë's work: her fragmentary autobiographical
diary papers, her graphic work, and her extraordinary French *devoirs,*
written in Brussels in 1842. While the four diary papers that Brontë
wrote between 1834 and 1845 report on events and circumstances in
the Brontë family, they also reveal significant features of Brontë's compositional methods; the papers are a diary of the fictional realm of
"Gondal" as much as of Brontë herself. By reproducing and discussing
illustrations from the papers, the present work shows how these autobiographical representations are related to the strategies of self-inscription
in Brontë's literary works. This study also examines selected images
from Brontë's graphic works—productions that, like her written
texts, dramatize and interrogate the limits of understanding and re-
presentability. Until now, critical discussions of Brontë have offered
commentary only on the most well known of her Brussels *devoirs*. In the
present work, I discuss all nine of the extant *devoirs* and show how they
can be seen as ironic interventions in and commentaries on the mores
and categories of nineteenth-century culture—as well as acts of textual
resistance on Brontë's part to the patriarchy that surrounded her.

In offering an account of Brontë's largely uneventful life, chapter 1
attempts to understand the patterns that nevertheless governed her
life—specifically, Brontë's recurrent descent into what was, apparently,
psychosomatic illness. Drawing on recent feminist work on self-starvation
in the Brontë family, the first chapter situates Brontë's illnesses in relation to a silent symbolic demand for emancipation, insofar as illness and
death become in her work—and, finally, in her consumptive body—
figures of a fatal liberation. Chapter 2 analyzes the conception and construction of "Gondal"—that kingdom of symbolic and imaginative
possibility whose tumultuous history Emily Brontë (along with her
sister Anne) fashioned and refashioned up until the year of her death.

The chapter uses the fluid fictions of Gondal to show how Brontë's poetic work is irreducibly *dramatic,* subscribing less to a poetics of self-revelation than of self-invention. The plural personae of Gondal thus become for Brontë a means and mode of self-emancipation.

Chapter 3 offers a sustained reading of Brontë's lyric verse and shows how her lyric poetry, like her Gondal poetry, embraces an aesthetic of self-dramatization. Across and between the poems, conflictual and often contradictory speaking positions are played out; these positions dramatize the dilemmas of utterance afflicting Brontë as a woman poet writing in a masculine literary tradition and as a dissident poet writing within an orthodox religious culture. Following feminist work on the poems, the chapter shows how Brontë was in struggle both with male Romantic poetry and with religious orthodoxy. The dissenting or heterodox Brontë stands forth again in the chapter's discussion of the Brussels *devoirs,* rebellious texts that flout the sanctities of polite Victorian culture.

Chapter 4 offers a comprehensive reading of *Wuthering Heights,* considering various aspects of the novel's own metaphor of "wuthering." The chapter shows how *Wuthering Heights* is about instability on many levels. It also demonstrates that, in relation to its contemporary literary culture, historical context and gender relationships, the novel induces a "wuthering" into its world, deconstituting bourgeois subjectivities and stabilities with a force of derangement and delirium. In this last connection, the chapter draws on the work of psychoanalytic theorist Julia Kristeva to reveal how the text's "wuthering" follows a logic of delirious desire.

Chapter 5 returns both to the poetry and to *Wuthering Heights* to address the vexed question of the spectral and the "ghostly" in Brontë's work. The chapter analyzes the various phantoms that populate the poems and the novel in order to explore the dynamics of loss and mourning that are inscribed across the body of Brontë's work. It shows how the ghosts that haunt Brontë's lyric verse are phantoms of poetic power and visionary sublimity. As fading phantoms, these elusive figures are traces both of power and of deprivation, who mark the spectral survival and irremediable loss in Brontë of Romantic visionary glory. The chapter suggests that a dynamic of mourning and refused mourning thus governs Brontë's relationship as a Victorian woman poet to the sublimity of visionary Romanticism. It also reveals a similar drama of mourning and refused mourning in the agon of Cathy and Heathcliff's relationship in *Wuthering Heights,* a drama in which what is lost is not power but the dream of unity and identity. To unfold the strange workings of loss, mourning, and haunting in Brontë's texts, the chapter draws on the recently translated work of psychoanalysts Nicolas Abraham and Maria Torok—in particular, their notion of a "crypt" in the psyche that encloses a scene both irrevocably lost and secretly preserved.

The book concludes in chapter 6 with a survey of the critical tradition surrounding Brontë—from naturalizing and metaphysical to Marxist and poststructuralist readings. The survey shows that to revisit Emily Brontë is, necessarily, never to revisit the same place; instead, it is to arrive somewhere that is never simply familiar, never simply recognized, but that keeps its strangeness and preserves its ghostliness. Perhaps, then, to revisit Emily Brontë is not to revisit her at all; perhaps it is rather to *be* revisited by what the final paragraph of *Wuthering Heights* calls "unquiet slumbers."

Acknowledgments

Most of this book was written during a period of sabbatical leave from the University of Wales, Swansea, from 1996 to 1997. I am grateful to Ian Bell, my Head of Department, for making that leave possible. Herb Sussman, my editor, was a helpful and encouraging reader of the chapters as they were written; I would like to thank him for his support. I am also grateful to the staff at the Brontë Parsonage Museum Picture Library for their ready assistance in providing images for reproduction, and also to Roger Davies at Swansea for providing photographs of images from published works. Thanks, too, to Jackie Amey, whose abilities with the computer always save me. Parts of chapter 4 were published as "The Wuther of the Other in *Wuthering Heights*" in *Nineteenth-Century Literature* 49 (1994): 339–59. I am grateful to the editors for their permission to incorporate that material here.

Chronology

1818   Emily Brontë born at Thornton, Bradford, Yorkshire, on 30 July.

1820   Brontë family moves to Haworth where Patrick Brontë, Emily's father, assumes perpetual curacy of Haworth.

1821   Maria Branwell Brontë, Emily's mother, dies of cancer on 15 September.

       "Aunt Branwell," Maria's sister, comes to live with the family.

1824   Maria and Elizabeth, Emily's elder sisters, enter Cowan Bridge School in July.

       Charlotte follows to Cowan Bridge in August, Emily in November.

1825   Maria leaves school ill in February and dies in May; Elizabeth leaves in May and dies in June.

       Patrick Brontë brings Charlotte and Emily home from Cowan Bridge on 1 June.

1826   Patrick Brontë returns from a conference in Leeds on 5 June with presents for the children: his gift of toy soldiers (the "Twelves") to Branwell, Emily's brother, inspires the Brontës to invent stories around these figures (or "Young Men") for the next six years.

1831   Charlotte leaves Haworth for Roe Head School in January.

1832   Charlotte returns from Roe Head.

1834   Emily and Anne write their first diary paper, which includes the first mention of the imaginary realm of "Gondal,"on 24 November.

1835   Charlotte and Emily arrive at Roe Head School in July, Charlotte as a teacher and Emily as a pupil.

       Emily's "failing strength" leads her to return to Haworth in October.

1836   Anne replaces Emily at Roe Head in January.

1837   Emily and Anne write their second diary paper on 26 June; it details the ongoing composition of the "Gondal" saga and links a coronation in Gondal to the coronation of Queen Victoria on 20 June.

1838   Emily takes up a position as teacher at Law Hill School, near Halifax, in September.

1839   Emily's declining health brings her home from Law Hill in March.

1841   Emily and Anne write diary papers on Emily's birthday; Emily reports on the sisters' plan of setting up a school at Haworth.

        Charlotte proposes that she and Emily study abroad to develop their languages in readiness for establishing the school.

1842   Emily and Charlotte journey to Brussels to the Pensionnat Heger.

        Between May and October Emily composes nine (extant) *devoirs* in French.

        Aunt Branwell dies on 29 October; Charlotte and Emily return to Haworth on 8 November.

1843   Charlotte goes to Brussels as a teacher in January.

1844   Charlotte returns from Brussels in January.

        Emily starts to transcribe her poems into two notebooks, one headed "Gondal Poems," the other left untitled.

        The plan to establish a school is revived in the summer; prospectuses are printed, but no inquiries are made.

1845   Anne and Emily visit York on 30 June. They write diary papers on 30 July; Anne reports that the Gondal characters are ailing, Emily that they "flourish bright as ever."

        Charlotte discovers Emily's poems (probably the "Gondal" notebook) in September.

1846   Charlotte negotiates with Aylott & Jones concerning the publication of a selection of her own and her sisters' poems under the pseudonym of the "Bell" brothers.

Poems by Currer, Ellis, and Acton Bell published in May.

1847   Thomas Newby accepts the publication of Emily's *Wuthering Heights* and Anne's *Agnes Grey* in July.

Wuthering Heights* and *Agnes Grey* published in December.

1848   Reviews of *Wuthering Heights* start to appear in January; Emily saves five of them in her writing desk.

Charlotte and Anne travel to London in July to prove the identities of the "Bells" to Charlotte's publisher, Smith, Elder & Company.

Charlotte writes to her publisher at the end of July to regret her disclosure that the Bells were "three sisters," recording the opposition of "Ellis Bell" to any such revelation.

Branwell dies on 24 September.

Poems by Currer, Ellis, and Acton Bell reissued by Smith, Elder & Company in October.

Emily dies on 19 December.

Emily's funeral on 22 December.

Chapter One
Living in Silence:
The Life of Emily Brontë

She lived in a sort of silence which, it seemed,
only literature could disrupt.[1]

Georges Bataille's description of Emily Brontë as living a life in "silence"
is echoed in the accounts of many of her contemporaries, biographers,
and critics; she is repeatedly figured by her interpreters as an enigma, a
secret, a cipher. Clement Shorter in *Charlotte Brontë and Her Circle*
(1896), for example, described Emily, in a phrase that would become
famous, as "the sphinx of our modern literature,"[2] while her first biographer, A. M. F. Robinson, drew this sharp response from Sidney Bidell (a
Brontë admirer) when Robinson announced in a letter to Ellen Nussey
her intent to write a "Life of Emily Brontë": "[W]ith such slight material to work upon, who could have suggested such a work? . . . No great
woman who ever lived has left so little behind her that can be written
about as Emily Brontë. . . . [W]hat do we know of the inner life of
Emily?"[3]

The "inner life of Emily" is enigmatic not least because the materials
that biographers conventionally draw upon to represent their subjects—
such as letters, diaries, and reported conversations—are in Brontë's case
remarkably scarce. Only three of Brontë's letters survive, for example,
and these are brief and businesslike missives to Ellen Nussey about
Charlotte's movements in her sojourns from Haworth.[4] Moreover, just
four brief texts of diary material —two "diary papers" and two "birthday papers"—exist;[5] while these are the closest one gets to autobiography in Brontë's writings, they remain, in Katherine Frank's words,
"curiously uninformative, fugitive pieces," offering briskly laconic "bulletins of daily life in the [Haworth] parsonage."[6] As Winifred Gérin
(Brontë's most well known biographer) notes, "Where personal statement is lacking . . . the want has to be supplied by the witness of others,
with the effect that, however trustworthy they may be, Emily Brontë is
heard through their medium, at second hand, seldom speaking in her

2

own voice."[7] It seems, then, that Emily Brontë insists on the inscruta-
bility of her sphinxlike reputation.

If Emily Brontë is seldom heard "speaking in her own voice" in her
extant writings, she was seldom heard speaking in life at all, outside of
her immediate family at Haworth. Ellen Nussey, for example, commented that Emily "did not often look at you," that she "talked very little,"[8] and, furthermore, that her "extreme reserve seemed impenetrable. . . . [There was] such a shyness of revealing herself—a strength of
self-containment seen in no other" (Shorter, 178–79). When Emily
traveled to Brussels with Charlotte in 1842 to study at the Pensionnat
Heger, the two retiring Brontë sisters were patronized by the Jenkinses,
an English family residing in the city, who dutifully invited them to Sunday tea for a period of several months—until, that is, the visits proved
too painful to endure; on these occasions Emily "hardly ever uttered
more than a monosyllable," while Charlotte, even when roused to con-
versation, had the habit of "gradually wheeling round on her chair, so as
almost to conceal her face from the person to whom she was speaking."[9]
Furthermore, Gérin writes of Emily's persona at Haworth, "She shunned
the people with whom her father's position in the parish brought her
into contact, refused to teach in the Sunday school, spoke to no one in
the village street on the unhappy occasions when she had to go to one of
the shops alone, and steadily averted her glance when a stranger spoke
to her" (46).

Brontë's social persona bespeaks a "profound secrecy" of self (Gérin,
4); her behavior seemed designed to protect her from public scrutiny, as
if it guarded an interior life that evaded even as it invited the inquiring
gaze of others. If Brontë herself turned an "impenetrable" face to the
world, her writings could also be said to eschew self-revelation, for they
reserve their secrets even as they solicit the reader's desire to know and
master their meanings. Even in her apparently most "personal" lyric
utterances, Brontë withholds the truth of her own "inner life," insisting
typically that "What my soul bore, my soul alone / Within itself may
tell!"[10]

Brontë's habitual secrecy, however, can be read as something other
than the concealment of a mystery or secret that, if only one knew
enough about her or could see her clearly enough, might be grasped and
understood. Brontë's secrecy can be read instead as an *act*—a gesture of
resistance and refusal that is designed to free her from the power,
scrutiny, and potential censure of others. Emily Brontë's secrecy is thus
an act of evasion and emancipation; living in "silence," she guarded a

perilous and precious freedom within. This secrecy was embodied, moreover, in the practice of all the young Brontës composing their miniature "books." The children produced these tiny volumes of tales and adventures in minuscule handwriting that, as Juliet Barker notes, "had the advantage of being illegible to their father and aunt, so the children enjoyed the delicious thrill of knowing that the contents of their little books were a secret shared only among themselves."[11] But, notably, it was "only Emily [who] seriously maintained" this tiny script into her adult compositions.[12] Specifically, this script for Emily was the "minute, cramped hand which . . . signalled the private world of Gondal" (Barker, 481): the imaginary realm of desire, adventure, and struggle that she invented as a child with Anne and whose fictional life she preserved well into her adult years. It was this script that Charlotte probably discovered when, in the autumn of 1845, she "accidentally lighted on a MS. volume of verse in my sister Emily's handwriting"—and read with rapt attention the "wild, melancholy, and elevating" music that the poems contained.[13] Although Charlotte reports that she knew her sister "could and did write verse," there was nevertheless an insistent reserve defining and delimiting these poems; for Charlotte had known nothing of their contents, and when Emily became aware of her sister's "unlicensed" intrusion into her silent world of composition, it took Charlotte "hours to reconcile her to the discovery I had made, and days to persuade her that such poems merited publication" (*WH*, xxvii). Even Anne—with whom Emily collaborated for years on the Gondal narrative—was excluded in the end, it seems, from the "secret room"[14] that Gondal became for Emily Brontë. Thus, in her 1845 diary paper, Anne refers to the "Gondal Chronicles," stating that "Emily is engaged in writing the Emperor Julius's Life"; she remarks that Emily has "read some of it" aloud but then comments, "She is writing some poetry, too. I wonder what it is about?" (*BLFC*, 2:52).

The pseudonyms that the sisters adopted when publishing *Poems by Currer, Ellis, and Acton Bell* in 1846 reveal another form of Brontëan secrecy. But, again, it was Emily—or "Ellis"—who insisted on preserving the pseudonyms, as if her fictive name was a saving mask that protected her from exposure. When Charlotte and Anne traveled to London in 1848 to meet Charlotte's publisher, George Smith, to clear up confusion that had arisen over the identities of the "Bells," Charlotte informed Smith that the Bell brothers were in fact three sisters. When the publishers subsequently wrote to Charlotte, alluding to her "sisters," Emily knew that her secret had been "betrayed." Afterward, Emily

raged at Charlotte for this unwarranted disclosure, and Charlotte was
forced to write back apologetically to Smith, Elder and Company: "Per-
mit me to caution you not to speak of my Sisters when you write to
me—I mean do not use the word in the plural. 'Ellis Bell' will not
endure to be alluded to under any other appellation than the '*nom de
plume.*' I committed a grand error in betraying [her] his identity to you.
. . . I find it is against every feeling and intention of 'Ellis Bell' " (quoted
in Barker, 563).

"Every feeling and intention of 'Ellis Bell' " was, instead, wedded to
secrecy and silence. As Juliet Barker says of the Brontës' pseudonyms,
"The fact that their authorship was such a close-guarded secret was a
form of empowerment . . . as it had been in the long-gone days of childhood. . . . [I]t was the three of them against the world" (575). But it was
"Ellis" who clung most obstinately to the empowerment that such
anonymity afforded. It was as if Emily Brontë's public silence installed
"Ellis Bell" in a position that was simultaneously unimpeachable and
empowering, for Ellis Bell might write and act as "he" thought fit, while
all the time refusing obdurately to give an account of himself, justify
himself, or declare himself to the world. The name was thus a mask of
silence and of power, a paradoxical assertion of self through the very act
of self-concealment and self-burial.

For Emily Brontë, the scene of writing was a silent scene of desire,
power, and possibility: it was a place where, in Stevie Davies's words, a
"transgressive writing record[ed] transgressive actions."[15] But, again,
Brontë's documented persona is constructed paradoxically: in one sense
Brontë's story is one of retiring and reclusive female domesticity; in
another, it is the history of a "chainless soul" (*CP,* 31) in conflict with the
categories of her culture and transgressing the limits of Victorian definitions of the feminine. Concerning the relationship of the Brontës to the
world beyond Haworth, Davies writes, "Out there, Emily had no face.
Whereas Anne successfully worked as governess in unhappy circumstances, the powerful author of 'No coward soul is mine' fled home from
comparable exiles to hide herself in domesticity and dreams" (1994, 28).
Emily's silence and withdrawal from the public world, however, can be
read also as a form of resistance to that world; as Lyn Pykett argues,
instead of corroborating prescribed notions of domestic femininity,
Brontë's retreat "ever further within the limits of domestic life . . . cre-
ate[s] a space from which to explore those limitations."[16] Ensconced for
the majority of her short life in her father's parsonage at Haworth,
Brontë's seemingly dutiful and daughterly silence nevertheless remains

a "parod[y of] the modest quietness of the good girl of the period" (Davies 1994, 30). In this sense she lived as an insurrectionist in the kitchen, an agitator in the parlor.

As the daughter of a relatively impoverished Yorkshire clergyman, the young Emily, like her sisters, faced a potentially perilous future. If their father were to die—in the absence of any dowries for marriage—the sisters would have faced the possibility of destitution or even the workhouse, since curates such as Patrick Brontë were unable to amass enough savings to provide for their children beyond their death, and the church itself made no provision for the widows and orphans of its clergy. The Brontë children, moreover, were motherless before any of them had reached the age of eight (Emily was three when her mother, Maria Branwell Brontë, died of cancer), and the children's subsequent guardian, the stern and punctilious "Aunt Branwell," was ill-equipped to manage the education of the Brontë girls. Yet education was a necessity for the sisters; in the event of their being orphaned they would need to be able to earn their own living in a harsh and precarious world. Consequently, in 1824, Patrick sent the two eldest Brontë sisters, Maria and Elizabeth, to a school for the daughters of impoverished clergymen at Cowan Bridge, about 50 miles from Haworth; later in that same year, Charlotte and Emily were also enrolled in the school. Emily was six at the time. The entry in the Clergy Daughters' School book detailing Emily's brief career at Cowan Bridge registers starkly the social destiny laid out for her—and, indeed, for her sisters (punctuation as in the entrance book):

> Emily Bronté   5 3/4   1824   Novbr 25th   H Cough
> Reads very prettily & Works a little
> Left School June 1st 1825   Governess
>   (Chitham, 37)

Failing marriage, "Governess"—or teaching at a school—was the inevitable fate in store for the Brontë girls, a life of often thankless and unremitting labor for little financial reward. Yet events overtook Emily's career at Cowan Bridge. In the spring of 1825, a typhoid epidemic descended on the school. Maria and Elizabeth Brontë fell ill, although they succumbed not to typhus but to a disease that would later claim other members of the Brontë family—tuberculosis. Within months, both older sisters died, and Patrick hurried to Cowan Bridge in June 1825 to fetch Charlotte and Emily home from what must have seemed a veritable seminary of death. The "double death" (Chitham, 50) that ended Emily's and Charlotte's first sojourn from Haworth would later come back to haunt Emily in her other excursions away from home; as will be shown, she subsequently repeated in the material and metaphoric form of her own body the literal "consumption" that racked her sisters at Cowan Bridge—freeing them from the "shattered prison" (*WH*, 160) of their frail corporeal being.

Even before Cowan Bridge, the invention of "plays" and stories had been part of the young Brontës' games; in 1826 these pastimes received a fresh impetus when Patrick Brontë returned from a conference in Leeds armed with presents for the children. These gifts included a box of toy soldiers for Branwell. The soldiers (each one adopted by a different Brontë) marked the beginning of the "Young Men" plays—fluid dramas whose forms would eventually modulate into the imaginary worlds of "Glass town" and, later, "Angria." But there were other plays, too, established by the children in the late 1820s—"Our fellows" plays, the plays of the "Islanders," and the "Bed plays" or "secret plays" performed by Emily and Charlotte alone (Barker, 151). These fictions came to dominate the sibling world of the parsonage, sharing a level of reality with the everyday events of the household.

In 1831 Charlotte left Haworth to begin her schooling at Roe Head, a small, new, select establishment some 20 miles from Haworth. Brontë scholars generally trace the inception of "Gondal"—the imaginary kingdom so crucial to Emily's poetic development—to around this time. With Charlotte's departure, Emily and Anne developed a new intimacy and a new imaginative collaboration: their creation of "Gondal" in the early 1830s was an act of secession from the masculine, military, and politically dominated worlds of "Glass Town" and "Angria" that were previously overseen by Charlotte and Branwell. Instead, "Gondal" was a female-governed kingdom riven by fierce passions and continual civil strife between royalists and republicans.

The first mention of Gondal is in Emily's and Anne's first diary paper of 24 November 1834 (written by Emily), in which Gondal is situated, rather disarmingly, as part of the everyday geography of life at the parsonage. In a busy kitchen scene in which family members come and go, Emily, Anne, and the servant Tabby are supposed to be peeling potatoes; a mischievous Emily instead brandishes a pen in dereliction of her duties. Emily writes:

> Taby said just now Come Anne pilloputate [pill a potato] Aunt has just
> come into the kitchin just now and said Where are your feet Anne Anne

answered On the floor Aunt. Papa opened the parlour door and gave Branwell a letter saying Here Branwell read this and show it to your Aunt and Charlotte. The Gondals are discovering the interior of Gaaldine. Sally Mosley is washing in the back kitchin.

. . . Taby said on my putting a pen in her face Ya pitter pottering there instead of pilling a potate. I answered O Dear, O Dear, O Dear I will derectly With that I get up, take a knife and begin pilling. (*BLFC*, 1:124)

Members of the family, the servants, and "The Gondals" all share the same chaotic space here, jostling with each other for literal and metaphorical room. As Barker notes, Brontë's text "moves from describing the practicalities of daily life to her imaginary world of Gondal as if there is no discernible difference between the two" (156). Instead, crucially, the diary paper dissolves the distinction between real and imagined worlds and places them on the same ontological plane. There is no stable difference or division between what Brontë later calls the "world without" and the "world within" (*CP*, 19); rather, in a fluid interchange, the Gondals are as busy "discovering the interior of Gaaldine" in the kitchen as Emily is peeling and writing, or as Sally Mosley is washing.

But if the 16-year-old Emily runs the worlds of Gondal and Haworth together—transgressing the distinction between reality and fantasy, the inside and outside of the self—the contrast between the "world within" and the "world without" at other times was starkly and painfully drawn. Charlotte left Roe Head in 1832, but in July 1835 she returned to the school with Emily. This time Charlotte was a teacher and Emily a pupil. Yet Emily lasted less than three months at the school. In 1850 Charlotte recalled Emily's career and mysterious "decline" at Roe Head:

Liberty was the breath of Emily's nostrils; without it, she perished. The change from her own home to a school, and from her own very noiseless, very secluded, but unrestricted and inartificial mode of life, to one of disciplined routine . . . was what she failed in enduring. Her nature proved here too strong for her fortitude. Every morning when she woke, the vision of home and the moors rushed on her, and darkened and saddened the day that lay before her. Nobody knew what ailed her but me—I knew only too well. In this struggle her health was quickly broken: her white face, attenuated form, and failing strength threatened rapid decline. I felt in my heart she would die if she did not go home, and with this conviction obtained her recall.[17]

Charlotte describes Emily's homesickness as a sickness for "liberty": a demand for the freedom denied to her by the austerities of the school regime. Moreover, as Juliet Barker argues, "home" for Brontë figured not just personal liberty but also the liberty to write, to imagine, and to invent. At Roe Head, the "pervasive nature of school routine effectively ensured that Emily had no time to spend in Gondal fantasies" (235). Starved of liberty and of Gondal, Emily, it seems, plunged into illness: an illness that was at once psychical and physical. Charlotte's description of Emily's "white face, attenuated form, and failing strength" emphasizes both a physical and an emotional wasting away, as if, by a perverse yet powerful logic, Brontë's body was symbolizing the anguish of her mind. "Her nature," Charlotte insists, "proved . . . too strong for her fortitude." Katherine Frank goes further, arguing that Brontë's condition at Roe Head was a form of psychosomatic speech:

> Emily hated the school and did nothing to conceal her antipathy. She spoke to no one other than Charlotte, and even with Charlotte she talked only when absolutely necessary. In addition to being silent and withdrawn, Emily was barely eating and growing thinner and thinner and more and more languid and unresponsive each day. The acts of speaking and eating were strangely intertwined in Emily's life. . . . At Roe Head, in the late summer and autumn of 1835, she refused, as far as possible, to eat or speak. But her refusal of food was, in fact, a kind of utterance. By pushing her plate away at breakfast, dinner and tea, day after day, she was clearly, if silently, speaking her mind: *I hate it here. I will not eat. . . . I will make myself ill, starve even, unless I am released.* (98–99)

Frank concludes that Brontë's illness at Roe Head was a form of silent protest: a self-destructive demand for release, a potentially fatal bid for freedom. Discussing Charlotte Brontë's 1849 novel *Shirley*—which includes, in the figure of Shirley Keeldar, Charlotte's commemorative portrait of her by then dead sister Emily—Deirdre Lashgari likewise understands self-starvation, or the refusal of food, as a gesture of protest. According to Lashgari, the nineteenth-century self-starver—or anorectic—is "part of a much larger picture, in which a dysfunctional society starves women, literally and metaphorically, and women internalize that dis/order as self-starvation." Thus, Lashgari says of *Shirley*'s two female noneaters, Caroline Helstone and Shirley Keeldar, "When each in turn finds herself blocked from any effective overt protest and barred from speaking her pain, she asserts control over her life in the only arena available, inscribing her hunger on her own body in a desperate plea to be 'read aright.' "[18] In this light the language of hunger is the language of the disempowered; it is the speech of the silent and the utterance of the dispossessed. For Emily Brontë at Roe Head, silence and hunger thus bespoke the starvation and deprivation of her existence—as she literalized in and on the frame of her own body the "desire and lack" (Lashgari, 150) that gripped her. Her body—as Hélène Cixous says of the symptomatology of female hysteria—"sp[oke] true"[19] and became the place where her starved desire was made materially visible. Shackled to a nineteenth-century female education and the destiny of the governess, Brontë declared her dissent by refusing to eat. The desire to be "read aright," in Lashgari's formulation, is in Brontë's case the desire to be *seen hungry:* to display—albeit silently—the deprivation that afflicted her being.

Yet the attenuations of hunger in Brontë are also, strangely and spectrally, the repetition of a death scene. As Juliet Barker notes, Emily's symptoms at Roe Head "forcibly recall[ed] the spectre of the consumption which had carried off Maria and Elizabeth" at Cowan Bridge (236), and it was this apparent recurrence that, sooner rather than later, hurried Emily home. Edward Chitham remarks, "At Roe Head, [Emily] literally drooped: her face was bloodlessly pale, she became thin. These symptoms surely had reference to the Cowan Bridge experiences" (33). It was as though Roe Head was the symptomatic repetition of the trauma of Cowan Bridge. If Brontë's "decline" at Roe Head was symptomatic, then, it symbolized more than one thing—and melded, in an overdetermined way, the drama of female disenfranchisement with that of sibling bereavement.

An 1837 diary paper records another scene of writing—"Anne and I writing in the drawing-room." Again, there is the documentation of the events and the writing of Gondal and again a disarming interpenetration of the imagined and the real: "Anne [is writing] a poem beginning 'Fair was the evening and brightly the stars'—I Agustus-Almeda's life 1st v. 1—4th page from the last Fine rather coolish then grey cloudy but sunny day Aunt working in the little room Papa gone out Tabby in the kitchen The Emperors and Empresses of Gondal and Gaaldine preparing to depart from Gaaldine to Gondal to prepare for the coronation which will be on the 12th of July Queen Victoria ascended the throne this month" (*BST* 12, no. 1 [1951]: 15). The accession to the English throne of the 18-year-old Queen Victoria on 20 June 1837 merges fluidly here with the coronation of the Gondalian emperors and empresses. Although there is a strange intertwining of fantasy and re-

FIGURE 1. Diary paper sketch of Anne and Emily, 26 June 1837. Reprinted courtesy of The Brontë Society.

ality in the diary paper, the text is also marked by a gesture of withdrawal and retreat. Barker points out, for example, that the diary paper is "startling evidence of the lack of impact the outside world had upon [Emily]" (271). This is the case even with regard to the events and circumstances affecting the Brontë family itself at the time—for example, Charlotte's unhappiness at Roe Head (where she had returned with

Anne), Anne's ill-health, and Branwell's increasing dissipation.[20] The text is accompanied by a tiny pen-and-ink sketch showing Anne and Emily composing the paper: Anne sits with her head resting on her hands while Emily, characteristically, writes with her back turned toward the viewer (see figure 1). It is as if the picture was drawn by someone standing a few paces behind Emily (Barker, 271).

A similar strategy is employed in the diary paper of 1845, in which Emily is shown composing the paper in the small upstairs bedroom in the middle of the parsonage; she is seated on a stool with her portable rosewood writing desk on her knees (see figure 2). She faces the window and, again, her back is toward the viewer. In one sense both illustrations situate the viewer's gaze in the position that Emily-as-writer occupies; the spectator sees more or less what Brontë sees. But in another sense the opaque figure of Brontë herself disrupts the viewer's mastery of the scene; while the spectator seems to command the perspective of the picture, Brontë's figure intrudes and steals the visual comprehension of the scene from the viewer. What Brontë sees is thus reserved to herself; furthermore, she turns her gaze away, as if to preserve the secrecy of her perspective. Like the texts of the papers themselves, the illustrations willfully withhold the dimension of interiority that the form of the "diary" seems to open up.

In September 1838 Emily took up a position as teacher at Law Hill School near Halifax. Little is known about how this appointment came about, but Barker deems it most likely that Emily answered an advertisement in the local press (294). As already discussed, there was constant pressure on the sisters to find paid employment. Shortly after Emily took up the post, Charlotte wrote to Ellen Nussey expressing her forebodings about Emily's fate at the school: "My sister Emily is gone into a situation as teacher in a large school of near forty pupils, near Halifax. I have had one letter from her since her departure; it gives an appalling account of her duties—hard labour from six in the morning until near eleven at night, with only one half-hour of exercise between. This is slavery. I fear she will never stand it" (quoted in Barker, 294). Emily, indeed, did not "stand it" for long, and in six months she was back at Haworth. But she seems to have endured the "slavery" at Law Hill during the autumn of 1838; during these months, Emily wrote a number of powerful poems, both Gondal pieces and poems of exile, achingly elegizing the "hearth of home" (*CP,* 88; see Chitham, 114–16). After the Christmas holidays, however, it seems that her health broke down. Despite her apparent attempts to bear the oppressiveness of Law

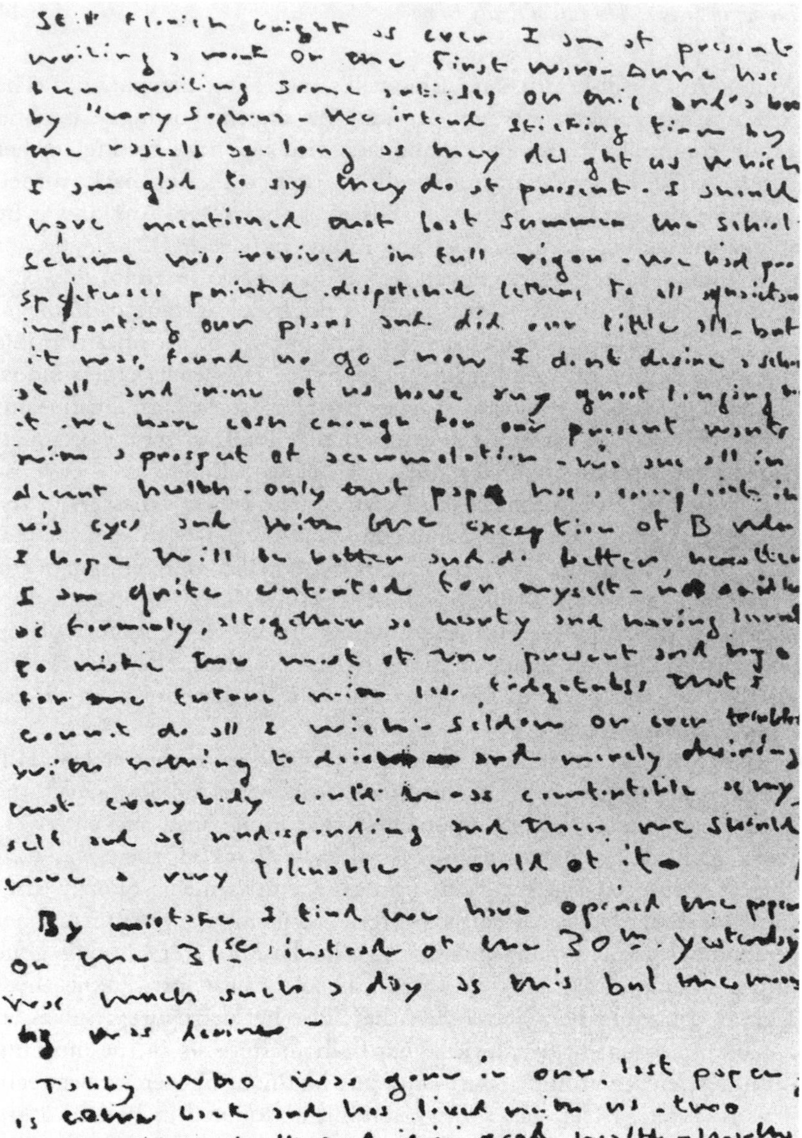
still flourish bright as ever I am at present
writing a work on the First Wars—Anne has
been writing some articles on this and a book
by "Henry Sophona"—We intend sticking firm by
the rascals as long as they delight us which
I am glad to say they do at present. I should
have mentioned that last summer the school
scheme was revived in full vigor—we had pro-
spectuses printed despatched letters to all aquaintances
imparting our plans and did our little all—but
it was found no go—now I don't desire a school
at all and none of us have any great longing for
it. we have cash enough for our present wants
with a prospect of accumulation—we are all in
decent health—only that papa has a complaint in
his eyes and with the exception of B who
I hope will be better and do better, hereafter
I am quite contented for myself—not as idle
as formerly, altogether as hearty and having learnt
to make the most of the present and hope
for the future with less fidgetiness that I
cannot do all I wish—seldom or ever troubled
with nothing to do and merely desiring
that everybody could be as comfortable as myself and as undesponding and then we should
have a very tolerable world of it—

By mistake I find we have opened the paper
on the 31st instead of the 30th. Yesterday
was much such a day as this but the morning was divine—

Tabby who was gone in our last paper
is come back and has lived with us—two
years and a half and is in good health—Martha
who also departed is here too. We have got
Flossy, got and lost Tiger—lost the Hawk. Nero
which with the geese was given away and

FIGURE 2. Emily Brontë's diary paper, 31 July 1845. Reprinted from Clement Shorter, *Charlotte Brontë and Her Circle* (1896)

is doubtless desk for which I came back
from Brussels I enquired on all hands and
could hear nothing of him — I saw did
early last year — Keeper and Flossey are well
also the canary bird 4 years since
we are now all at home and likely to
be there some time — Branwell went
to Liverpool on Tuesday to stay a week
Tabby has just been teasing me to turn
as formerly to "pillopatate" — Anne and I
should have picked the black currants
if it had been fine and sunshiny. I must
hurry off now to my turning and ironing
I have plenty of work on hands and
writing and am altogether full of business
with best wishes for the whole
House till 1848 July 30th and as
much longer as may be I conclude

Emily Jane Brontë

Hill, "her body," in Frank's words, "revolted against her resolution" (125). As Barker puts it, "[D]epression of mind . . . made writing impossible. . . . Deprived of the time to indulge in Gondal fantasies by the rigidity and all-pervasive nature of boarding school life and deprived of the power to write by her homesickness and unhappiness, Emily broke down. In a repeat of her brief days as a schoolgirl at Roe Head, her health gave way and she was obliged to return to Haworth" (306). Law Hill was the first and last attempt by Emily Brontë to achieve economic independence.

Emily's birthday paper of 1841, however, reports on a collective plan by the sisters to establish a school at Haworth. She writes, "A scheme is at present in agitation for setting us up in a school of our own; as yet nothing is determined, but I hope and trust it may go on and prosper and answer our highest expectations. This day four years I wonder whether we shall still be dragging on in our present condition or established to our hearts' content. Time will show" (BLFC, 1:238). As a preliminary to the establishment of the Brontës' school, Charlotte and Emily—at Charlotte's instigation—resolved to study at a foreign seminary for about a year in order to acquire the necessary proficiency in European languages. The sisters departed in February 1842 for Brussels to begin a course of study at the Pensionnat Heger, a school of 40 day-pupils and 12 boarders that catered mainly to young, Catholic, Belgian girls. The two retiring Protestant English sisters were propelled into a new world in which lessons were taught exclusively in French and in which, in Charlotte's words, there was "a broad line of demarcation between us and all the rest," leaving the sisters "completely isolated in the midst of numbers" (BLFC, 1:260).

Emily's response to this "isolation" was to retreat still further. Although, as Charlotte put it, Emily "work[ed] like a horse" (quoted in Barker, 382), her demeanor in this foreign land was even more painfully reclusive than it had been previously. For example, when Charlotte and Emily walked together in the school garden, Emily clung to her sister's arm in frightened yet insistent dependency. The sisters' beds were at the end of a long dormitory, separated from the others by a white curtain; interaction with others could therefore be studiously avoided. Emily, moreover, monopolized her sister, effectively preventing Charlotte from becoming involved in school life; Emily herself behaved toward others either with aloofness or with barely concealed hostility. Furthermore, Charlotte said that Emily's relationship with their tutor in French literature, Monsieur Heger himself, was strained at best: "Emily and he don't draw well together at all," she wrote (quoted in Barker, 384). For his part, Heger judged Emily to be "egotistical and exacting," exercising "a kind of unconscious tyranny over [Charlotte]."[21] At the same time, however, Heger's appreciation of Emily's intellect and strength of will has become part of Brontë legend. "She should have been a man," Heger confided to Mrs. Gaskell, "a great navigator. Her powerful reason would have deduced new spheres of discovery from the knowledge of the old; and her strong, imperious will would never have been daunted by opposition or difficulty" (Gaskell, 230). Heger's view of Emily is based in large measure on his reading of her French *devoirs,* the literary exercises he set for his two English pupils (see chapter 3 for a discussion of these essays); Heger saw in Emily's writing "a head for logic, and a capability of argument, unusual in a man, and rare indeed in a woman" (Gaskell, 230).

As Lyn Pykett has observed, commentators on Emily Brontë frequently resort to a masculinized language in order to account for her powers, since "Male discourse is not simply the dominant discourse, it is also a discourse of domination in which originality, argumentative *power, force* of reason etc. are linguistically represented as masculine qualities" (16). But one need not accept C. Day Lewis's phallocentrism, a characterization of Brontë as a man in a woman's skin—having "a masculine cast of mind in a woman's body"[22]—to acknowledge that Emily Brontë, both in her social persona and her writing, transgressed nineteenth-century definitions of femininity. Indeed, Brontë's subversion both of social codes and, as we will see in chapters 3 and 4, of conventional literary idioms is a key element in the recent feminist revaluation of her work.

Brontë's resistance to sanctioned definitions of femininity seems to have extended even to her clothing; she did not, according to the criticisms of her fellow pupils in Brussels, look as a well-dressed woman "should." For example, Laetitia Wheelwright, an English day-boarder at the school, commented to Clement Shorter when solicited for information about Emily, "I am afraid my recollections of Emily Brontë will not aid you much. I simply disliked her from the first; her tallish, ungainly ill-dressed figure contrasting so strongly with Charlotte's small, neat, trim person, although their dresses were alike; always answering our jokes with 'I wish to be as God made me' " (Gérin, 130). Gaskell, moreover, reports that Emily persisted in sporting gigot or "leg-of-mutton" sleeves, which had long gone out of fashion, and in wearing petticoats that lacked fullness and that, clinging to her legs, emphasized her tallness and gaunt frame (230; see also Barker, 393). In these ways Emily flouted the protocols of nineteenth-century feminine dress.

Laetitia Wheelright, again, described Emily as "thin and sallow," while Louise de Bassompierre—the only friend Emily made in Brussels—remembered her as "very pale and thin" (Frank, 170). These descriptions of Emily as "pale and thin" in Brussels resonate more darkly than do the insults about her dress, since they eerily echo Charlotte's 1850 account of her sister's drift toward decline at the Pensionnat Heger. After her description of Emily's illness at Roe Head, Charlotte recounts the similarly fateful course of her sister's stay in Brussels:

> After the age of twenty . . . [Emily] went with me to an establishment on the Continent: the same suffering and conflict ensued [as at Roe Head], heightened by the strong recoil of her upright, heretic and English spirit from the gentle Jesuitry of the foreign and Romish system. Once more she seemed sinking, but this time she rallied through the mere force of resolution: with inward remorse and shame she looked back on her former failure, and resolved to conquer in this second ordeal. She did conquer: but the victory cost her dear. She was never happy till she carried her hard-won knowledge back to the remote English village, the old parsonage-house, and desolate Yorkshire hills. (Jack, 370)

According to Charlotte, Emily's experiences at Roe Head were repeated compulsively at the Pensionnat Heger; and, if we recall the traumas of Cowan Bridge and Law Hill, it seems that all Emily's ventures into the world engendered the same "strong recoil" or "sinking," a psychical flight that sent her back to Haworth and self-seclusion, to the retreat in which her writing happened, and to the solitude out of which she spoke. It seems, in the end, that Brontë was only willing to live in silence.

As it was, Charlotte and Emily were recalled from Brussels late in 1842 by external rather than internal circumstances: the death of Aunt Branwell. In 1843 Charlotte returned to Brussels, this time without Emily. Instead, Emily resumed her previous role as parsonage housekeeper. More crucial for Emily, she resumed her writing, producing an "outpouring" of verse that decisively ended the "creative fast" (Frank, 181) of her period abroad. In February 1844 she carefully transcribed all her poems into two separate notebooks—one headed "Gondal Poems" and the other left untitled. She continued to add new poems to the books until 1848, the year of her death. Her final birthday paper, dated 1845, reports on the continued buoyancy of her Gondal fictions, as well as on the eventual fate of the school scheme for which she and Charlotte had journeyed to Brussels several years earlier. The paper also includes a fascinating insight into Brontë's relationship to her own fictional personae. Recording a trip to York with Anne in June 1845, she writes:

> Anne and I went our first long journey by ourselves together, leaving home on the 30th of June, Monday, sleeping at York, returning to Keighley Tuesday evening, sleeping there and walking home on Wednesday morning. Though the weather was broken we enjoyed ourselves very much, except during a few hours at Bradford. And during our excursion we were, Ronald Macalgin, Henry Angora, Juliet Angusteena, Rosabella Esmaldan, Ella and Julian Egremont, Catharine Navarre, and Cordelia Fitzaphnold, escaping from the palaces of instruction to join the Royalists who are hard driven at present by the victorious Republicans. The Gondals still flourish bright as ever. I am at present writing a work on the First Wars. . . . I should have mentioned that last summer the school scheme was revived in full vigour. We had prospectuses printed, despatched letters to all acquaintances imparting our plans, and did our little all; but it was found no go. Now I don't desire a school at all. . . . I am quite contented for myself: not as idle as formerly, altogether as hearty, and having learnt to make the most of the present and long for the future with the fidgetiness that I cannot do all I wish. . . . I have plenty of work on hands, and writing, and am altogether full of business. (*BLFC*, 2:49–50)

If the school scheme collapsed, it seems that its "vigour" was transferred to the "flourishing" life of the Gondals—and to the sustained writing in which Brontë was engaged. The corresponding 1845 diary note by Anne, however, tells a different story. It laments: "The Gondals in general are not in a first-rate playing condition. Will they improve?" (*BLFC*, 2:53). If Emily, for her part, enthused that "during our excursion we *were*, Ronald Macalgin, Henry Angora, Juliet Angusteena," for Anne there was a mournful distance rather than ecstatic mergence between herself and the *dramatis personae* of the Gondal chronicles. Emily's relationship to the theatrical concert of the Gondals was, by contrast, radically self-transformative; in her birthday paper she "is," or becomes, the fantasy figures that she plays in an act of dramatic self-reinvention. Stevie Davies writes of Emily's account of the York trip:

> York Minster, the City Walls and the river do not merit comment, as being presumably merely a theatrical backdrop against which the travelling actors could play out their improvisations. Indeed it might be fair to say that Emily and Anne did not visit York at all, in their own persons.

Ronald, Henry, Juliet, Rosabella . . . went in their stead, "escaping from
the palaces of instruction" as their creators were escaping from the constraints social life places on the individual woman. . . . From Emily's
identity spilt a plenitude of people. The self was plural, protean, her-
maphroditic. (1994, 36)

Davies's insightful comments disclose the ways in which the fictions of
Gondal were a mode of self-refashioning for Brontë. In this sense writing was for her a form of emancipation, a release from the constraints of
the self. As Teddi Lynn Chichester puts it, "trying on different selves,
different genders, different philosophies" allowed Brontë to elude the
confinements of her feminine material position—and to transfigure limitation into the play of possibility.[23]

Like the literary pseudonym "Ellis Bell," the fictional masks of
Gondal were a mode of self-empowerment; playing them, Brontë transformed herself. Moreover, their fictionality preserved the silence and
secrecy of "Emily Brontë"; vanishing into her fictions, she disappeared
from view altogether. As shown earlier, Charlotte's discovery of her sister's poems in 1845 provoked outrage from Emily (for it had violated a
secret), and although Emily was won over to the idea of publishing the
sisters' poems, it was on condition that—as she insisted with Anne—
pseudonyms be adopted (Barker, 479). But Emily's demand for secrecy
continued unabated. She clung to the mask of "Ellis Bell" against all
attempts to let it drop: it was, paradoxically, her way of preserving her
silence.

Poems by Currer, Ellis, and Acton Bell was published in May 1846, but
the collection met with mixed reviews and no commercial success: a year
after publication only two copies had been sold. It was clear—even
before the poems' publication—that literary success, if it was to be had,
would come through fiction rather than verse. The sisters had, in fact,
already embarked on works of fiction—Charlotte on *The Professor,* Anne
on *Agnes Grey,* and Emily on *Wuthering Heights*—before *Poems* was published. It seems that Emily embraced the project of publishing the
"Bell" fictions more readily than she ever did the poems. The majority of
Wuthering Heights was written between the autumns of 1845 and 1846;
it was published in December 1847. Yet even here Brontëan secrecy was
maintained. For the composition of these new fictions, the sisters
returned to their childhood practice of collaborative production.
"[P]utting away their work at nine o'clock, and beginning their study,"
writes Gaskell, "[they paced] up and down the sitting room . . . [and

o]nce or twice a week, each read to the others what she had written, and heard what they had to say about it" (307). Remarkably, this vibrant workshop of literary creation remained a secret both to their father and probably to Branwell. It was only after the publication of *Jane Eyre* at the end of 1847, for example, that Patrick learned the identity of "Currer Bell" (Barker, 546). Branwell, on the other hand, was spared the news of his sisters' literary ventures for more material reasons; Charlotte wrote of the project for the 1846 *Poems,* for example, that "we could not tell him of our efforts for fear of causing him too deep a pang of remorse for his own time misspent, and talents misapplied" (Barker, 489).

Branwell Brontë sunk into despair, dissipation, and finally death from tuberculosis in the summer of 1848—his miseries hurried forward by disappointment in love as well as professional failure and physical sickness. Throughout his decline, it was Emily who was closest to him and most tolerant of him. During 1848, it is evident that Emily was working on a second novel;[24] Juliet Barker has suggested that Branwell's deterioration and then Emily's own illness conspired to prevent her from completing and revising the text. Branwell died on 24 September. After the funeral, all the family suffered aching coughs and colds precipitated by the fierce easterly winds across Haworth hills. By the end of October, Charlotte feared that something much more serious was wrong with her younger sisters. She wrote to Ellen Nussey of Emily, "[Her] cough and cold are very obstinate; I fear she has pain in the chest—and I sometimes catch a shortness in her breathing when she has moved at all quickly—She looks very, very thin and pale. Her reserved nature occasions one great uneasiness of mind—it is useless to question her—you get no answers—it is still more useless to recommend remedies—they are never adopted" (*BLFC,* 2:268).

Charlotte's letters during Emily's last illness, as her consumption advanced, make poignant reading; indeed, Charlotte's letters are a tragic record of her sister's final struggles. As Charlotte indicates to Ellen Nussey, Emily obdurately refused to answer questions about her health throughout her illness, rejecting all offers of advice or help, whether from family or doctors. It was as if Emily's habitual reserve now tightened its hold upon her and enclosed her in a secret and deadly realm that she fiercely, even perversely, defended against all invasion. It seems that she literally guarded her illness: keeping it to herself, she held it in a fatal embrace.

On 2 November Charlotte wrote, "[Emily] will not yield a step before pain or sickness till forced; not one of her ordinary avocations will she voluntarily renounce: you must look on, and see her do what she is unfit to do, and not dare to say a word" (*BLFC*, 2:269). Indeed, despite the ravages of her illness, Emily persisted in doing what she had always done. She rose at 7:00, as was her wont, and sat up until 10:00 at night; she continued to dress herself, even on the last morning she was alive; she fed her beloved dogs, Keeper and Flossy, as she always did. On her last evening, performing this latter task, she staggered in the stone-flagged passage of the parsonage and almost fell against the wall but waved away Charlotte and Anne as they hurried to support her, completing the task alone. Her "spirit," in Charlotte's memorable words, was "inexorable to the flesh" (*WH*, xxxi); her obduracy, to quote Georges Bataille, was the "approval of life, up until death" (16).

The pattern of Emily's illness, of course, grimly recalled the earlier deaths in the Brontë family; but it also uncannily repeated her own "sinkings" at Roe Head, Law Hill, and the Pensionnat Heger. "Never in her life had she lingered over any task," wrote Charlotte, "and she did not linger now. She made haste to leave us" (*WH*, xxxi). Charlotte's remarks come near to suggesting that Emily in some way willed her own demise—or at least embraced the death that claimed her. And there does, indeed, seem to be a "haste" about Emily's decline, as if she hurried to merge with the vacancy that was taking possession of her body. As consumption wasted her frame, she appeared to identify with its deadly work, refusing medicine, food, and sympathy in the austere and strange discipline of self-starvation—as though repeating, finally, not just her own earlier deprivations but the deaths of her fierce heroine and hero from *Wuthering Heights,* Catherine and Heathcliff, who starve themselves to death, symbolizing in the wasting of their bodies the illimitable hunger of their desire.[25]

Similarly, Brontë inscribed her desire on her flesh as hunger—and her body became, in the absence of speech, the very text of her deprivation. She died on 19 December 1848 and was buried three days later. Her coffin maker, William Wood, had to construct the narrowest coffin he had ever made for an adult; it measured just 16 inches across (Gérin, 259). If Emily Brontë died the death of a "hunger artist" (Frank, 257), then, she died in an inexorable evacuation of the flesh—an emptying that, strangely, both bespoke her own famishing and displayed her body as a "shattered prison" whose bars, finally, failed to contain their prisoner.

Chapter Two
Writing Worlds: Gondal

The Gondals are discovering the interior of Gaaldine.

This remark from Emily's and Anne's diary paper of 1834 is the first mention of the turbulent fictional world of "Gondal" in the work of the Brontës. Once begun, however, the tumultuous emotional and political history of Gondal (described by Anne as "a large island in the North Pacific"[1]) and of its colony Gaaldine, a South Pacific island, would preoccupy Emily Brontë's writing up until the year of her death—although the exploits of the Gondalians would in the end pale for Anne.

Disarmingly, Brontë presents the Gondals' colonization in 1834 of Gaaldine simultaneously with "Sally Mosley . . . washing in the back kitchin," thereby collapsing any distinction between real and imagined worlds. But it is not just the case that Gondal is constructed on the same ontological plane as everyday reality in Brontë; Gondal is constructed in the *now*, as part of a temporal continuum. A report on the Gondals, indeed, appears in each of Brontë's four diary papers of 1834, 1837, 1841, and 1845; just as the papers are bulletins of the everyday life of the Brontë family and household, so they are a diary of the ongoing life of the Gondals. Thus, both histories—the Brontëan and Gondalian, the real and the fictional—unfold in the same temporal dimension. In this sense they are both "real" and occur as a simultaneous process. In the 1841 paper, Brontë writes:

> The *Gondalians* are at present in a threatening state, but there is no open rupture as yet. All the princes and princesses of the Royalty are at the Palace of Instruction. I have a good many books on hand, but I am sorry to say that as usual I make small progress with any. However, I have just made a new regularity paper! and I mean verb sap to do great things. And now I must close, sending from far an exhortation, "Courage, courage," to exiled and harassed Anne, wishing she was here. (*BLFC*, 1:238)[2]

"[A]re at present," "there is . . . as yet": the narrative of the Gondalians is represented here as a continuous, immediate unfolding in the present and in the present tense, a story dissolved into a temporal process rather than finalized in any finished pattern. The Gondals are "threatening," Anne is "exiled and harassed": both narratives, real and imagined, thus occur as ongoing events.

The "Gondal Chronicles" (*BLFC*, 2:52)—that is, the prose stories that surrounded and connected the Gondal poems written by Emily and Anne—are unfortunately now lost or destroyed, and the history of Gondal exists only as an epic fragment. But even if the prose narratives still existed, it is likely that the Gondal saga would *remain* a fragmentary and fractured composition rather than be revealed as a unified whole. As J. Hillis Miller remarks, "The primary characteristic of the Gondal saga was its unfinished quality, its openness. Characters and events proliferated endlessly."[3] Indeed, the records that survive of Emily's and Anne's compositional methods for the Gondal narrative indicate that the tale was written as an open-ended work-in-progress, lacking any teleological direction other than the aleatory passing of time itself. In fact, it seems that the Gondal story spawned itself almost alarmingly—in the note quoted above, Emily indicates that she has "a good many books on hand"—and it is likely that Anne's eventual disaffection with the saga, as Stevie Davies states, sprung from a sense that the Gondal Chronicles were "getting out of hand": that the "endlessly unfolding cycle of Gondal . . . was beginning to loom as an uncontrollable labour rather than a spontaneous joy."[4] But for Emily, as illustrated in her 1845 diary paper, the Gondal characters continued to "flourish bright as ever"— and so we find her declaring, despite Anne's evident disillusionment, "We intend sticking firm by [our Gondal] rascals as long as they delight us, which I am glad to say they do at present" (*BLFC*, 2:51).

If the Gondal story eventually became, then, "as multitudinous as life itself"—a polyphonous, multidirectional, kaleidoscopic texture rather than "a single, linear narrative" (Davies 1983, 33)—it is all the more extraordinary that efforts have been made by some literary critics to reconstruct the Gondal narrative into a unified whole, despite the fact that all that remains of that fragmentary composition is itself a series of fragments: Emily's "Gondal Poems" and the poems written by Anne on Gondalian themes. Three serious attempts have been made by Brontë scholars to rebuild the ruins of Gondal. The most celebrated of the Gondal reconstructors is Fannie Ratchford, who in *The Brontës' Web of Childhood* (1941) and then in *Gondal's Queen: A Novel in Verse* (1955) contended that "many, perhaps all, of [Brontë's] poems, including those most exploited by theorizing biographers as subjective, [are] actually

units in a flaming epic of a purely imaginary world and its people"—
that is, the universe of Gondal.[5] Ratchford describes Gondal itself as "an
island in the North Pacific, a land of lakes and mountains and rocky
shorelines, with a climate much like Emily's native Yorkshire. Its people
were a strong, passionate, freedom-loving race, highly imaginative and
intensely patriotic. Politically, Gondal was a confederacy of provinces or
kingdoms, each governed by an hereditary ruling family. Between the
House of Brenzaida, in the kingdom of Angora, and the House of Exina
existed a deadly rivalry which gave direction to the developing play."[6]

If this was the geography of Gondal, the saga itself, asserts Ratchford, was similarly a carefully organized unity: "a compact and well-
integrated whole, rather than the sprawling, formless thing some would
make it." Evidencing an "over-all design comparable to the clear-cut
blueprint of *Wuthering Heights*," the Gondalian epic could be reconstructed, Ratchford claimed, so as to display unimpaired and undecayed
the "glorious fruitage" of Emily Brontë's imagination (1955, 23, 12).
Gondal's Queen: A Novel in Verse is Ratchford's bizarrely self-assured narration of the Gondal story, derived and deduced from the fragments of
narrative in Brontë's lyric-dramatic Gondal poems; its approximately
120 pages are made up of Ratchford's narrative prose punctuated by
Brontë's Gondal poems. Arguing that "all of Emily's verse, as we have
it, falls within the Gondal context" (1955, 32), Ratchford also contends
that Gondal was not a "sprawling" thing but the story of a single
woman, A.G.A., or "Gondal's Queen," told "from dramatic birth,
through tempestuous life, to tragic death" (1955, 27). Ratchford spells
out the "argument" of this birth, life, and death as follows: "A.G.A. [is]
born under the predominating auspices of the planet Venus. From a
'glorious child,' loving and generous, courageous and truthful, a messenger of joy and gladness, she developed into a true daughter of her
brilliant star, ardent in temperament, poetic in thought, fickle and
changeable in love. Worshiped [sic] of all men who came under her
charms, she brought tragedy to those upon whom her amorous light
shone" (1955, 41).

The narrative unity that Ratchford manages to produce from the
Gondal materials depends, however, on a drastic reduction of the multi-
fariousness of the Gondalian characters. In the list of dramatis personae
given at the beginning of her "reconstructed" novel, Ratchford introduces the principal character, Gondal's Queen, A.G.A, in the following
way: "AUGUSTA GERALDINE ALMEDA, variously designated as A.G.A.,
A. G. ALMEDA, GERALDINE, ROSINA, ROSINA OF ALCONA, ALCONA" (43).

Ratchford's strategy is to resolve at least three potentially distinct Gondalian characters—A.G.A., Geraldine S., and Rosina Alcona—into a single dramatic figure, thereby producing (rather than reconstructing) a narrative unity out of narrative fragmentation. The other two reconstructions of the Gondal story—Laura Hinkley's *The Brontës: Charlotte and Emily* (New York, 1945) and W. D. Paden's *An Investigation of Gondal* (New York, 1965)—keep distinct the figures that Ratchford unites and thus generate narratives that are radically different in shape and emphasis.

Against Ratchford's impulse to unify, David Musselwhite reminds us that Gondal *remains* a textual fragment. And this fragmentariness is, for Musselwhite, a crucial indicator of the radical or feminist force of Brontë's writing, that is, of the subversive nature of Gondalian textuality. It is precisely in Gondal's *resistance* to harmonious narrative appropriation that, according to Musselwhite, its significant energies lie. Gondal, he argues, becomes a fluid place of play, symbolic subversion, and transgressive—even self-contradictory—invention that resists the strictures of "what Lacan has called the 'Symbolic Order': [the] . . . socially sanctioned order of gender allocation" that ascribes fixed identities to human subjects, containing and constraining gendered selves within acceptable, self-identical positions. In the context of the fluidity of Gondal's voices—in which it is often impossible to know the speaker's name, let alone his or her gender—Musselwhite says of Ratchford's reconstructive project:

> [O]ne is . . . led to question whether Mrs Ratchford's endeavours, admirable and ingenious as they are, are not radically misguided. The mistake is to have even sought for a coherent scheme: *the poems and their titles are not the epiphenomena of a lost narrative—they are an aggregative ensemble "anterior to" and resistant of narrative appropriation.* Consider the titles given to the poems by Emily herself:
> A.G.A. to A.E; A.G.A. to A.S.; A.S. to G.S.; D.G.C. to J.A.; E.W. to A.G.A.; E.G. to M.R.; M.G. for the U.S.; I.M. to I.G., etc, etc.
> . . . The pleasure is in the making of connections, any connections, with blithe disregard for the rules of selection and exclusion, for the identifications that narrative requires. It is, in other words, the mode of a wilfulness and perversity that eludes the strictures and structures of the Symbolic Order.[7]

Whereas Ratchford seeks for identification and definition, Musselwhite insists that the Gondal poems are "not about 'identified' events," since "it is identity that they are an escape from" (1987, 85). Indeed, the disruption of stable or fixed identity is part of Gondal's subversive feminist poetics: "[O]ver and against the imperative 'be feminine' what the Gondal material manifests is the revelry of endless connections and miraculous conjugations: here one can be male and/or female, boy and/or girl, father and/or daughter, mother and/or son *all at once*." Gondal's labile names are thus the "indices of an imperious androgyny" in which gender identities are refused and endlessly redefined: "Here one is not a single subject but an assemblage of singularities" (1987, 84, 85). Gondal is thus an arena of textual subversion and experimentation rather than a fixed entity.

But if Ratchford's monolithic Gondal is restrictive and ideologically stultifying in these ways, in other ways her version of Gondal has proved politically productive for feminist critics. It is significant, for example, that Ratchford insists—against the "subjective" or biographical reading of some of the poems—that Brontë's poetic output is irreducibly dramatic; that is to say, Brontë's poetry is a play (for Ratchford, an entirely Gondalian play) of voices and personae, none of which can be unproblematically identified with Emily Brontë herself (Ratchford 1955, 32). For feminists, the importance of this view is that it demonstrates the ways in which Brontë's poetry in general, and Gondal in particular, offers an emancipatory feminist aesthetic in which the female self is a site of symbolic transformation rather than of stable identification. As Brontë's remarkable 1845 diary paper, discussed in chapter 1, illustrates, the world of Gondal and the personae of Gondal operated as a means of self-remaking in Brontë: a gallery of identifications in which Brontë could take on and put off what Teddi Lynn Chichester calls "alternative selfhoods," inscribing a "mercurial poetic identity" that simultaneously embraced both her Gondalian and non-Gondalian verse (1, 4; for more on the poems see chapter 3). For Chichester, Brontë is thus a Keatsian poet of "Negative Capability" who is able "to imaginatively coalesce with a variety of characters of both genders, many in situations utterly foreign to her own" (4). As a crucible of self-invention, then, Gondal is a place where Emily Brontë is transformed into the various personae that she ventriloquizes—the endemic "objectivity and impersonality of the poems," in Miller's words, transposing her "to another plane . . . [in which] the author herself has disappeared in her creation" (1963, 161). "Emily Brontë" is thereby remade in the turbulent image of Gondal.

Crucial here, of course, is Gondal's character as a predominantly female realm: a realm in which male characters are not infrequently disenfranchised in the face of the imperious designs and desires of powerful women, not least the imposing figure of A.G.A. Gondal, as Stevie Davies argues, spurns the "bellicose masculinities" of the world of Glass town presided over by Branwell Brontë; instead, it is "a place of female power where patriarchy (despite frequent incarcerations of princesses) [is] not admired" (1983, 35). Furthermore, as a textual space, Gondal is a "theatre of power—a power denied to females so that they must . . . open out a private space in which to legitimise it" (1994, 35–36). On one level, then, Gondal is a compensatory world overturning female disempowerment in nineteenth-century society; but on another, it is an affirmatory world that imagines female power into existence. As Lyn Pykett observes: "In Gondal Emily Brontë created a series of dramatic situations, personae, and masks by means of which she could escape some of the restrictions of the culturally conditioned female voice: heroic warriors calling their troops to battle, adventurers wandering the high seas, and, most interesting of all, proud, powerful and assertive women such as Angelica and A.G.A., who are often portrayed through the perspective of their desperate and spurned lovers whom they inspire to commit terrible deeds" (Pykett, 45–46).

As well as a theater of female empowerment, though, Brontë's poems also present Gondal as a scene of female imprisonment; indeed, emancipation and incarceration are bound together in an inescapable dialectic throughout Brontë's work. For all their imperiousness, Brontë's Gondal women are often exiles and prisoners whose lyric utterances bespeak a condition of privation that, beyond any Gondalian narrative, seems freighted with the burden of nineteenth-century femininity itself. Davies remarks that it is the "elegeic voice, rather than the noise of military or political encounters, [that] characterizes the Gondal world" (1983, 35); and, indeed, whether the individual speakers are identified as men or women, many of the Gondal poems seem to resonate with a peculiarly *female* dilemma of marginality, liminality, and dispossession. Pykett states, for example, that despite their apparent dominance, Brontë's "powerful women offer female versions of the Romantic exile, that outcast, outlawed, or otherwise isolated figure, the lonely bearer of the truth who rejects or rebels against the society from which he has been exiled," and that in this way Brontë dramatizes her "sense of her own freakishness and exceptionality" (46, 47). To this extent, it is possible to read Brontë's Gondalian dramas as complex and multiple acts of self-inscription.

A characteristic Brontëan cameo of power and loss appears in "Written in Aspin Castle" (*CP,* 139–42). In this poem, a solitary speaker muses on a still and starless night on the ancestral history of "Aspin Castle," the feudal seat of the Gondal character "Lord Alfred S." The history that the speaker conjures, however, is not just ancestral but spectral: for on the "wild walk" (17)[8] by Aspin's side, says the speaker, "wanders . . . a phantom pale / With spirit-eyes of dreamy blue" (32–33):

> It always walks with head declined
> Its long curls move not in the wind
> Its face is fair—divinely fair;
> But brooding on that angel brow
> Rests such a shade of deep despair
> As nought divine could ever know
> (34–39)

The perilous mixture of divinity and the demonic ("angel brow . . . deep despair") in this portrait makes Aspin's phantom a walking subversion of categories. Belonging neither to earth, hell, or heaven, the specter is an exile from definition, a wanderer from identity. The poem presents its ghost as part of a scene in which "evening's pensive hour / Hushes the bird and shuts the flower / And gives to Fancy magic power / O'er each familiar tone" (26–29); it is a moment in which truth cedes to "Fancy," nature gives way to imagination, and the "familiar" surrenders to the unfamiliar. In this witching hour, the dead walk, the phantom rises, and the exile returns. In the hall, a portrait hangs of the dead man alive; but this, too, is a ghost, for "when the moonbeam chill and blue / Streams the spectral windows through / That picture's like a spectre too—" (56–58). Spectral scene, spectral picture, and spectral exile: these phantom effects prepare the way for the presentation of a final ghost in the poem—Lord Alfred S.'s lost lover, A.G.A.:

> . . . turn towards the western side
> There stands Sidonia's deity!
> In all her glory, all her pride!
> And truly like a god she seems
> Some god of wild enthusiast's dreams

And this is she for whom he died!
For whom his spirit unforgiven,
Wanders unsheltered shut from heaven
An outcast for eternity—
                                                    (75–83)

Alfred's desire for A.G.A., it seems, has fatal consequences; loving
her, he is banished and spurned, a banishment that finally turns into the
disbarment of death. Even beyond death he lives the exiled life of the
"phantom." But if Alfred is cast out of "heaven" because of his love for
A.G.A.—if his desire for her in this sense *induces* his exile—then A.G.A.
herself is a figure of exile as well. She, too, is an outcast from "heaven"
and a wanderer from the securities of nature. In "A.G.A. to A.S." (*CP*,
150–51), A.G.A. sings of her love for Alfred, hymning her desire in
exultant terms that exceed conventional categories. She speaks of a
"heaven . . . reigning in my thought" (7) that surpasses the beauties of
nature and the promises of religion, finding heaven instead in the object
of her love:

That heaven which my sweet lover's brow
Has won me to adore—
Which from his blue eyes beaming now
Reflects a still intenser glow
Than nature's heaven can pour—
                                                    (10–14)

Naming her lover and herself "divine" (15)—and so usurping the language of orthodoxy—A.G.A. scorns those who seek for "beams divine"
and "heaven's sun" in "cell and cloister drear" (33–35); for hers is a
creed of longing that constitutes its object of bliss through the very force
of desire itself. In this way, A.G.A. exiles herself from all security: rejecting the comforts of nature and religion, she generates a perilous and
mutable heaven from the energies of her own love.

A.G.A.'s desire is thus exorbitant and transgressive; like her dead
lover, Alfred, she is an outcast from both orthodoxy and nature. In
"Written in Aspin Castle" the speaker, having encountered both the
phantom wanderer and the specter of A.G.A., admonishes himself,
"Come leave these dreams o'er things of yore / And turn to Nature's face

divine—" (94–95), as if nature is a power that banishes "Fancy," phantoms, and visions and restores the "familiar tone" of the world. Yet, in effect, both Alfred S. and A.G.A. are identified as disturbances of nature. As exiles from nature, they are restless and errant spirits who in both life and death dissolve the stability and perdurability that nature represents and to which the speaker of the poem wishes to return. Similarly, in her longest poem, "The Death of A.G.A." (*CP*, 158–68), Brontë depicts Lord Eldred standing over A.G.A.'s body under an open sky:

> . . . he sees the stars
> Their quiet course continuing
> And, far away, down Elmor scars
> He hears the stream its waters fling:
>
> That lulling monotone did sing
> Of broken rock and shaggy glen,
> Of welcome for the moorcock's wing,
> But, not of wail for men!
>
> Nothing in heaven or earth to show
> One sign of sympathizing woe—
>   (296–305)

A.G.A., severed here from the "sympathizing" power of nature, ends her history an exile from the world. Moreover, she ends as an apostate from the creed propounded in Romantic poetry whereby the human mind finds its reflection and completion in the realm of nature—in what Coleridge called the "dim sympathies" ("Frost at Midnight," 18) between the self and nature. When such Romantic "sympathies" are lacking, the self becomes an exile or phantom—wandering, restless, and unmoored: the "Surplus of Nature's dread activity," in Coleridge's words ("Human Life: On the Denial of Immortality," 10)—and the type of the Romantic exile that A.G.A. embodies.

But if A.G.A. and other Gondal females are in this sense Romantic exiles, their femininity renders them doubly transgressive. As Margaret Homans notes, Romantic tradition consistently identifies femininity with nature and nature's influence;[9] consequently, for femininity to be severed or exiled from nature is to consign it to darkness, even to

demonism. Two of Brontë's Gondal poems strikingly dramatize such
demonic transgression of naturalized femininity. In "A Farewell to
Alexandria" (*CP,* 106–7), a female speaker—possibly, but not definitely,
A.G.A.—chillingly abandons her child to certain death in a snowstorm.
The first five stanzas of the poem conjure a "dell in July's shine" (1), presenting a natural scene that is benevolent, beautiful, and divinely superintended:

> Then, then I might have laid thee down
> And deemed thy sleep would gentle be
> I might have left thee, darling one
> And thought thy God was guarding thee!
> (17–20)

Mother, nature, and God exist in mutually supportive conjunction
here. Collectively constructing a fantasy of maternal, natural, and providential care, it is as if the child's well-being was guaranteed merely by
the combination of these three terms. But in the second half of the
poem, each of the initially protective terms vanishes. As the mother prepares to exit, she hails a nature turned pitiless and a God gone truant:

> But now, there is no wandering glow
> No gleam to say that God is nigh:
> And coldly spreads thy couch of snow
> And harshly sounds thy lullaby.
> (21–24)

With God and nature emptied of Romantic beneficence—their influence literally buried in "palling" snow—no "guardian crest" of heather
or protective spirit remains to protect the child. In a valediction to the
doomed child and maternal love itself, the mother moans as she leaves,
"I cannot bear to watch thee die!" (30, 31, 36). The poem's infanticide
brutally explodes the ideological bond between nature, femininity,
maternity, and God; in this way, Brontë's text perversely disrupts sanctioned definitions of femininity. The text itself, in fact, is an act of transgression.

Another poem that pushes the category of the feminine to its limit is
"Geraldine" (*CP,* 133–34). Here, a speaker reports on her "lady"'s (13)

nighttime vigil or self-exile in a "cavern wild" (17) where, separated
from her revelling comrades, she bends over her "beauteous child" (19)
as it sleeps and sings a "witching" (16) song that, it seems, is the prelude
to an act of infanticide.[10] The poem's narrative tells us that this scene
takes place in the wake of the death of Geraldine's lover, Julius Brenzaida (their relationship recalls that between A.G.A. and Lord Alfred in
"Written in Aspin Castle" and "A.G.A. to A.S."—as noted earlier,
Ratchford identifies Geraldine with A.G.A.); and that the sleeping child
is Geraldine and Julius's. Singing over her child, however, Geraldine
"d[oes] not mourn" (14), says the speaker. Instead, a transgressive and
finally murderous logic unfolds from her desire. Geraldine sings:

> "Why sank so soon the summer sun
> From our Zedora's skies?
> I was not tired, my darling one,
> Of gazing in thine eyes—
>
> "Methought the heaven whence thou hast come
> Was lingering there awhile
> And Earth seemed such an alien home
> They did not dare to smile.
>
> "Methought each moment something strange
> Within their circles shone
> And yet, through every magic change
> They were Brenzaida's own . . ."
>
> (21–32)

As the poem proceeds, Geraldine divinizes the child and melds the
"heaven" from which the infant comes with her lover, Julius Brenzaida—for the two shine indistinguishably together in the child's eyes.
Heaven and lover are inseparable in Geraldine's song, since the fading
divinity that lingers in the child's eyes is at the same time the trace of
Geraldine's lost love. However, as Chichester has shown, Brontë's poem
is not merely a local Gondalian drama. It is also an intertextual revision
of Wordsworth's "Ode: Intimations of Immortality from Recollections
of Early Childhood" (1807): "[I]t is "an eerie retelling of Wordsworth's

[poem in which Geraldine] decides to prevent 'shades of the prison-house' from closing upon her daughter by sending her right back to 'that imperial palace whence [she] came' " (8). Geraldine's desire—wedded both to the visionary "heaven" from which the child emerges and the "immortal love" (*WH,* 321) that she has lost (and with which that visionary heaven is identified)—embraces infanticide in a perverse attempt both to keep the child in its heavenly state and to keep Brenzaida's image safe in the child. Geraldine utters an "ardent prayer" (36) that the child will be "preserved" as it now is:

> "Bless it, my gracious God, I cried,
> Preserve thy mortal shrine
> For thine own sake, be thou its guide
> And keep it still divine!
>
> "Say, sin shall never blanch that cheek
> Nor suffering charge that brow
> Speak, in thy mercy maker, speak
> And seal it safe from woe!
>
> "Why did I doubt? In God's control
> Our mutual fates remain
> And pure as now, my angel's soul
> *Must* go to heaven again!"
>   (37–48)

At the end of the poem, having heard this strange lament, the narrator watches "o'er [her lady's] slumber" and weeps "[a]s one who mourns the dead!" (51–52), as though consigning both child and mother already to the grave. For, insofar as each of them is wedded to the "divine," mother and child both find earth an "alien home," a place of banishment or exile. The speaker seems to recognize as he or she mourns them that, in a sense, mother and child are already dead, already elsewhere. Despite her appeal to God, the "witching" song that Geraldine utters is a demonic orison that "d[oes] not mourn" but refuses to accept the separation or barrier between birth, death, and heaven; indeed, it obliterates such barriers in a transgressive contemplation of murder, a hubristic reappropriation of "heaven." If Wordsworth's "Intimations Ode" mourns the loss of the "imperial palace" of heavenly vision, then Brontë's Geraldine seems—imperiously and criminally—about to re-seize that heaven for her "divine" child. Geraldine's longing is an anti-Wordsworthian lament in which the benevolence of nature is repudiated in the name of visionary transcendence, and in which a woman's desire to embrace "heaven" involves rejecting mortal and maternal nature. Doffing the role of mother and the rule of nature, Brontë's speaker is a transgressor who exceeds the nineteenth-century sanctities of maternity and of natural feeling. In transgressing them, Geraldine's song makes explicit the confines within which nineteenth-century femininity was defined and constrained. Indeed, Brontë's text in effect identifies female transcendence or visionary aspiration with crime—or with what Chichester calls a "transgression . . . of the natural order" (9). It is as though the poem suggests that female desire itself can only be understood as transgressive—as a subversion of "nature."

Whether or not Geraldine is A.G.A., she certainly echoes the latter as a figure of exile and excess. A.G.A.'s defining characteristics, however, are change and betrayal; she seems dissolved in an element of alteration and instability that conditions both her own "changeful life" (*CP,* 99) and, as we saw earlier, the realm of Gondal itself as a shifting, mutable, and inconstant kingdom. Poems that mark out A.G.A. as a betrayer include "A.G.A. to A.S." (*CP,* 156), in which A.G.A. acknowledges her faithlessness to her lover ("I know that I have done thee wrong— / Have wronged both thee and Heaven"; 9–10); "F. De Samara to A.G.A." (*CP,* 82–83), in which A.G.A.'s lover, Fernando, slaughters himself as he bids her farewell ("There, go, Deceiver, go! My hand is streaming wet, / My heart's blood flows to buy the blessing—To forget"; 21–22); and "The Death of A.G.A." (*CP,* 158–68), in which Angelica, A.G.A.'s "childhood's mate" (79), speaks of her betrayal by her ("What recked she of another's pain?"; 88) and of A.G.A.'s driving into "Exile's doom" (96) Lord Alfred S., another paramour. But A.G.A.'s own losses are also relentlessly marked in the landscape of Gondal. In "There shines the moon, at noon of night—" (*CP,* 36–38), for example, A.G.A. recalls the death of her lover Alexander, Lord of Elbë, years before—and reveals herself as a subject of alteration and dispossession, as well:

> And Earth's the same but Oh to see
> How wildly Time has altered me!

> Am I the being who long ago
> Sat watching by that water side
> The light of life expiring slow
> From his fair cheek and brow of pride?
>   (15–20)

A.G.A.'s reflections, "Am I the being . . . ," suggest that the self is as radically alterable as "Time" itself and that there is a logic of betrayal and changeability inscribed in the very passage of time according to which the self abandons its loves as part of the relentless mutability of the world. This is confirmed at the end of the poem by Alexander of Elbë himself as he miserably contemplates his abandonment by A.G.A. after his death:

> Augusta—you will soon return
> Back to [my] land in health and bloom
> And then the heath alone will mourn
> Above my unremembered tomb
> For you'll forget the lonely grave
> And mouldering corpse by Elnor's wave—
>   (63–68)

Alexander's complaint about being forgotten by A.G.A. ("You'll forget") amounts to a fear of betrayal by her. Yet betrayal is a function here less of a specific individual than of time and mutability as such. Indeed, as Nina Auerbach persuasively argues, Brontë's "Gondal" can be seen as "an epic about mutability" in which time and change—in contrast to the dominant accents of nineteenth-century writing—are not shunned but are instead ambiguously embraced. For Auerbach, Brontë's Gondalian poetry rejects any Wordsworthian affirmation of constancy— for example, Wordsworth's adherence to the self's "restoration through permanence of setting"—and instead offers "fluid dramatic utterances" that "embrace [the] fluctuation of scene, time, and being itself." Gondal's turbulence in terms of its political, personal, and natural land- scape, then, forms part of a sustained Brontëan poetic of alterability: "Gondal's land finds its being in its storm: changes—psychic, seasonal, and political—appear to rock its world forever." Furthermore, over this tumultuous world presides A.G.A. herself—whom Auerbach describes as a queen of mutability, a monarch who "embodies time and feeds on change," displaying a "commitment to mutability" that dissolves every bond and betrays every love (212, 214, 215, 217, 224, 226). A.G.A., then, is treacherous to the extent that she is mutable: and Gondal is a world of brutal conflicts, rivalries, and betrayals for the same reason.

Embedded in A.G.A.'s perfidy, however, is another Brontëan energy: that of emancipation. There is a sense in which A.G.A.'s cruel treacheries—and even the infanticidal desires of "Farewell to Alexandria" and "Geraldine"—embody a demonic yet anguished demand: a demand that the female self be free to shed the bonds or bounds that otherwise confine it, chaining it to man, maternity, nature, or fidelity. As a queen of betrayal, then, A.G.A. is at the same time a queen of female liberty, lording it over her world as an animate embodiment of female power. Thus, for Christine Gallant, Gondal's histories of "dominant and passionate women" elaborate "a mythic world emphatically excluding the real world known then by women"; but Gallant suggests, too, that Brontë's creation of the Gondalian world was in itself an act of rebellion through which Brontë "resisted the experience of the contemporary womanhood which others around her were obliged to undergo."[11]

Perhaps the most obvious index of confinement and containment in Gondal, however, is the frequency with which actual prisons or dungeons appear in the saga. Poems that take prisons as their literal scene include, for example, "Gleneden's Dream" (*CP*, 69–71), "Written in the Gaaldine Prison Caves to A.G.A." (*CP*, 121–23), "From a Dungeon Wall in the Southern College" (*CP*, 170–71), "M.A. Written on the Dungeon Wall—N.C." (*CP*, 175–76), and "Julian M. and A. G. Rochelle" (*CP*, 177–81; see chapters 3 and 5 for a discussion of this last poem). As Robin Grove remarks, Brontë's poems in general have "images of captivity [as] practically their identifying mark,"[12] and in this way they seem to be *written* from a vantage point of imprisonment. As Pykett argues, images of incarceration in Brontë are readable as a sign of her "frustration with the cultural limitations which constrained women," since "[a]lmost all of Emily Brontë's writings are centrally concerned with the transcending of these and other limitations, and with the dissolving of boundaries. Imprisonment and the yearning for release, restraint and freedom are key oppositions which provide a central dynamic of both her novel and poems" (20). This dynamic of incarceration and freedom in Brontë emerges with peculiar clarity in a stanza from "Gleneden's Dream," in which a captive Gondalian converses with a "watcher," interrogating him about the world beyond the dungeon. But the captive then reports,

> Watcher, in this lonely prison,
> Shut from joy and kindly air
> Heaven, descending in a vision
> Taught my soul to do and bear—
> (17–20)

Here, the glories of "vision" descend *because* of the speaker's imprisonment, while the bright prospect of "Gondal's liberty" (44) held out by the poem is conditioned by the incarceration under which Gleneden labors. To this extent, "prison" generates "vision" in the poem in the same way that Brontë's social and cultural confinement as a nineteenth-century female writer generates the kingdom of "Gondal" itself as an imperious and queenly realm of liberty, self-invention, and self-emancipation.

According to Auerbach, "prison is always prison [for Emily Brontë], because like the fixity of eternity it locks its inhabitant away from change" (227). Despite the suggestiveness of this reading, however, Auerbach ignores the ways in which Brontë's texts engender visions of change, mutability, and transformation *on the basis of* confinement, containment, and constraint. For Brontë, "prison" gives birth to "vision" because it is the role of "Imagination" ("To Imagination"; *CP,* 19–20) to "call a lovelier Life from Death" (28)—to visit the lonely prisoner as a "messenger of Hope" and to descend to the dungeon as a "transient voyager of heaven" (*CP,* 15, 57). Whether dissolved in mutability or chained in captivity, then, Brontë's Gondalian speakers restlessly look away from their "present entity" (*CP,* 7) to change—as though to embody in their own fluid stories the fractured epic of alteration of which they are a part.

Chapter Three

Anchors of Desire:
Poems, *Devoirs,* Drawings

"Looking for *What Is to Be*": The Poems

The first poem by Emily Brontë to appear in the 1846 volume *Poems by Currer, Ellis, and Acton Bell,* "Faith and Despondency" (*CP,* 3–5), is a dialogue on death and hope between a despondent father and a desiring daughter. Calling his daughter away from her books and "mateless play" (3), the father mourns the loss of "those that I have loved of old" (21). Quelling his own fears of death, he draws his daughter to him in "happy quiet on my breast" (13), as though to restore in this embrace the love that he has lost. After he has lamented the absence of those who he "shall greet . . . ne'er again" (24), his daughter speaks, but she answers her father with a rebuke. At first she says that in her "early infancy," when the father was "far beyond the sea" (25–26), she, too, was prey to the dread of death, but then she turns the tables on paternal despondency. She declares:

> But this world's life has much to dread,
> Not so, my Father, with the dead.
>
> Oh! not for them, should we despair,
> The grave is drear, but they are not there;
> Their dust is mingled with the sod,
> Their happy souls are gone to God!
> You told me this, and yet you sigh,
> And murmur that your friends must die.
> Ah! my dear father, tell me why?
> For, if your former words were true,
> How useless would such sorrow be . . .
>
> (36–46)

In one sense the daughter's response is an orthodox call to her father to
return to Christian "faith" and to embrace belief in an afterlife. But, at the
same time, the poem subtly undoes this conventional emphasis, exerting
a pressure on the Christian code that it seems to promote. The daughter's
rebuke throws the father's religious creed into self-contradiction: "You
taught me this," she says of her desire for heaven, "and yet you sigh," as
though the extent of the father's mourning plunged the idea of an afterlife into disarray and extinguished the promise of heaven. In this sense the
father's mourning introduces "despondency"—the irremediability of
loss—into the very heart of "faith" and undoes the certitude of Christian
immortality. According to this logic, to mourn is to lose the vision of
heaven. The daughter's response to this orthodox self-contradiction, however, is to banish despondency itself: to erase the very possibility of loss,
and to refuse to mourn. She says:

> But, I'll not fear, I will not weep
> For those whose bodies rest in sleep,—
> I know there is a blessed shore,
>   Opening its ports for me, and mine;
> And, gazing Time's wide waters o'er,
>   I weary for that land divine,
> Where we were born, where you and I
> Shall meet our Dearest, when we die;
> From suffering and corruption free,
> Restored into the Deity.
>
>   (53–62)

While the daughter's speech sustains the categories of orthodox faith,
it also impels them toward dissolution. In her rhapsody, the belief in an
afterlife is transmuted into an anxious *longing* for it; and doctrinal
abstraction is engulfed by the force of desire. "I weary for that land
divine," the daughter asserts; and to ache for heaven is, in this childhood
credo, to be commanded by affect rather than truth. Indeed, the wish
for death that the daughter's speech embraces subtly transgresses the
limits of Christian orthodoxy; the daughter defers to visionary anticipation rather than sanctioned doctrine. Her vision exceeds the Christian
catechism on life and death. The father, however, derives an appropriately orthodox message from his daughter's words:

Well hast thou spoken, sweet, trustful child!
And wiser than thy sire;
And worldly tempests, raging wild,
Shall strengthen thy desire—
Thy fervent hope, through storm and foam,
Through wind and ocean's roar,
To reach, at last, the eternal home,
The steadfast, changeless, shore!

(63–70)

Despite this concluding conventional sentiment, the father's reply acknowledges that the daughter speaks from "desire" rather than dogma. Thus, by the end of the poem, a subtle shift has occurred, whereby the discourse of paternal truth ("if your former words were *true* . . . ") has been displaced into a discourse of daughterly desire. In this sense the father's orthodox words—his paternal lessons on the faith of heaven—are returned to him reinvented, reconfigured, and reinterpreted; but now they have their origin in desire rather than doctrine. The "faith" of the poem's title is reinvented in the process, as well; it now suggests an imaginative rather than an orthodox creed. Heaven is recast in terms of visionary desire, not religious truth.

"Anticipation" (*CP,* 12–13), another poem from the 1846 volume, extrapolates this Brontëan credo of desire in terms that suggest a specifically feminist reshaping both of religious convention and of literary tradition. Once again, the poem is a dialogue between a despondent and a desiring speaker. The first speaker—who voices the opening two stanzas—addresses the second in a tone of bemusement, inquiring how it is that the second speaker can preserve youthful "happiness" and "glory" (2, 5) in the face of the disillusionments of age and experience, and in the face of the loss of "youth's delight" (9) in others. The second voice answers with a lesson in desire:

Because, I hoped while they enjoyed,
And, by fulfilment, hope destroyed;
As children hope, with trustful breast,
I waited bliss—and cherished rest.
A thoughtful spirit taught me, soon,

That we must long till life be done;
That every phase of earthly joy
Must always fade, and always cloy . . .

(19–26)

Remarkably, the second speaker generates a creed of bliss on the basis
of nonfulfillment and nonsatisfaction: because she "hoped" and did not
enjoy, she insists, she saved the vision of fulfillment from destruction by
experience. Beyond any imperative of fulfillment, the speaker's hope
exceeds all given bounds, and the self is constructed as a subject of desire
whose bliss inheres in an ecstasy of deferral, in a sublime of incomple-
tion. Hoping "[a]s children hope," the speaker echoes the daughter of
"Faith and Despondency"; but now the dynamics of desire construct a
female subject who refuses the allurements of the world with all the
force of affective rebellion. Speaking of the world's disappointments, the
speaker says:

This I foresaw—and would not chase
    The fleeting treacheries;
But, with firm foot and tranquil face,
Held backward from that tempting race,
Gazed o'er the sands the waves efface,
    To the enduring seas—
There cast my anchor of desire
Deep in unknown eternity;
Nor ever let my spirit tire,
With looking for *what is to be*!

(27–36)

In "Anticipation" the subject of desire is constructed as radically *other*
in relation to any possible realization of its hopes, for it utterly transgresses the accommodations and fulfillments that the world can offer.
The self's desire remains restless, unappeased, unassuaged; retreating
from the world, it comports itself in a radical elsewhere. As recent feminist critics have noted, this Brontëan resistance to the given world does
not amount simply to a metaphysical gesture. It is also a chafing at the
confines of Victorian womanhood and is readable as a symbolic rejection

of the restrictions imposed on Victorian femininity. Commenting, for example, on C. Day Lewis's baffled question in a 1957 lecture, "[W]hy . . . all this beating of wings? What was this cage, invisible to us, which she felt herself to be confined in?"[1] Lyn Pykett concludes:

> Throughout her poetry, through the dramatic personae of the Gondal poems, or through the lyric "I" of the non-Gondal verse, Emily Brontë constantly articulates a sense of constraint, limitation, and restriction. . . . [This provides] an impetus for an intense focus on the inner life, and in particular for an exploration of those inner resources of vision and imagination which might be a means of rising above the external limitations of the female condition. . . . [The poems] consistently articulate those fears, frustrations and sense of weakness which the poet felt to be peculiarly her own, but which our hindsight might see as being more widely shared by nineteenth-century women. (69–70)[2]

In this context, the radical excessiveness of Brontëan desire or "anticipation" can be read as a refusal of Victorian femininity itself: a political repudiation of the constraints—and, indeed, "treacherous" fulfillments—that governed nineteenth-century womanhood.

Stevie Davies notes that the speaker of "Anticipation," casting her "anchor of desire / Deep in unknown eternity," ties herself to an "an element that is without stability or measurement" (1983, 84); indeed, the self in the poem embraces an ethic of unrealization, repudiating confinement in the name of possibility. The speaker is constituted in and as a gesture of excess, a radical movement *beyond.* The identity of the desiring self dissolves in a turn toward alterity, toward the otherness in and of the self. Tirelessly "looking for *what is to be,*" the subject refuses that which *is*—the given or constituted world—and plunges into possibility: a possibility that is realizable, however, only through endlessly exceeding all possible realization. The self sustains itself in nonsatisfaction, and desire maintains itself through the deferral of its dreams. The Brontëan subject exceeds limitation by refusing to be satisfied.

The sublime of female desire in "Anticipation" contrasts revealingly with the expansive—or, in Keats's words, "egotistical"[3]—sublime of the imagination that rises up in Wordsworth's well-known Simplon Pass episode from book 6 of *The Prelude* (1850). Wordsworth's sublime resides in a moment of self-recognition in which the subject meteorically realizes the "glory" (6.600) of its own soul, and in which the "Imagination" (6.593) of the self transcends the dictates of "sense" (6.601). Born in a moment of disappointed expectation—Wordsworth and his walking companion have "*crossed the Alps*" (6.592) unknowingly and have thus missed the sublime moment that they were anticipating—the power of the "Imagination" rises up to relocate the subject's sublimity not in fulfillment but in desire:

> Imagination—here the Power so called
> Through sad incompetence of human speech—
> That awful Power rose from the Mind's abyss
> Like an unfathered vapour that enwraps
> At once some lonely Traveller. I was lost,
> Halted without an effort to break through;
> But to my conscious soul I now can say,
> "I recognize thy glory"; in such strength
> Of usurpation, when the light of sense
> Goes out, but with a flash that has revealed
> The invisible world, doth Greatness make abode,
> There harbours, whether we be young or old;
> Our destiny, our being's heart and home,
> Is with infinitude, and only there;
> With hope it is, hope that can never die,
> Effort, and expectation, and desire,
> And something evermore about to be.
>   (6:593–609)

Though the subject is constituted here on the basis of desire and possibility—of the "something evermore about to be"—this Wordsworthian sublime remains one of narcissistic self-recognition and self-aggrandizement. The desiring self in Wordsworth, that is to say, comes into its own in a sublime moment in which it imperiously claims its kinship with infinitude: "But to my conscious soul I now can say, / 'I recognise thy glory.' " In Brontë's "Anticipation," however, the subject of desire fails to return masterfully to itself in this way. Instead of staging its own narcissistic splendor, the self pursues a perilous discipline of alterity. In Brontë's poem, the speaker addresses "anticipation" as a power that comes from *elsewhere*, from the other. That is, anticipation in

Brontë is not a power that belongs securely to the self—as it does in Wordsworth—or that can be commandingly "recognized" as the self's glory. Instead, Brontë's speaker addresses "anticipation" in a supplication, and Wordsworth's hymn to the self is displaced into a secular orison to the beyond:

> "Glad comforter! will I not brave,
> Unawed, the darkness of the grave?
> Nay, smile to hear Death's billows rave—
> Sustained, my guide, by thee?
> The more unjust seems present fate,
> The more my spirit swells elate,
> Strong, in thy strength, to anticipate,
> Rewarding destiny!"
>
> (45–52)

A suppliant rather than a celebrant, the self here implores its "comforter" to sustain it in the face of its own irremediable defeat. Indeed, the self's victory *inheres* in its ruin, for its elation is founded on its abjection: "The more unjust seems present fate, / The more my spirit swells elate." In this way, the Brontëan subject constitutes itself on the basis of unknown "anticipation" rather than present *realization*; and Wordsworthian narcissistic glory transmutes into the restless sublime of a Brontëan female self whose "destiny" resides in the realm of the possible, not the actual.

Margaret Homans argues that Brontë's poetic invocations to visionary glory often figure that beatitude as the numinous power of a spiritual visitant: a sublime visitant who, gendered as masculine, "bring[s] visionary experience to her" (1980, 104). Homans contends that, in these scenes of invocation, the submission of the Brontëan self to a masculine muse or visitant betokens her alienating subjection as a woman poet to the power of the male literary tradition, specifically that of male Romanticism; for poetic power, in such gestures, is located outside the female self, not in it. It is as though, in those scenes, the Wordsworth of book 6 of *The Prelude* silently visited Brontë and tantalizingly held out to her the nimbus of Romantic visionary power. Homans writes: "The visionary visitant of [Brontë's] poems takes many forms, but he is always masculine, and he is threatening as well as inspiring, dangerous as well as beloved. He is threatening more because, being external, he can withdraw her poetic powers at will than because of any dangerous content in the visions he brings" (1980, 110). Insofar as this leads to a situation in which the Brontëan speaker becomes uncertain of her own utterance, Homans observes that the "poet's fear that she neither originates nor controls her own speech . . . arises from her being a woman writing in a masculine tradition" (1980, 128). For Homans, then, Brontë as poet is burdened by the weight of a poetic tradition that identifies powerful lyric utterance overwhelmingly with male subjectivity.

In contrast to Homans, one can argue that Brontë's lyric uncertainties are less a mode of subjection than of evasion. For, although Brontë's poetic reveries fall short of Wordsworthian self-certainty, they project a desiring subjectivity that transgresses the limits of Victorian femininity and that embraces oceanic possibility in the name of an emancipatory (and implicitly feminist) promise: "[I g]azed o'er the sands the waves efface, / To the enduring seas— / There cast my anchor of desire / Deep in unknown eternity." The Brontëan self, in this sense, eludes the world of the existent (and, indeed, its own existent being) in order to find its home in the other, in "anticipation."

But if "Anticipation" houses the female self in the beyond, it also makes that self an exile in the world. Two poems that meditate on the burden and benediction of this exile are "The Night-Wind" (*CP,* 126–27) and "Shall Earth no more inspire thee" (*CP,* 130). Homans persuasively argues that both poems, which are acts of resistance, are allegories of Brontë's struggle against the patriarchal dimensions of Romantic nature poetry. Homans contends that, in male Romanticism, woman is typically fused with nature and that this identification robs her of poetic utterance, as femininity merges with nature in the speechlessness of a being prior to language (1980, 124–29). Woman is thus placed in the position of a silent object rather than a speaking subject. Both "The Night-Wind" and "Shall Earth no more inspire thee," concludes Homans, are invitations by a patriarchal voice to a solitary female listener to merge with nature; yet this mergence ends in the death of female speech, the collapse of the woman's "linguistic powers," and her decline into silence (1980, 125, 127). In "The Night-Wind," for example, the speaking wind solicits the poet's love and strives to end her solitary "musing" (5) by drawing her into the "dark . . . woods" (12)— where, presumably, reflection will dissolve into sensation, and thinking will deliquesce into feeling:

> The Wanderer would not leave me
> Its kiss grew warmer still—
> "O come," it sighed so sweetly
> "I'll win thee 'gainst thy will—"
>   (25–28)

The suggestion of seduction and rape here eroticizes the female poet's powerlessness and aligns the force of nature with the power of patriarchy in a baleful violation of female vision, a masculinist interdiction on female "musing." But the female subject of the poem resists this imposition. Similarly (though silently), the female subject addressed in "Shall Earth no more inspire thee" eludes the blandishments of nature. In this poem, the Earth petitions a "lonely dreamer" (2) to abandon the "useless roving" (7) of her mind and to "Return and dwell with me" (28):

> I know my mountain breezes
> Enchant and soothe thee still—
> I know my sunshine pleases
> Despite thy wayward will—
>   (9–12)

The speaking Earth aims to annul the dreamer's visionary aspirations, to still her "ever moving" mind by reincorporating her in the permanence of "Nature" (4–5). But if the changelessness of nature is a positive value for poets such as Wordsworth,[4] Nina Auerbach demonstrates that this immutability takes on a specific ideological meaning in Emily Brontë; while the "two great engines of eternity transmitted by Wordsworth and his acolytes [are] 'nature and the language of the sense,' " in Brontë these "gifts from the great patriarch of Rydal become . . . a poisoned fruit that strangles the soul it is supposed to feed, threatening with immutability the 'changeful dreams' of the multitudinous self" (220–21). Patriarchal permanence, in this sense, imprisons female changeability; and the treacherous consolations of nature threaten to stifle the transformative energies of the female self, immuring them in changelessness. To be exiled from nature constitutes, in this light, a perilous but precious freedom, and the self's enclosure within nature represents its death.

The speaker of "Shall Earth no more inspire thee" mounts an argument against mutability, recommending the surrender of female desire to stasis, and of visionary adventure to return. In poetic terms, "Earth" in the poem offers a deadly inspiration. Contradictorily, however, Earth *also* proffers a desired inspiration: in this poem, the self dreams silently of extinction as well as aspiration, as though Earth's invitation answered a longing in the self for its own demise. This aspect of the poem is extrapolated in another of Brontë's texts, "I see around me tombstones grey" (*CP*, 131–33). In this poem, the speaker is a dweller on the earth who refuses the spiritual consolations of the Christian afterlife. Remarkably, the poem outlines a contest between "Earth" and "Heaven" (25, 27) for possession of Earth's "children" (36), a conflict that is presented as a struggle between an earthly mother and a heavenly father (see Homans 1980, 149). Throughout the poem, Earth is identified as an agency of death; but this death is now figured as the home of the self, as the origin and end of the self's desire. Earth is depicted as a "mother" (29) who jealously guards the mortality of her children against the "dazzling" (35) claims of a spiritual—and paternal—Heaven. Consequently, in eager yet mortal embrace of the maternal body of Earth, the speaker asserts, "We would not leave our native home / For *any* world beyond the Tomb" (41–42). In this deadly conflation of womb and tomb as the self's "native home," the poem constructs Heaven itself as a place of exile, not Earth; in this way, the speaker anticipates Catherine Earnshaw's heretical dream in *Wuthering Heights,* that "heaven did not seem to be my home; and I broke my heart with weeping to come back to earth . . . " (*WH*, 80). The fusion of the speaker in "I see around me tombstones grey" with Earth is therefore a transgressive identification with the mortal "mother" against the immortal or heavenly Father. As such, it refuses to surrender the illicit maternal object to the paternal signifier of Heaven. The self's deadly mergence with Earth is, in this sense, an act of female resistance to the heavenly Father of orthodoxy, albeit a self-defeating and self-destroying one.

The speaker's resistance to heavenly orthodoxy receives a more troubled articulation in one of Brontë's most celebrated lyrics, "No coward soul is mine" (*CP*, 182). Throughout this poem, orthodoxy and its subversion coexist in heady and unstable conjunction. The poem begins:

> No coward soul is mine
> No trembler in the world's storm-troubled sphere
> I see Heaven's glories shine

And Faith shines equal arming me from Fear

> O God within my breast
> Almighty ever-present Deity
> Life, that in me has rest
> As I Undying Life, have power in thee . . .
>
> (1–8)

The poet's apostrophe to the "God within my breast" hovers between an address to a divinity beyond the self and to the divinity *of* the self: for the "God within" inhabits the breast both as an alien visitant and as the very being of the self. To this extent, the stanza hymns both the self's power and a Godhead transcending the self. In a radical sense, however, the language of the poem refuses to decide whether the "ever-present Deity" is to be lodged in the self or beyond it. The text perversely conflates categories that, from an orthodox perspective, should be rigorously distinguished. For example, in its lack of subordinating syntactical structures and hierarchizing punctuation, "O God within my breast / Almighty ever-present Deity" fuses "God" and "breast" together, so that, in a flicker of the syntax, it is possible to read the "Deity" of the second line as referring either to God or to the breast, or to both together. Similarly, in one sense, "Life, that in me has rest / As I Undying Life, have power in thee" hierarchizes the relationship between the individual "I" and the universal "Life," situating "rest" in the self and "power" beyond the self; but the syntactical fluidity of the lines fleetingly identifies the "I" *with* "Undying Life," mingling the two instead of separating them. In this sense the stanza dismantles the hierarchies that it seems to instate. The measure of this unsettling of hierarchies in the poem can be gauged by comparing the second stanza with the version that was finally published by Charlotte Brontë in 1850 (*CP,* 220–21)—and that was significantly revised by her—presumably with a view to making her sister's unorthodox language acceptable to the Victorian reading public:[5]

> O God within my breast,
> Almighty, ever-present Deity!
> Life—that in me has rest,
> As I—undying Life—have power in thee!
>
> (5–8)

In her revision, Charlotte rigorously reerects the hierarchies that Emily's stanza threatens to dissolve, dividing the self from the divine as surely as Emily's stanza undoes the difference between them. The conventional punctuation that Charlotte introduces conventionalizes the sense of the stanza, as well. The God of orthodoxy, the "Almighty" (the word now functions as a noun as well as an adjective, in contrast to Emily's version), is addressed as a power distinct from the self, while "Undying Life" is separated from "I" by means of subordinating and hierarchizing dashes. If Emily's poem destabilizes orthodoxy, then Charlotte's 1850 version recuperates it, and what Lawrence J. Starzyk calls the earlier poem's drive to "undifferentiated existence" is edited out.[6]

"No coward soul is mine" figures the "Undying Life" of the soul ambivalently; while the "I" in the poem is in one sense hailed as an undying life, in another it is lauded only in its annihilation. In this way, the Brontëan self becomes a site both of affirmation and of dissolution, of sovereignty and of disempowerment. This ambiguity is staged with striking power in another of Brontë's manuscript poems, "Aye there it is! It wakes tonight" (*CP*, 131). In this poem, the speaker addresses a silent, passive listener. Irene Tayler argues convincingly that the poem "describ[es] a death scene as a scene of visionary ecstasy," for the addressee exhibits all "the signs of death's approach—the altered cheek, the kindled gaze, the eager energy of a spirit being released from captivity."[7] The poem begins:

> Aye there it is! It wakes tonight
> Sweet thoughts that will not die
> And feeling's fires flash all as bright
> As in the years gone by!—
>
> And I can tell by thine altered cheek
> And by thy kindled gaze
> And by the words thou scarce dost speak,
> How wildly fancy plays—
>
> Yes I could swear that glorious wind
> Has swept the world aside
> Has dashed its memory from thy mind
> Like foam-bells from the tide—
>   (1–12)

The subject in this poem seems simultaneously to be approaching transfiguration and an ecstasy of annihilation, for the world is "swept . . .
aside" in an ambivalent gesture of transcendence and obliteration:

> And thou art now a spirit pouring
> Thy presence into all—
> The essence of the Tempest's roaring
> And of the Tempest's fall—
>
> A universal influence
> From Thine own influence free—
> A principle of life intense
> Lost to mortality—
>
> Thus truly when that breast is cold
> Thy prisoned soul shall rise
> The dungeon mingle with the mould—
> The captive with the skies—
>
> (13–24)

At the beginning of the poem, the "it" or wind waking "Sweet
thoughts" is both the force of nature and the force of spirit; the breath of
wind and the breath of mind. Throughout, the poem refuses to separate
subjectivity from nature, joining natural and spiritual inspiration
together in a paean to the indistinguishability of self and universe. But
the ambivalence of the poem depends on the meaning of this mergence.
In one sense the self's identity with the universe effects a transfiguring
fusion of subject and object in favor of the sovereignty of the self, as
though the poem sought to fulfill what Kathryn Burlinson calls "the
high romantic dream of obliterating the distinction between subject and
object."[8] But at the same time, the force of this Romantic mergence
annihilates the subject along with the object. In this sense Brontë's
poem dramatizes the ambivalent Romantic logic in which the self's
union with universal nature entails its own disappearance.[9] Thus, when
the subject in the poem becomes "a spirit pouring / [Its] presence into
all," that ecstatic outpouring can be read as either transcendence or deli-
quescence, a triumph or a death. The poem's subject, in this light, incorporates "all" within itself *and* dissolves into "all" in utter self-loss.

Similarly, the self's transmutation into "A universal influence / From Thine own influence free" is ambivalent, for the self might be freed "from" itself in that it loses its egocentric limitations, or freed "from" itself in the sense that it projects itself into infinity by means of its own power. Again, the sovereignty of the self is both affirmed and denied, and "Thine own influence" is at once injurious and efficacious to the self's boundlessness.

The division in the meaning of the self in "Aye there it is!" is repeated by the poem's critics. Tayler, for example, argues that the line "Lost to mortality"—describing the self's departure from mortal life—seems at first to be "applied to the departer," but that it in fact "points the other way" and suggests that "mortality is the loser" (44), not the self. Homans, by contrast, asserts that " 'Lost to mortality' suggests 'lost to life' as much as 'lost to death' " and that the poem's ecstatic contemplation of the self's mergence with "an intellectual breeze . . . promotes thoughts of death, not of power" (1980, 124, 129). This disagreement among Brontë scholars serves to underscore the uncertainty that powers Brontë's poem itself, for the lyric offers a contradictory vision in which the self simultaneously dreams of apotheosis and quietus.

In the final stanza, the "prisoned soul" is seen as rising up in freedom from mortality and from enchainment to the body. Chichester argues that in Brontë's poetry there is an equation of "death . . . with the female body" that presents femininity as the powerless prisoner of mortality and that sees the dying body of nature as fatally feminized (2). The imprisonment of femininity in bodiliness in Brontë involves her, as we have seen, in a struggle to transcend material limitations in the name of vision, a struggle that is readable as an unappeased feminist demand. Thus, Brontë's lyric passion, Chichester states, stems "less from sublime egotism and more from dissatisfaction with her 'present entity,' her material—and feminine—selfhood" (12). But insofar as this emancipation of the prisoned soul is a release from the female body itself, it is an escape that ends in death rather than fulfillment. The freedom that looses the self in this sense also loses it, and the transcendence of imprisoned identity spills over into the nonidentity of death. Consequently, although in the last stanza of "Aye there it is!" the chained soul "rises" from its material grave into the sky, its emancipation is a dissolution; and although the "dungeon" of the body mingles with the "mould" of the earth, the "captive" spirit is inseparable from wind and tempest. It is as though female being in Brontë was unable to find a place for itself aside from the rigors of incarceration or disintegration, and as though desiring Brontëan femininity found its language only in contradiction.

The conflictual composition of Brontëan selfhood is dramatized searchingly in a poem from the 1846 collection, "The Philosopher" (*CP,* 7–8). In this poem, a philosopher and a poet-seer debate the energies of vision, division, and death in the self. If the philosopher in the poem is gendered as "man" (27), the visionary poet-seer seems to speak from a position of desiring femininity; for this voice echoes the uncompromising desires of the daughter in "Faith and Despondency" and the main speaker in "Anticipation." That said, however, the two speakers are seen in the poem as aspects of one another, as conflicting possibilities of the self. As Isobel Armstrong states, "The Philosopher . . . is an aspect of the speaker's self, and the 'I' which resounds through the poem splits and fragments into separate experiences and definitions."[10] The unified lyric subject is, in this sense, fragmented into a dramatic and discontinuous play of voices. The poem starts with a rebuke spoken by the poet-seer to the philosopher, bidding him abandon his "Unenlightened" (3) musing and quoting back to him the "conclusion" (6) of his reflections:

> Oh, for the time when I shall sleep
> Without identity,
> And never care how rain may steep,
> Or snow may cover me!
> No promised heaven, these wild desires,
> Could all, or half fulfil;
> No threatened hell, with quenchless fires,
> Subdue this quenchless will!
>
> (7–14)

The philosopher is divided between celebrating his "wild desires"— fierce and unquenchable as they are—and dreaming of the extinction of desire in a sleep "Without identity," in the quiescence of death. Insofar as the philosopher's desires are unfulfillable, they are not confined to the categories of orthodoxy, whether the prospect of heaven or the threat of hell. The philosopher's desire cannot find a home in this world or the next and instead longs for its own death. This aching wish for loss of identity is expressed as a longing to "forget" (21) the self's contradictions and to banish "war" (18) from the self:

"So said I, and still say the same;
    Still, to my death, will say—
Three gods, within this little frame,
    Are warring night and day;
Heaven could not hold them all, and yet
    They all are held in me;
And must be mine till I forget
    My present entity!
Oh, for the time, when in my breast
    Their struggles will be o'er!
Oh, for the day, when I shall rest,
    And never suffer more!"

                                    (15–26)

The "three gods" warring within the philosopher's "frame" unframe his being and constitute his identity on the basis of contradiction. As Joseph Bristow remarks, the " 'wild desires' . . . and 'quenchless fires' . . . that he continually suffers actually constitute who he is. Identity, in other words, is internally structured by these violent impulses."[11] To be without identity is, in this sense, to be without contradiction, to lose the internal dissension that forms and undoes the self in the turbulent drama of the Brontëan lyric subject. The identity of the "three gods" is, nonetheless, appropriately withheld in the poem, and both self and poem struggle unnervingly with metaphors and meanings in a "war" of lyric self-definition. Isobel Armstrong suggests that the philosopher, refusing heaven and defying hell, nevertheless remains committed to an "epistemology of opposition": to the austerity of a "universe founded on rigid categories of binary difference [that] constantly excludes the third term" (335). This excluded "third term," however, is invoked in the astonishing vision of the poet-seer staged in the third stanza:

I saw a spirit, standing, man,
    Where thou doth stand—an hour ago,
And round his feet three rivers ran,
    Of equal depth, and equal flow—
A golden stream—and one like blood;
    And one like sapphire seemed to be;

> But, where they joined their triple flood
> It tumbled in an inky sea.
> The spirit sent his dazzling gaze
> Down through that ocean's gloomy night
> Then, kindling all, with sudden blaze,
> The glad deep sparkled wide and bright—
> White as the sun, far, far more fair
> Than its divided sources were!
>
> (27–40)

For Armstrong, the poem at first brings " 'spirit' and 'man' into relationship but exclude[s] 'woman,' the unmentioned term of the poem"; but now it "offers a revelation of another universe, a world of 'three rivers' 'Of equal depth, and equal flow.' The rigid antitheses are broken." She continues: "The specific symbolism of these rivers, reaching back to *Revelation,* matters less, perhaps, than their triple nature, their capacity to include the third term. Gold, sapphire and blood could signify Father, Son and ungendered Holy Ghost, or spirit, matter and the human, or divine, satanic and human, or androgyne, male and female. What matters is that the violence of a universe constituted through rigid categories of difference, whether spiritual, moral or sexual, needs to be 'lost' " (I. Armstrong, 336). On this argument, to lose rigid differentiation and violent exclusion is to dissolve the subject's "present entity," not into nonentity but into a visionary confluence of opposing forces that transgresses the philosopher's orthodox commitment to dualism, to the terrible divisions of "heaven" and "hell." And for Armstrong, "woman" is the silent or third term in the poem that has the power to reinvent the philosopher's world, to exceed his bondage to binarism and generate a vision of relatedness rather than of "warring." At the same time, however, Brontë's poem, argues Armstrong, remains tied to the categories it strives to exceed, for "the powerful energies of Emily Brontë's poetry, which push the hymn-like form of her stanzas towards violence, tend to reaffirm terrible alternatives despite the move to the third term—heaven or hell, spirit or man, male or female, a gendered or an ungendered world" (I. Armstrong, 336).

To this extent, the poet-seer in the poem is implicated in the divisions—the "warring"—that the philosopher laments, and the two speakers remain aspects of one another. The poet-seer, indeed, seems to "hold" contradiction within the self in the same way that the philosopher does.

The difference is that while the philosopher rejects conflict in the name of "rest," the seer includes contradiction in a vision of ambiguity. For the seer presents a vision—"I saw a spirit . . . "—that both tumbles into an "inky sea" *and* brightens into a "sudden blaze," and that is simultaneously benighted and blessed. In this sense the vision of the seer is not identified with the spirit's—with unity—but rather dramatizes a contrary vision that maintains the heterogeneity of the lyric self, incorporating both inkiness and whiteness.[12] As such, the poem restates the contradiction between division and unity that the philosopher laments. But the seer affirms the heterogeneity—or, in Armstrong's terms, the inclusiveness— that the philosopher bemoans. Insofar as the Brontëan subject is one of dramatic fragmentation rather than lyric unity, it transgresses identity in the name of multiplicity; and the "I" becomes a theater of possibilities that fractures the philosopher's (male) dream of "one repose!" (56)

"Plead for Me" (*CP,* 22–23) is a poem that similarly fragments the self in an unstable lyric drama. As the final stanza reveals, the poem is an extended address to a mysterious "God of visions" (39), to the power of Brontëan imagination itself. Throughout the poem, the Brontëan self is literally on trial; as Tayler notes, the poem is set in "a kind of celestial courtroom" (49) in which the speaker calls on her God of visions to "plead" for her against the accusations of "Stern Reason" (6), who charges her with abandoning the world in favor of an illicit deity. From the beginning, the poem's speaker is presented as a theater of struggle:

> Oh, thy bright eyes must answer now,
> When Reason, with a scornful brow,
> Is mocking at my overthrow!
> Oh, thy sweet tongue must plead for me
> And tell, why I have chosen thee!
>
> (1–5)

The self in this poem is scattered across multiple and incompatible speaking positions: "thy" eyes (the God's), "Reason's" brow, and the overthrow of "me" all shatter the self into a play of shifting identifications, and the self becomes an unstable composition of roles rather than a realized identity.

If Reason mocks at the self's "overthrow," the speaker's "advocate" (8) in the poem—her "radiant angel" (9) of vision—is called on to defend her against that impeachment and to affirm the self's visionary vocation in the face of its indictment under the law of reason. Strikingly, the Brontëan poetic self is therefore figured as a law-breaker. As a subject of transgression and illegality, the poem's speaker—like the main speaker in "Anticipation"—refuses the rules of the world, spurning the "common paths that others run," "wealth and power," "glory's wreath," and "pleasure's flower" (12–14). In a turn toward visionary otherness, the speaker embraces a God of her own making, exceeding the comportments of reality:

> So, with a ready heart I swore
> To seek their altar-stone no more;
> And gave my spirit to adore
> Thee, ever-present, phantom thing;
> My slave, my comrade, and my king . . .
>   (21–25)

As an elusive shade, the "phantom thing" adored by the speaker can barely be placed by her—and even less by the court of "Reason"—for this restless spirit acts as a figure for the transgressiveness of the Brontëan self as such: for its undoing of orthodox identities and sanctioned selfhoods. Neither a subject of Reason nor of the "world" (10), the speaker echoes the rebellious and demonic resolve of Milton's Satan in *Paradise Lost,* who, defying the rational regime of heaven, determines to govern a world elsewhere and to make of the mind "its own place" (*Paradise Lost,* 1667, 1.254). But in Brontë's poem, the visionary kingdom that the self institutes against Reason's law is in a state of perpetual revolution or crisis; in it, power is dispersed and diffused, rather than centered. The Brontëan self becomes a moving arena of desire, power, and overthrow, and it internalizes, within the narrow space of the lyric, in Homans's valuable phrase, the "mobile adoption of fictive roles" that marks Brontë's early literary ventures before the invention of the Gondal narrative (1980, 109). Simultaneously characterized as a "slave," "comrade," and "king," the speaker's visionary God is a fluid persona that tropes the self in a changing political drama. The poem depicts its blessed phantom as

> A slave, because I rule thee still;
> Incline thee to my changeful will,

And make thy influence good or ill:
A comrade, for by day and night
Thou art my intimate delight,—

My darling pain that wounds and sears
And wrings a blessing out from tears
By deadening me to earthly cares;
And yet, a king, though Prudence well
Have taught thy subject to rebel.
                                             (26–35)

The kingdom of the self here is as "changeful" as the "will" by which it whimsically governs its visionary God; and the drama of these internal players both invests and divests the subject of sovereignty. As a figure of the self's shifting incarnations—the form of its alterable existence—the poem's "phantom thing" phantomizes the subject, too, and constructs it as a fugitive from symbolic fixity. Refusing the law of unchanging identity (and the stern demands of "Reason" that she conform to the world), the speaker pursues a "strange road" (13) that renders her an outcast and rebel in relation to the dominant idioms of her world. Like the desiring self in "Anticipation," the speaker exceeds any sanctioned form of identity; she is constituted as a subject of excess in a painful play of possibilities—a "darling pain that wounds and sears"—and is arraigned in a court of law that pits her against both the world and her own rational or social self (she dubs her dangerous God "a king, though Prudence well / Have taught thy subject to rebel"). The speaker's "advocate," in this sense, argues for the "changefulness" of the self, for the self as a site of struggle and transformation. To this extent, to explain "why I have chosen thee" is to explain the self's identification with alteration—with a "God of visions" whose mutability (as in the Gondal poems) is the ground of the self's freedom. Consequently, in order for Reason's accusations not to succeed in this poem, the speaker must be allowed her transgressive love: a love that undoes her even as it makes her what she is. If the speaker's advocate in the poem prevailed, the court of Reason would find itself in disarray, and the self would be conditioned by a law of alteration rather than of identity. It is not hard to see in this poetic logic the feminist demand that was implicit in "Anticipation"; for Brontë's poetry finds emancipation in the affirmation of mutability.

One of Brontë's most well known poems, "The Prisoner (A Fragment)" (*CP,* 14–16), dramatizes visionary changefulness in an explicitly political context.[13] If Reason in "Plead for Me" argues for the speaker's indictment and (one supposes) imprisonment, "The Prisoner" takes this logic one step further, presenting a female prisoner who is languishing in the "dungeon-crypts" (1) of two decidedly patriarchal jailors: a "bland and kind" master whose heart is "hardest flint" beneath his mellifluous manner (25–26), and a "rough and rude" warder whose being is the home of a pitiless "hidden ghost" (27–28). Both master and man here are figures from the world of eighteenth- and nineteenth-century gothic, a world in which grim patriarchal powers frequently incarcerate female victims.[14] However, "The Prisoner" works to unsettle the structures of power dramatized in its own narrative scene—despite the fact that, at the end of the poem, the woman remains imprisoned. The encounter between the two male jailors and the visionary woman in the poem disorients the jailors' world—disarming them of "power" (62) and leaving them silent and "unanswering" (61) in the face of her strange speech.

The poem begins with master and warder tramping idly through the dungeon-crypts in malicious mockery of their prisoners' plight. Then the master, who narrates the poem, encounters the imprisoned woman, and the strange meeting begins:

> Then, God forgive my youth; forgive my careless tongue;
> I scoffed, as chill chains on the damp flag-stones rung:
> "Confined in triple walls, art thou so much to fear,
> That we must bind thee down and clench thy fetters here?"
>
> (9–12)

The woman's reply to the master's question can be read as an extended explanation of why she might be "so much to fear," for her answer hymns the uncontainability of female vision. From her position of imprisonment she asserts her emancipation:

> The captive raised her hand and pressed it to her brow;
> "I have been struck," she said, "and I am suffering now;
> Yet these are little worth, your bolts and irons strong,
> And, were they forged in steel, they could not hold me long . . . "
>
> (17–20)

Insisting that her jailors' bolts of steel could not "hold" her any more
than do their bolts of iron, the prisoner envisions her dungeon as a scene
of liberty. While her jailors believe she is incarcerated, she reveals that
her cell is a place of visionary tryst:

> Still, let my tyrants know, I am not doomed to wear
> Year after year in gloom, and desolate despair;
> A messenger of Hope, comes every night to me,
> And offers for short life, eternal liberty.
>
> He comes with western winds, with evening's wandering airs,
> With that clear dusk of heaven that brings the thickest stars.
> Winds take a pensive tone, and starts a tender fire,
> And visions rise, and change, that kill me with desire.
>
> (33–40)

The dark prison house becomes a site of visionary ecstasy, and the
prisoner's "messenger of Hope," who is also a harbinger of death, brings
the prospect of "eternal liberty." However, the prisoner's freedom is
not realized in the form of any "present entity" but in desire. Indeed,
the captive's present entity is constituted (as in other Brontë poems) on
the basis of possibility and anticipation; her selfhood is formed by the
"desire" that courses through her, and her subjectivity is fashioned by
the "visions" that desire generates. The logic of this is that identity is
produced in an opening on to alterity, and selfhood in a movement
toward otherness; the "visions" that "rise, and change" in the visionary
self also "kill" that self in an annihilation of its present entity, plunging
it into death in a reinvention of being. The visionary woman is born in a
movement that destroys her, making her a subject of excess who transgresses her present being in a passage toward the "Invisible," the
"Unseen." The life and death of the visionary Brontëan self inheres in
the excessive, unimaginable leap of (and beyond) the "final bound":

> Then dawns the Invisible; the Unseen its truth reveals;
> My outward sense is gone, my inward essence feels:
> Its wings are almost free—its home, its harbour found,
> Measuring the gulf, it stoops, and dares the final bound.
>
> (49–52)

However, the visionary goes on to lament the return to the body:

Oh, dreadful is the check—intense the agony—
When the ear begins to hear, and the eye begins to see;
When the pulse begins to throb, the brain to think again,
The soul to feel the flesh, and the flesh to feel the chain.

(53–56)

This return shackles the self again to limitation, returning the soul to the body and the woman to the prison. In the context of Brontë's depiction of female desire, the prisoner's visions—her flouting of the bounds of bodiliness—can be understood as a dramatization and repudiation of enchained femininity. The poem's scene in this sense stands as a critique of the imprisonment of woman by patriarchy.

If in "The Prisoner" the visionary's ecstasy carries her beyond imprisonment, such transport is also the subject of "Stars" (*CP,* 5–6); but now the focus is explicitly on the disempowerment and exile of the female imagination. "Stars" presents a struggle between the powers of night and day, between the "stars" and the "sun" (1), with the stars gendered as female and the sun as male. The poem begins by lamenting the arrival of day because the light of the sun extinguishes that of the stars. Halfway through, the rising of the sun is depicted in phallically violent terms:

Blood-red, he rose, and, arrow-straight,
    His fierce beams struck my brow;
The soul of nature, sprang, elate,
    But *mine* sank sad and low!

(21–24)

Here, as elsewhere, an opposition opens up between nature and the visionary Brontëan self; while nature springs "elate" in response to the sun, Brontë's speaker rejects nature's kingdom. Instead of deferring to nature and her fierce masculine master, the speaker cherishes the nocturnal fulfillments of vision, bathing in the "cool radiance" (20) of the stars:

All through the night, your glorious eyes
    Were gazing down in mine,

And with a full heart's thankful sighs,
I blessed that watch divine.

I was at peace, and drank your beams
    As they were life to me;
And revelled in my changeful dreams,
    Like petrel on the sea.

Thought followed thought, star followed star,
    Through boundless regions, on;
While one sweet influence, near and far,
    Thrilled through, and proved us one!
                        (5–16)

In a rebel kingdom of nighttime dream, the "stars" fuse with the
speaker in the bonds of exile and become "one" with the Brontëan self in
an identification that dissolves the tyranny of the day in which a phallic
sun lords over nature. Stars and self merge into one another in nocturnal—and maternal—opposition to nature and her God. As Tayler notes,
the image of the speaker gazing up into the stars' eyes and "drinking"
their beams suggests "an infant nestled in her mother's arms" (34). The
relationship between stars and self is thus feminized, offering a fragile
female alternative to the patriarchal reign of the day. Rejecting any language of mastery, the poem does not draw a distinction between the
light of the stars and that of the self but joins their beams in a radical
reciprocity. Thus, "your glorious eyes / . . . gazing down in mine" suggests both the look of the stars and what appears "in" or to the eyes of
the speaker, and "that watch divine" is both the watch of the stars and
the watch of the self.
    This nocturnal-maternal reciprocity, however, is violated by the
dawning of the day; and the poem's feminized stellar sublime—founded
on mutuality—is usurped by a phallic, solar sublime of mastery. The sun
erases both the night and female vision with what Denis Donoghue calls
"the admonishing voice of daylight and law."[15] As Stevie Davies puts it,
the poem enacts "a rape, of night by day; stars by sun; female by male . . .
the creative 'feminine' world . . . by the masculine" (1983, 82). The sun
of patriarchy subjects all things to its rule. To the extent that Brontë's
poem presents its speaker's imagination as belonging to the night, then,

it dramatizes both the subversiveness and the disenfranchisment of female vision; while the speaker's "changeful dreams" revel in their freedom, their liberty is based on confinement. As day dawns, the many "stars" surrender to the masterful sun, and plurality is closed down by singleness. Once again, visionary Brontëan femininity finds itself in exile and in anticipation; separated from power, it transgresses the law of the day in a tremulous flight from the "blinding reign" (47) of the phallus. Evading patriarchal power and consigned to the night, "Stars" projects a fugitive feminist sublime whose life—finding its blessing in darkness—anticipates the death that, for Brontë, remains the "final bound" of the female self.

"Her Name Is Civilization": The Brussels *Devoirs*

If Brontë's poems construct a lyric self whose desires and dreams unsettle the limits of given being—plunging the self into boundless "anticipation"—her remarkable French essays, composed in Brussels during six months in 1842, similarly challenge the limits of Victorian culture. While the poems, albeit perilously, project their speakers beyond the bounds that confine them, the essays push the categories of Victorian culture into crisis and expose the fragile or contradictory nature of what "The Palace of Death" calls "Civilization."[16]

Brontë's 1842 essays, or *devoirs*—written as formal exercises in French composition for Charlotte and Emily's literature tutor in Brussels, Constantin Heger—are texts that strain against their own restricted idiom. Heger's practice with his more able pupils was to read to them a passage of French literature and, having discussed with them the virtues and faults of the piece, require them to write an essay based on their own reflections in a similar style. Emily's response to Heger's proposal of this exercise for herself and Charlotte was initially hostile, since she believed that it would destroy "all originality of thought and expression" (Gaskell, 231).[17] Although the plan went ahead, her surviving essays bear the traces of that resistance; even where they appear to take up conventional, dutiful, or moralizing positions, the essays put such attitudes under pressure and push orthodox ideas toward irony. In this sense the tone of Brontë's essays is remarkably unstable, and the texts seem to undo from within their own status as polite or moralizing discourses.

"L'Amour Filial" ("Filial Love," 5 August 1842), for example, is ostensibly a didactic piece on the virtue of children's love for their par-

ents. From the start, however, the shape of Brontë's argument raises as
many questions as it answers. The text begins:

> "Honour thy father and thy mother if thou wouldst live." It is by such a
> commandment that God gives us knowledge of the baseness of our race,
> of how it appears in His sight. To fulfill the gentlest, the holiest of all
> duties man must be threatened; it is through fear that the maniac must
> be forced to sanctify himself. In this commandment is hidden a more bit-
> ter reproach than any open accusation could contain, a charge against us
> of absolute blindness or of infernal ingratitude. (*BE*, 156)

Filial love—that love that should, by nature, "sanctify" those who feel
it—is enjoined on humankind through "fear": love your father and your
mother, God says, or you will die. Disturbingly, the love that *ought* to be
the most natural of feelings turns out to be an occasion for the most
unnatural of feelings: what the text calls "infernal ingratitude." The
problem this presents is that, although filial love is a "principle of
nature," that principle is everywhere transgressed. Therefore, the order
of nature as instituted by God begins to break down.

The essay goes on: "Parents love their children; this is a principle of
nature. The doe does not fear the dogs when her little one is in danger;
the bird dies on its nest. This instinct is a particle of the divine spirit we
share with every animal that exists. Has God not put a similar feeling
into the heart of the child? Truly there is something of the kind, yet still
the voice of thunder cries out, 'Honour your parents or you will die!' "
(*BE*, 156). At the level of orthodoxy, the reason for this situation is the
sinfulness of humankind (as the essay, indeed, goes on to argue); but the
force of Brontë's meditation lays bare the contradiction between the idea
that, on the one hand, nature is divinely governed and that, on the other,
a "moral chaos without light and without order" takes over when filial
ingratitude occurs (*BE*, 156). As Winifred Gérin notes, Brontë's thinking therefore draws attention not only to "sinful man's share in [the universe's] imperfections" but also expresses a "[d]iscontent with the way
the universe is run" (ultimately by God) (125). It is in this discontent
that the unorthodoxy of the essay lies.

Brontë's skepticism about the divine ordering of nature is extrapolated in what is perhaps the most remarkable of the Brussels *devoirs*, "Le
Papillon" ("The Butterfly," 11 August 1842). The essay begins with the
speaker wandering one summer evening "at the edge of a forest" in "one
of those moods that everyone falls into sometimes, when the world of

the imagination suffers a winter that blights its vegetation; when the light of life seems to go out and existence becomes a barren desert where we wander, exposed to all the tempests that blow under heaven, without hope of rest or shelter" (*BE,* 176). The summer scene loses all its beauty for the speaker in such a mood, and it appears instead as a scene of murder and rapine:

> [T]he sun was still shining high in the west and the air resounded with the songs of birds. All appeared happy, but for me, it was only an appearance. I sat at the foot of an old oak, among whose branches the nightingale had just begun its vespers. "Poor fool," I said to myself, "is it to guide the bullet to your breast or the child to your brood that you sing so loud and clear? Silence that untimely tune, perch yourself on your nest; tomorrow, perhaps, it will be empty." But why address myself to you alone? All creation is equally mad. Behold those flies playing above the brook; the swallows and fish diminish their number every minute. These will become, in their turn, the prey of some tyrant of the air or water; and man for his amusement or his needs will kill their murderers. Nature is an inexplicable problem; it exists on a principle of destruction. Every being must be the tireless instrument of death to others, or itself must cease to live, yet nonetheless we celebrate the day of our birth, and we praise God for having entered such a world. (*BE,* 176)

Brontë's speaker rejects the orthodox and Romantic creed that nature is benevolent, scorning the view that it is either providentially superintended or harmoniously designed. Instead, nature is a panorama of destruction. Stevie Davies notes that the "language of zoology came down to Emily Brontë impregnated with the language of natural theology, imbued with the idea of design, purpose and divine pattern" (1994, 107); but in "Le Papillon" Brontë explodes that providential principle and presents the Darwinian prospect of a nature ruled by rapacious conflict. Davies goes so far as to say that "[h]ad this essay been composed in English, it would certainly have stood as one of the classic texts in post-Romantic and post-humanist thinking about the dilemma of life on a violent planet" (1994, 106).

But if Brontë's text dissolves Romanticism's faith in nature's benignity and the glories of humankind—relegating humanity to the status of animality and even abolishing the distinction between the two—its relation to orthodoxy remains unstable. On the one hand, the text fumes against orthodoxy and speaks with a force that approaches blasphemy; but on the other, it curtails its own heretical energy by relativizing the bitter voice that damns the goodness of God and complains, "the universe appeared to me a vast machine constructed only to produce evil" (*BE*, 178). For the text attributes these views, as Davies puts it, to a "blighted mood" (1994, 107) and in fact energetically refutes them in the second part of the essay. Crushing a caterpillar underfoot as it destroys a newly opened flower, the speaker says:

> I had scarcely removed my foot from the poor insect when, like a censoring angel sent from heaven, there came fluttering through the trees a butterfly with large wings of lustrous gold and purple. It shone only a moment before my eyes; then, rising among the leaves, it vanished into the height of the azure vault. I was mute, but an inner voice said to me, "Let not the creature judge his Creator; here is a symbol of the world to come. As the ugly caterpillar is the origin of the splendid butterfly, so this globe is the embryo of a new heaven and a new earth whose poorest beauty will infinitely exceed your mortal imagination. And when you see the magnificent result of that which seems so base to you now, how you will scorn your blind presumption, in accusing Omniscience for not having made nature perish in her infancy." (*BE*, 178)

J. Hillis Miller notes that the "transformation of the caterpillar into a butterfly is a traditional symbol of resurrection, or of the liberation of the soul" (1963, 163); but although Brontë's text invokes this traditional symbol, it also puts its authority in question. If the heretical vision staged in the first half of the text is qualified as a "mood," the orthodox vision at the end of the essay is likewise part of an internal debate—"an inner voice said to me . . . " says the speaker—and, to this extent, the speaker's orthodox symbol belongs less to sacred tradition than to a play of the "imagination." The blighted "world of imagination" with which the essay begins is thus transformed into a blessed vision by the restoration of the self's imaginative power; but, as in her poetry, Brontë shifts the ground of hope from dogma to desire.

The contrary vision of "Le Papillon" suggests, in fact, that the opposing worlds of rapine and rapture *depend* on one another; just as the beauty of the butterfly is born from the corruption of the caterpillar, so the glorious "world to come" issues from the universe of death. The figure of metamorphosis from caterpillar to butterfly, then, hints that if the butterfly begins as a caterpillar, heaven has its origins in corruption, too. Yet heaven excludes the "inexplicable problem" of nature's rapacity from itself and discards nature in the name of its own transcendence: having been metamorphosed, heaven forgets nature as the butterfly forgets the caterpillar. To this extent, the orthodox vision of beatitude represses its own abject beginnings. Yet the subversive strategy of Brontë's text is to restore to view this orthodox repressed and to dramatize its continuing force. Thus, the Darwinian and providential visions of "Le Papillon" exist in unstable and warring conjunction.[18]

The force of the repressed is also the subject of "Le Chat" ("The Cat," 15 May 1842), but what is at stake now is the category of the "human." "Le Chat" is a ferociously ironic exercise in social and cultural critique. The speaker begins by declaring (with a "sincerity" that is indistinguishable from mockery): "I can say with sincerity that I like cats; also I can give very good reasons why those who despise them are wrong." The essay then goes on to insist that, contrary to conventional wisdom, it is not the "most wicked men" who most resemble cats but rather the generality of humankind. For although polite society deprecates cats— "despising" them for their self-seeking indifference to human master and animal prey alike—cats in fact hold up a truer image of humanity than any other creature. "A cat," says the speaker,

> is an animal who has more human feelings than almost any other being. . . . [T]he cat, although it differs in some physical points, is extremely like us in disposition.
> There may be people, in truth, who would say that this resemblance extends only to the most wicked men; that it is limited to their excessive hypocrisy, cruelty, and ingratitude. . . .
> I answer that if hypocrisy, cruelty, and ingratitude are exclusively the domain of the wicked, that class comprises everyone. Our education develops one of those qualities in great perfection; the others flourish without nurture, and far from condemning them, we regard all three with great complacency. (*BE,* 56)

The essay contends that, far from threatening or undermining society, the vicious qualities of the cat—its "hypocrisy, cruelty, and ingratitude"—are in fact human society's foundation:

> A cat, in its own interest, sometimes hides its misanthropy under the guise of amiable gentleness; instead of tearing what it desires from its master's hand, it approaches with a caressing air, rubs its pretty little head against him, and advances a paw whose touch is as soft as down. When it has gained its end, it resumes its character of Timon; and that artfulness in it is called hypocrisy. In ourselves, we give it another name, politeness, and he who did not use it to hide his real feelings would soon be driven from society. (*BE,* 56)

Hypocrisy is the basis of human society; but this hypocrisy is renamed "politeness" and becomes the founding falsehood that enables genteel or civilized society to function. This foundation is, however, repressed from sight. As in "Le Papillon," the strategy of Brontë's essay is to retrieve that repressed image and to confront polite or civilized society with what it wishes to forget. To this extent, the cat is the site of humanity's repressed. The symbol of what civilization wishes to banish from itself, the cat's qualities are in fact what allows civilization to function in the first place. "[H]e who did not use [hypocrisy/politeness] to hide his real feelings," the essay says, "would soon be driven from society."

"Le Chat" concludes with the vignette of a "delicate lady" (*BE,* 56) who, professing aversion to the hunt pursued by her husband, nevertheless embraces her child rapturously when he brings her "a beautiful butterfly crushed between his cruel little fingers." The speaker observes: "[A]t that moment, I really wanted to have a cat, with the tail of a half-devoured rat hanging from its mouth, to present as the image, the true copy, of your angel. You could not refuse to kiss him, and if he scratched us both in revenge, so much the better. Little boys are rather liable to acknowledge their friends' caresses in that way, and the resemblance would be more perfect" (*BE,* 58). In an ironic image, the lady kissing the cat with the rat's tail in its mouth presents a "true copy" of the lady embracing her child; and, confronting humanity with what it excludes, Brontë's text thus revisits on polite behavior the violence that underpins it. In this way, "Le Chat" critically discloses the barbarity that grounds civility itself.

Emily and Charlotte both penned essays in Brussels entitled "Le Palais de la Mort" ("The Palace of Death"; Charlotte's was written on 16 October and Emily's on 18 October 1842). Clearly working from the same model, the sisters followed their source quite closely; in each case the narrative presents an allegorical tableau in which Death seeks out a new minister to do her work, Old Age finding the task "too much to do" (*BE,* 224). Having rejected a series of arguments from rival claimants for the job—Rage and Vengeance, Envy and Treason, Famine and Pestilence, Sloth and Avarice, Ambition and Fanaticism (in this last case Charlotte chose War)—Death finally chooses Intemperance. But, although Emily was required by her source to elect Intemperance, the speech in which Intemperance presents her case shifts attention away from herself and toward "a friend," a figure whose baleful power, it seems, is the condition even of Intemperance's strength. Intemperance says to Death:

I arrive later than the others, but I know that my claim is certain. Some of my rivals are formidable, I admit, and I may perhaps be surpassed by several in striking deeds that draw the admiration of the mob, but I have a friend before whom this whole assembly will be forced to succumb. Her name is Civilization: in a few years she will come to dwell on this earth with us, and each century will amplify her power. In the end, she will divert Ambition from your service; she will put the brake of law on wrath; she will wrest the weapons from Fanaticism's hands; she will chase Famine off among the savages. I alone will grow and flourish under her reign; the power of all the others will expire with their partisans; mine will exist even when I am dead. If once I make acquaintance with the father, my influence will extend to the son, and before men unite to banish me from their society, I will have changed their entire nature and made the whole species an easier prey for your Majesty, so effectively, in fact, that Old Age will have almost a sinecure and your palace will be gorged with victims. (*BE,* 229–30)

"I alone will grow and flourish under her reign," Intemperance says of Civilization. If Civilization is Intemperance's "friend," she is also, it seems, her ruler—and Intemperance's service to Civilization earns her the right to become Death's "viceroy" (*BE,* 230). In nefarious complicity, Intemperance is shown to be Civilization's secret coworker; or, more abstractly, Intemperance is revealed as Civilization's silent logic. By conjuring a vision of Civilization as one of excess, exorbitance, and immoderacy, Brontë throws the category of Civilization into contradiction with itself, suggesting that it is not a power of enlightenment but of death, not of improvement but of barbarization. Like a rabid imperialist, Civilization grasps everything in its maw and subjects everything to itself; before it, every malign power will, says Intemperance, be "forced to succumb."

A gluttonous and engulfing tyrant, Civilization brooks no difference from itself and subdues all things to its influence. It is in this expansionism or excess that Brontë locates Civilization's "intemperance." Against its declared intentions, Civilization becomes immoderate in its drive for dominion. As Juliet Barker notes: "An apparent belief in the power of civilization to tame the savageries of mankind, which was not uncommon in the nineteenth century, is . . . given a cynical twist: Intemperance becomes the vice particularly associated with civilization, flourishing outside the state of nature, and it alone will continue to kill" (390). Pushed into self-contradiction by the irony of Brontë's text, Civilization becomes a despotic ruler whose project of colonization is underpinned by violence. For example, each aspect of Civilization's empire mentioned in Brontë's text is sustained by power. "[S]he will put the brake of law on wrath," Intemperance says of Civilization, suggesting the power of the law to incarcerate and subdue (as we saw in her poems, imprisonment is a key metaphor in Brontë for political subjection and disenfranchisement). The phrase "she will wrest the weapons from Fanaticism's hand" suggests not only reason's empire over religion but the suppression of dissent and difference by reason's law. In the next phrase, "she will chase Famine off among the savages," Civilization, in a colonial cameo, conquers hunger but also subdues the "savages," imperiously mastering the one along with the other. The force of Civilization is thus a force of dominion—outstripping the powers it conquers with its own intemperance. Furthermore, Civilization murders to secure its power, feeding "Death" with its victims. As in "Le Chat," Brontë's irony thus critiques the pious self-images of nineteenth-century culture, twisting them into self-contradiction and disclosing their dark underside.

Other of Brontë's Brussels essays, rather than being analytical, moralizing, or philosophical arguments, are dramatic vignettes of the self. One of these is the historical portrait "Portrait: Le Roi Harold avant la Bataille de Hastings" ("Portrait: King Harold on the Eve of the Battle of Hastings," June 1842), a meditation on the heroic self. As its title indicates, the essay depicts Harold on the night before Hastings, confronting the prospect of the following day's battle. The text muses on the difference between Harold's daily and heroic self, his commonplace and sublime being. Poised before Hastings, with the hostile fires of the enemy ranged below him, Harold is redefined—transfigured from ordinary to heroic selfhood. This transfiguration is an effect of his kingly isolation—of his transcendent separation, in this heroic moment, from the entanglements of political intrigue and courtly machination. After sketching the political world of flattery and self-interest from which Harold is now separated, Brontë writes:

> Harold, on the field of battle, without palace, without ministers, without courtiers, without pomp, without luxury, having only the sky of his country above him for a roof, and that land beneath his feet, which he holds from his ancestors, and which he will only abandon with his life; Harold, surrounded by that crowd of devoted hearts, the representatives of millions more, all entrusting to him their safety, their liberty, and their existence as a people—what a difference! As visible to men as to his Creator, the soul divine shines in his eyes; a multitude of human passions

awake there at the same time, but they are exalted, sanctified, almost deified. (*BE,* 102)

Brontë here defines Harold's heroic selfhood—"Harold . . . without"—as the denuding of his social being and its refinement into godlike singleness. Earlier, she says that "a sublime expression lit up his face" (*BE,* 100); this divinized selfhood is produced in large measure through Harold's radical separation from all surrounding circumstance—his transcendence of all contingency. To this extent, Brontë's portrait projects an idealized myth of the self, a self raised heroically above history into divinity and standing separate from the commonness of the world. This heroic self is, however, an embattled one, defined in and as a gesture of opposition, in and as a field of embattlement. In fact, in "King Harold" the self's endangering is double; on the one hand, Harold is threatened by the massed enemy, but on the other, he is threatened by domestic political intrigue. Indeed, the danger to Harold's heroic selfhood has more to do with familiar than with foreign forces. Brontë heroizes Harold in the following terms:

> At that moment, the spirit of Harold gathered within itself the energy, the power, and the hopes of the nation. Then, he was no more king; he was a hero. The situation had transformed him. For in peace he would doubtless have been, like almost all other princes seated on a tranquil throne, a nothing, a wretch entombed within his palace, sunk in pleasures, deceived by flatterers, knowing, provided he be not wholly imbecile, that of all his people he is the least free; that he is a creature who dares not act, who scarcely dares to think for itself. That all those who surround him try to entangle his soul in a labyrinth of follies and vices; that it is the universal interest to blind his eyes, so that his hand cannot move without being directed by a minister, and so that his body is a true prisoner, having his kingdom for prison and his subjects for guards. (*BE,* 101–2)

Remarkably, Harold the "king" here is Harold the prisoner; and it is only as military "hero"—free of palace, ministers, court, and comforts—that he acquires sublime selfhood, for the beguiling complacencies and compromises of domestic politics rob him of heroic self-definition. Stripped of autonomy, Harold is reduced to the puppet of a political world that denudes him of freedom. Acquiring heroic identity only through separation, his isolation is nevertheless a kind of exile, an ironic

banishment from kingly being—"he was no more a king." Although
Harold becomes the symbol of a newly heroized nation—his spirit
"gathering within itself" the hopes of his people—he is also divided
from the nation he symbolizes, refined into an isolation that makes his
final adversary neither his own "flatterers" nor the invading army, but
"Death" itself. The essay concludes: "He is inwardly convinced that a
mortal power will not fell him. The hand of Death, alone, can bear the
victory away from his arms, and Harold is ready to succumb before it,
because the touch of that hand is, to the hero, what the stroke that gave
him liberty was to the slave" (*BE,* 102).

If Harold's heroization, then, emancipates him from the commonplace world, his final emancipation—or transcendence—is achieved
only through death. In this way, Harold finds freedom in death just as
Brontë in her lyric poetry locates liberty beyond what she calls the "final
bound." Thus, the heroism of Harold becomes an idealized Brontëan
self-image: the depiction of a soul—facing fear—that is "no coward"
but that embraces death as a route to transcendence. As in the poetry,
however, the freeing of the self through death is an obliteration as well
as an emancipation of being; as a metaphor of release, death measures
both the self's glory and its powerlessness. On the eve of Hastings,
Harold is poised before defeat and death, and his heroic nature fulfills
itself, as in the poetry, in a sublime self-extinction. The heroic self in
Brontë thus becomes a fugitive from the world, realizing itself only in
annihilation.

Traces of Brontë's resistance to Heger's *devoirs* project in her essays
can be read in the mischievous irony of "King Harold." Stevie Davies
describes the essay as a "perverse, ironic and probably Francophobic
praise of King Harold before Hastings" (1994, 182), while Fannie
Ratchford makes the point that the two sisters—and "particularly
Emily"—"chose their subjects in line with strong English and Protestant prejudices, forced to the surface by life in a foreign and Catholic
school."[19] Other of Brontë's essays offer ironic barbs that seem directly
to satirize the patriarchal attitudes and teacherly imperiousness of
Heger himself. Sue Lonoff, for example, points out that in the two essays
entitled "Le Siège d'Oudenarde" ("The Siege of Oudenarde," [undated],
BE, 68–74), written by Charlotte and Emily, Charlotte "writes a
response sure to please [Heger]" (*BE,* lix), depicting the women of the
besieged city in a supportive role in relation to the men, while Emily
takes aim directly at the patriarchal disablement of women's power:
"Even the women, that class condemned by the laws of society to be a

heavy burden in any situation of action and danger, on that occasion cast aside their degrading privileges, and took a distinguished part in the work of defense" (*BE,* 68).

In one of the briefest *devoirs,* "Lettre [et] Réponse" ("Letter [and] Reply," 16 July 1842)—in which a music student invites her teacher to play at a soirée—Brontë ironizes the supposedly respectful relationship between a pupil and teacher by exploding the polite social formulas between them. Tersely, the pupil informs the teacher that she has been "directed to invite" her to the soirée and that a contribution to the "evening's amusements" is "expect[ed]" of her. The teacher begins her reply formally, but then turns savagely on the pupil after having informed her she is too busy to come:

> [W]hen I suffer a disappointment, I ordinarily seek some compensation in return; and at present, I console myself with the thought that if I am denied the opportunity to exhibit my small talent, at least, I will not undergo the mortification of witnessing the poor results of my work with you; because I have heard that you are to play a piece on this occasion, and forgive me if I advise you (out of pure friendship) to choose a time when everyone is occupied with something other than music, for I fear that your performance will be a little too remarkable.
>
> Still, I would not want to discourage you . . . (*BE,* 141–42)

The acerbity of the music teacher's reply is both impish and impassioned. Indeed, in an overdetermined way, the text's ironies seem obliquely to allude both to Brontë's position at the Pensionnat Heger and to Heger himself. Emily was herself a music teacher at the Pensionnat Heger (having been asked by the Hegers to instruct the younger girls in piano playing), and the evidence suggests that she complied with this request reluctantly (*BE,* 148)—perhaps even acerbically. Consequently, it seems that there is Brontëan irony *and* self-irony here. On another level, however, the portrait seems a barb directed at Heger himself, for in the spare exchange between exacting teacher and tight-lipped pupil, the text mischievously satirizes the position of the imperious tutor.

A further, more troubled trace of Brontëan resistance is readable in an extraordinary text penned on 26 July 1842, "Lettre: Ma chère Maman" ("Letter: My dear Mama"). The genesis of this piece was the bizarre instruction from Heger that Emily and Charlotte should compose a letter home to their absent "Maman," informing her of their welfare and their progress at school—even though, as Katherine Frank says, Heger "was fully aware that their mother had died while they were small children" (165). Even taking into account the "mirthless farcical-ity of [this] exercise" (Davies 1994, 182)—flooded as it is by irony— Brontë's text is a remarkable production. Despite the requirements of polite convention that daughterly affection should be expressed in such a letter, it amounts to a reproach to the missing mother for her silence, her distance, and her absence:

> My dear Mama,
> It seems to me a very long time since I have seen you, and a long time even, that I have not heard from you. If you were ill, they would have written me; I am not afraid of that, but I am afraid that you think less often of your daughter in her absence. Lately, I am saddened by very lit-tle things, and at this thought above all, I cannot help crying. They say that my health is frail; and they have made me keep to my room and give up my studies and my companions. It is perhaps for this reason that I am so sad, because it is very tiresome to be confined the whole day in a soli-tary chamber, where I have nothing to do, from morning until night, but to daydream and to listen, from time to time, to the joyous cries of the other children, who play, and laugh without thinking of me.
> I long to be at home, once again, and to see the house and the people that I love so much. At least if you could come here, I believe that your presence alone would cure me.
> Come then, dear Mama; and forgive this letter; it speaks only of me, but I myself would speak to you of many other things.
>   Your devoted daughter, (BE, 152)

Remarkably, Brontë's fictional letter reads as if it were a textual symptom: the symptom of an emotional and psychical malaise induced by the mother's absence. Her text simultaneously thematizes and symp-tomatizes the mother's loss. It is as though, despite Heger's injunction that the letter dedicate itself to the fiction of the mother's presence, "Ma chère Maman" perversely—even melancholically—commemorates her absence. Musing on the mother's distance, the writer of the letter depicts herself as melancholic ("I cannot help crying"), ill ("my health is frail"), solitary, even imprisoned ("they have made me keep to my room and give up my studies and my companions"). This pathological self-representation is on one level, of course, an ironic riposte to Heger; if Emily is supposed to write home and tell of how well she fares and how much she learns at school in Brussels, she in fact complains that she is sick, isolated, and confined. On another level, however, the text records a depressive speech that turns compulsively toward silence and seclusion; to this extent, it offers a speech of comfortless mourning in hopeless search of a maternal object. "I believe that your presence alone would cure me," the speaker says to her mother.

Beyond the frame of the letter's fiction, however, this daughterly act of mourning is impossible—the demand that "your presence" be restored would amount to a restoration of the dead, namely, Emily's mother, Maria Branwell, who was buried at Haworth in 1821, when Emily was three. In another fictional epistle written in Brussels, "Lettre: d'un frère à un frère" ("Letter: from one brother to another," 5 August 1842), a remorseful brother separated from his sibling through conflict writes, "A letter (received) from me will be for you as a letter received from the tomb" (*BE,* 168); but the situation in "Lettre: Ma chère Maman" reverses this, delivering an address *to* the tomb. Apostrophizing vacancy, "Ma chère Maman" situates its speaker as a daughter of the dead—for she calls up her mother melancholically as if dreaming of not addressing absence. Held by loss, however, the speaker's language remains a melancholic framing of the void. To this extent, the text prepares itself mournfully for its own silence, its own death. Margaret Homans reads the letter's fiction in the following suggestive terms: "If the girl is in quarantine, nineteenth-century experience and literary convention make it likely that she is dying; suppressing her reproaches against the mother, the girl instead identifies with her, with fatal results: the mother's abandonment will issue in the child's death" (1980, 150). To identify with the mother, then, is to identify with death and with loss; in this way, the letter echoes the self-destructive dynamics of Brontë's "I see around me tombstones grey," in which the speaker fatally fuses with a mortal and maternal nature in opposition to a spiritual and paternal heaven.

According to psychoanalysis, melancholy is a pathological form of mourning in which the self, instead of accepting the loss (or death) of a loved object, fuses or identifies with that object and, as a result, falls into silence, sadness, and death with the object. The melancholic self, in this sense, embraces within itself the fate that has befallen the object. According to Julia Kristeva, melancholics remain "painfully riveted" to the "object (the Thing) of their loss, which is just what they do not manage to lose";[20] instead, they live the object's death in the living grave of their own sadness. Kristeva, moreover—following Freud—sees in melancholy what she calls an "impossible mourning for the maternal object": a mourning for the first object (the mother's body) from which the child is irrevocably separated (1989, 9). As a cameo of maternal loss, Brontë's "Ma chère Maman," too, enacts a melancholic bonding to the dead mother, a bonding that glues the self to loss and renders it inexhaustibly sad ("I believe that your presence alone would cure me . . . ").

To the extent that it impels its speaker toward death, then, in a ruinous maternal identification, Brontë's text rejects the world, scorning both the protocols of filial relationship (it accuses instead of deferring to the mother) and the demands of public duty (it retreats from education into illness). Moreover, the letter resists Heger's teacherly injunction by presenting him not with a dutiful or conventional daughterly letter but with a stark figure of female melancholy. Remarkably, Heger's stringent corrections to Brontë's text culminate in an admonitory note at the end of the piece in which he takes up a reproving—and paternal—attitude to Brontë's lament for the mother: "Aucune marque de souvenir pr papa—*c'est une faute*. C. Heger" ("No token of remembrance for papa?—*that's a mistake*. C. Heger" [*BE*, 152–53]). Homans glosses this remark: "Himself a figure of paternal authority, Heger is the appropriate defender of deference to the father" (1980, 150). Brontë's text thus resists inscription in Constantin Heger's paternal and patriarchal world and, refusing assimilation, embraces a self-destructive logic of female exile, namely, the illness of melancholy. Like the poems, then, "Ma chère Maman" turns female subjectivity toward a radical beyond: a beyond that—whether signified by desire or illness—weds the self to liberty and to death.

"Powerfully Sketched": The Drawings

Together with the pen-and-ink sketches illustrating her diary papers of 1837, 1841, and 1845 (discussed in chapter 1), Brontë also produced graphic work throughout her life, ranging from copies of engravings to boldly executed drawings from "life." Of the 29 paintings and drawings that survive, more than half concern natural subjects—perhaps the most well known of these being the sketches and watercolors of the Brontë household animals.[21] Many of these pictures, however, were produced as formal exercises in composition, and, as Christine Alexander notes, they are thus "relatively public performances, monitored by teachers and admired by family." Nonetheless, as Alexander also notes, Brontë's "drawings and rough sketches are as fragmentary, and as elusive of interpretation, as her surviving poetry. They are inclined to raise more

questions than answers" (Alexander and Sellars, 100–101, 102). Like the "rudely yet powerfully sketched" figures of herself in the diary papers,[22] the most striking of the pictures engage the viewer by *not* giving themselves up to exhaustive interpretation; instead, they challenge the viewer's gaze by the very force of what they withhold.

A very early sketch from 1829, for example—*Mullioned Window*—is in one sense a standard compositional exercise (Alexander and Sellars, 370; see figure 3). As part of their training, young artists were required to master the elements of landscape at increasing levels of complexity—subjects for exercises included bridges, stiles, rocks, lintels, trees and towers—and Brontë's *Mullioned Window* belongs to this rudimentary training. But while tasks of this kind were frequently done by copying existing illustrations, Alexander argues that the execution of Brontë's sketch is

> individual enough (in the inaccuracies in lighting and perspective) to suggest that it may have been copied from life. Such stone mullions and lattice panes are still common throughout Yorkshire and beyond; and the broken pane would not be uncommon in a district of neglected farmhouses, dotted along the heights of the rolling moorland and deserted by their inhabitants for work in the factories in the valleys below. These are the same lattices found at the Heights in Emily's novel. They are the same lattices, easily broken by a terrified Lockwood as Catherine Earnshaws's ghastly little hand reaches in for refuge. . . . [W]e may never know the exact source of this picture. Like her enigmatic poems, which often defy definition of time or place, "Mullioned window" warns us from the start that it is impossible to be dogmatic about any of Emily Brontë's art works: all interpretation must to a large extent be suggestive. (Alexander and Sellars, 109)

But if this is the case, Brontë's picture is itself "suggestive"; while in or sense it offers itself passively to the viewer for inspection, in another disrupts the viewer's masterful gaze and resists even as it invites spectator's understanding. The central section of the window is brok if this means that a dimension of interiority is thereby opened up, it i interiority that nevertheless repels the eye's attempts to penetrate further. The broken area of window may be covered over with sla paper, but this covering is in turn broken by a ghostly hand that th through the pane—the shadowy suggestion of a face hanging b it.[23] Suddenly, then, in a moment of disturbance, the viewer's ʃ invaded by an alien presence, and a specter or apparition inhab

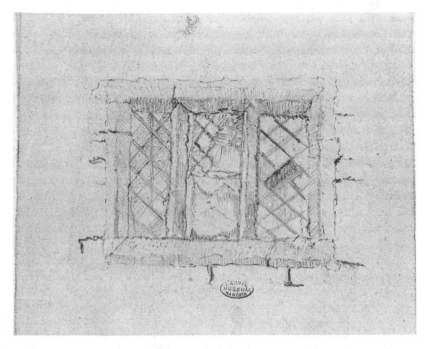

FIGURE 3. *Mullioned Window* (1829). Reprinted courtesy of The Brontë Society.

visual field that the gaze believed it commanded. As Alexander notes, Brontë's spectral window anticipates the nightmare experienced by Lockwood in chapter 3 of *Wuthering Heights*—in which his sleep at the Heights is invaded by the screaming ghost of the first Catherine thrusting her tiny hand through the windowpane (*WH*, 25–26). However, like Lockwood, it is impossible for the viewer of *Mullioned Window* to be sure exactly what it is that confronts him or her, for the ghostly or uncanny presence appearing in the frame of the picture disturbs all security, estranging the viewer's gaze from itself.

A different kind of disturbance is staged in a much later watercolor—probably executed in Brussels in 1842—titled by Brontë *The North Wind* (Alexander and Sellars, 386; see figure 4). As *Mullioned Window* foreshadows Lockwood's dream, *The North Wind* also anticipates *Wuthering Heights;* at the same time, it seems to echo the lyric and dramatic personae of the poems, as well. The painting shows a half-length female figure whose hair and cloak are blown powerfully to the left of the picture as she herself advances boldly to the right, the wind buffeting her

body. Her strong face and eyes are turned to the left, too, as if "her attention has suddenly been caught"; but her whole form plunges in the opposite direction as if "caught in flight" (Alexander and Sellars, 386). The image freezes for a moment an energy of escape; but the precipitate movement of the figure hurls it offstage and reminds the viewer that, notwithstanding this moment of arrest, the woman-in-flight is not to be contained. Like the speakers and visionaries of Brontë's poems, this figure seems to flee the world (Alexander and Sellars, 117). More than this, however, she rebuffs the wind in a reminder that the female self in Brontë is itself a site of struggle and contest, whether with internal or external powers. In *Villette* (1853), Charlotte Brontë speaks of the " 'wuther' of wind amongst trees."[24] Emily's *The North Wind*—again in anticipation of *Wuthering Heights*—is also an image of "wuthering": the wuthering of a female self shaken by the power of desire and deliverance. Alexander thus sees in the woman's "piercing gaze, translucent skin, and flowing dark hair" the fiercely desiring first Catherine of *Wuthering Heights,* while in the "liberating wind" that convulses her she sees an "embodied form" of the emancipatory energies dramatized in the poems (Alexander and Sellars, 116–17).

Another picture Brontë completed in Brussels in 1842 is the remarkable pencil drawing from life *Study of a Fir Tree* (Alexander, 387; see figure 5). Alexander notes that "[a]n examination of Charlotte's 'Landscape with fallen trees' . . . reveals that the two sisters sketched the same bedraggled fir tree from opposite sides" (Alexander and Sellars, 118; Charlotte's drawing is reproduced on p. 259), but she points out that aesthetically the two pictures are diametrically opposed. She writes:

> The remarkable thing about these two drawings is their difference in conception; Charlotte's conventional picturesque interpretation of the whole scene and Emily's dramatic foregrounding of the decayed tree itself clearly articulate their different attitudes to nature and art. Even when sketching from nature, Charlotte's view is seen to be dictated by a learnt way of "seeing": she has produced a "pretty" scene as if from a nineteenth-century Annual . . . Nature is framed, balanced and benign. In contrast, Emily's view of the scene is strikingly different. The tree predominates in all its decayed glory. . . . There is fluidity and movement in the whole scene, with the suggested swirl of the rocks in the foreground, the stark vertical tree trunk rising through the centre of the picture balanced by the horizontal fallen trunks behind, and the branches that reach diagonally across the page, stretching their limbs "as if craving alms of the sun." (Alexander and Sellars, 119)

FIGURE 4. *The North Wind* (1842). Reprinted from Winifred Gérin, *Emily Brontë*, Oxford University Press, 1971, by permission of Oxford University Press.

This drawing's depiction of ravaged nature recalls that other somber production of Brontë's stay in Brussels, "Le Papillon," with its grim vision of life "exist[ing] on a principle of destruction." Like the Darwinian cameo in the first half of that essay, *Study of a Fir Tree* envisions nature as a scene of dissolution, a panorama of decay. Nevertheless, if nature is a spectacle of death here, Brontë's tree rises with a sublime

FIGURE 5. *Study of a Fir Tree* (c. 1842). Reprinted courtesy of The Brontë Society.

grandeur that—like the disempowered and desiring speakers of the poems, or Harold poised perilously before Hastings—resides in its ruination.

Chapter Four

The Wuthering of
Wuthering Heights

"Wuthering Heights," explains Lockwood in the opening chapter of *Wuthering Heights*, "is the name of Mr Heathcliff's dwelling" (*WH*, 4). Although Lockwood is, as he tells us, seeking a spot far "removed from the stir of society" (*WH*, 3), Wuthering Heights seems altogether too far removed. The name of the house compounds geographical inaccessibility with linguistic unfamiliarity, and Lockwood has to explain the name—as if to counter the strangeness that it opens up:

> . . . "Wuthering" being a significant provincial adjective, descriptive of the atmospheric tumult to which [the house's] station is exposed in stormy weather. Pure, bracing ventilation they must have up there, at all times, indeed: one may guess the power of the north wind, blowing over the edge, by the excessive slant of a few stunted firs at the end of the house; and by a range of gaunt thorns all stretching their limbs one way, as if craving alms of the sun. Happily, the architect had foresight to build it strong: the narrow windows are deeply set in the wall, and the corners defended with large jutting stones. (*WH*, 4)

Wuthering Heights is a house under stress; its very stability is the result of a climatic "tumult," which means that its windows are sunk, desperately and defensively, deep into its walls, and its clean corners broken up by obtruding stones. But if the house is less slanted, stunted, and stretched than the firs and thorns that gather round it, its strange grotesqueries—disappearing windows, jutting walls—nevertheless betray the turbulence that conditions it. As a dwelling, Wuthering Heights is skewed by extremity; it is an architectural torsion wuthering between stability and instability, solidity and dissolution. The "height" of the house, moreover, itself suggests extremity, as if the house is located at the limits of the habitable—and as if, in these sublime extremes, the domestic is always about to pass into the "atmospheric," and Heathcliff's solid dwelling into an indeterminate "wuthering."

According to the Oxford English Dictionary, 2nd edition (Oxford: Clarendon Press, 1989), a "wuther" (a variant of Scots and dialect English "whither") can mean an "attack, onset; a smart blow, or stroke" (the house, in this sense, is constantly under attack from the outside); but it can also mean "to tremble, shake, quiver," so that "wuthering" names "a quivering movement" or "a tremble" that convulses from within rather than attacks from without. In this sense the house's wuthering is taken inside instead of remaining on the outside, and the Heights wuthers *internally:* the remorseless buffeting that threatens the house's exterior structure is found to condition its interior, as well. The house's wuthering itself "wuthers" between the internal and external, the domestic and the climatic. Thus, a little later in chapter 1, Lockwood suffers an "assault" from the interior of the house as he is rounded on by the house-dogs—being rescued from this "storm" only by Zillah the housekeeper, who is left "heaving like a sea after a high wind" from the disturbance (*WH*, 7).

If Wuthering Heights wuthers, then—and if the idea of wuthering destabilizes the distinction between interiority and exteriority—there can be no secure difference between the inside and outside of Heathcliff's dwelling. Instead, his house is a location of tumult, a site of simultaneous stability and storm as, in the logic of the wuther, the difference between interior and exterior, attack and convulsion, becomes indeterminate, and the within comes to share the properties of the without. Trembling between internality and externality, wuthering is in a certain sense a movement of *othering:* a passing of boundaries or limits that takes the outside in and the inside out, where the familiar is made strange (as the domestic interior Lockwood encounters is riven by the storms it should exclude) and the strange comes to inhabit the familiar. If wuthering is an othering, *Wuthering Heights,* as we will see, powerfully dramatizes the conflicts and dissensions that open up seeming stabilities to the wuther of the other and submits sexual, psychical, textual, and ideological identities to the tumult that constitutes them. As a wuthering text, *Wuthering Heights* itself wuthers the categories of the world that it enters—and disrupts symbolic quietude with the force of the excluded and the unassimilable.

Wuthering the World

Fittingly, when *Wuthering Heights* was first published in 1847, it raised a storm. What is striking about the responses of the first reviewers is that they themselves seem to have been *struck*—as though, stunned, they did not possess any terms within which they could accommodate or rationalize the strange force of the novel before them. As *Douglas Jerrold's Weekly Newspaper* remarked, *Wuthering Heights* "baffl[es] all regular criticism."[1] G. W. Peck in the *American Review* intoned:

> That the book is original all who have read it need not be told. It is *very* original. And this is the reason of its popularity. It comes upon a sated public [as] a new sensation. Nothing like it has ever been written before; it is to be hoped that in respect of its faults, for the sake of good manners, nothing will be hereafter. Let it stand by itself, a coarse, original, powerful book,—one that does not give us true characters, but horridly *striking* [emphasis added] and effective ones. (quoted in Allott 1974, 240–41)

"Struck" by the book, Peck is impacted by the force of the new—by the onset of something that for him is unprecedented in literary terms, something that ought to remain a striking novelty rather than establish a literary tradition or spawn a fictional brood. If *Wuthering Heights* has, for Peck, the power of the unprecedented and of "originality," it has so because it possesses the power to disturb and to antagonize the polite reader's constituted literary tastes, disrespecting his or her "good manners." *Wuthering Heights* invades the polite culture of its readers with a force of disturbance—in the book's own idiom, a force of "wuthering."

Two main lines of response characterized the initial reactions to the novel. On the one hand, the book was judged to be crude, rude, and excessive; on the other, it was seen as harboring a strange and unaccountable power. Thus, the reviewer in the *Literary World* saw *Wuthering Heights* as "a book that seizes upon us with an iron grasp, and makes us read its story of passions and wrongs whether we will or no. Fascinated by strange magic we read what we dislike, we become interested in characters which are most revolting to our feelings, and are made subject to the immense power, of the book,—a rough, shaggy, uncouth power. . . . [In] spite of the disgusting coarseness of much of the dialogue, and the improbabilities and incongruities of the plot, we are spell-bound, we cannot choose but read" (quoted in Allott 1974, 2:233–34). Intriguingly, the reviewer here refers implicitly to another dark Romantic tale of obsession, Coleridge's "The Rime of the Ancient Mariner" (1798), in which the Ancient Mariner delivers a tale of endless penance to an unwilling listener, a Wedding-Guest, who, held by the

Mariner's "skinny hand" (9), "cannot choose but hear" (18) his story. At the end of Coleridge's poem, the Wedding-Guest departs "like one that hath been stunned, / And is of sense forlorn" (622–23); similarly, the *Literary World*'s reviewer is grasped by *Wuthering Heights* as if by an "iron" hand, and is left "of sense forlorn." The "dark fascination" (Allott 1974, 2:234) of the novel, it seems, possesses and disorganizes the reader's good sense and good manners, rendering him helplessly "subject" to its baleful power and plunging him into an element of turbulence where the only response that can protect the integrity of bourgeois taste is that of "revulsion." And, indeed, a good deal of revulsion was expressed about *Wuthering Heights* when it first appeared. "We know nothing in the whole range of our fictitious literature which presents such shocking pictures of the worst forms of humanity," declared the *Atlas* (quoted in Allott 1974, 2:231). "We rise from the perusal of *Wuthering Heights* as if we had come fresh from a pest-house," said *Paterson's Magazine,* concluding: "Read *Jane Eyre* . . . but burn *Wuthering Heights.*"[2] And in 1851 the *Eclectic Review* roundly pronounced *Wuthering Heights* to be "one of the most repellent books we ever read" (quoted in Allott 1974, 2:296). If Brontë's text, then, raised a storm, it raised that storm in the polite cultural world of its Victorian readers—deranging the protocols or canons of middle-class literary taste. Possessing the uncanny power to fascinate and disturb, *Wuthering Heights* shook the securities of the cultural world into which it entered. To this extent the text, we might say, induced a wuthering in its readers: challenging, flouting, and disorganizing readerly expectations, it destabilized the constituted cultural horizons of its bourgeois readers.

It was the power of wuthering, or disturbance, embodied in *Wuthering Heights* that required Charlotte Brontë to defend her sister's novel from its critics when she wrote her "Biographical Notice of Ellis and Acton Bell" (*WH,* xxvi–xxxii) and "Editor's Preface" (*WH,* xxxiii–xxxvii) to accompany the republication of *Wuthering Heights* and of Anne's *Agnes Grey* in 1850. (Charlotte was, of course, also protecting and preserving the endangered memory of her sisters; both had died between 1847 and 1850.) In 1847 *Wuthering Heights* had provoked either polite opprobrium or the grudging acknowledgment of its power; but Charlotte wanted to make the novel positively and properly acceptable to the very readers who had before reviled it. "Critics," wrote Charlotte, "failed to do [*Wuthering Heights* and *Agnes Grey*] justice." Of the reception of *Wuthering Heights* she said:

Too often do reviewers remind us of the mob of Astrologers, Chaldeans, and Soothsayers gathered before the "writing on the wall," and unable to read the characters or make known the interpretation. We have a right to rejoice when a true seer comes at last . . . who can accurately read the "Mene, Mene, Tekel, Upharsin" of an original mind (however unripe, however inefficiently cultured and partially expanded that mind may be); and who can say with confidence, "This is the interpretation thereof." (*WH,* xxix–xxx)

As her comments suggest, Charlotte had indeed found—she believed—a "true seer" among the mob of reviewers, standing solitary and sage in the throng. The reviewer was Sydney Dobell, who wrote on *Wuthering Heights* in the *Palladium* in 1850. Dobell characterized Emily's novel in the following terms: "We look upon [*Wuthering Heights*] as the flight of an impatient fancy fluttering in the very exultation of its young wings; sometimes beating against its solitary bars, but turning, rather to exhaust, in a circumscribed space, the energy and agility which it may not yet spend in the heavens—a youthful story, written for oneself in solitude, and thrown aside till other successes recall the eyes to it in hope" (quoted in Allott 1974, 2:278).[3] Evidently, Dobell's florid remarks either confirmed or crystallized the position that Charlotte had already decided to take on her sister's novel in 1850; that is, that *Wuthering Heights* was the product of a "homebred country girl" (*WH,* xxxiv) who lacked either extensive experience or knowledge but who possessed what Dobell called a power of "unconscious art" (Allott 1974, 2:280) and, in Charlotte's words, "wrought with a rude chisel . . . from no model but the vision of [her] meditations" (*WH,* xxxvii). Charlotte's account of Emily presents her as an untutored rustic genius far removed from "what is called 'the world' " (*WH,* xxxiv): a cultural unsophisticate who, having fashioned her "moorish," "wild," and "knotty" novel, "did not know what she had done" (*WH,* xxxiv, xxxv). The effect of Charlotte's strategy was both to protect Emily from the censorious eye of the metropolitan literary culture ("the world") that had scorned her and, at the same time, to defer to the values of that world by depicting Emily as an unlettered moorland innocent who could not—and did not—know any better than to do as she had done. Emily's novel, then, says Charlotte, "must appear . . . rude and strange" to its polite metropolitan readers—as rude and strange, we might say, as the name "Wuthering Heights" itself appears to the sophisticated Lockwood in the novel. By insisting that *Wuthering Heights* belonged to a world far removed from, or "alien" and "unfamiliar" to its audience (*WH,* xxxiii),

Charlotte consigned her sister's work to cultural marginality, while at the same time insulating its readers from the novel's disturbing or "wuthering" effects—those effects that, as she put it in a letter, "shock more than they attract" (*BLFC,* 2:165; see chapter 6 for further discussion of Charlotte's strategy concerning the interpretation of her sister's novel).

But the "shock" or wuther of *Wuthering Heights* was in fact closer to the world of polite culture than Charlotte's repressive apologia for the novel would suggest. Indeed, the force with which *Wuthering Heights* was rejected by some reviewers can be seen as the very measure of its power to disturb. On the first publication of *Jane Eyre, Agnes Grey,* and *Wuthering Heights* (authored by the mysterious "Bell" brothers), many reviewers assumed that the Bells were not three, but in fact one. One such reader was the celebrated Elizabeth Rigby, or Lady Eastlake, writing in the Tory *Quarterly Review* in December 1848. In her essay, which concentrated on *Jane Eyre* and *Wuthering Heights,* Rigby showed no interest in possible or arguable distinctions between the works of the Bells. She instead lumped them all together as evidencing what she called "ignorance of the habits of [polite] society," "coarseness of taste," and a "heathenish doctrine of religion." The only significant difference between *Jane Eyre* and *Wuthering Heights,* she claimed, was that the latter should be singled out for "more individual reprobation," since the spectacle of "Catherine and Heathfield [*sic*]" together was "too odiously and abominably pagan to be palatable even to the most vitiated class of English readers" (Allott 1974, 2:111). Rigby's aristocratic, high Tory language—"habits of society, . . . coarseness, . . . heathenish, . . . vitiated class"—reveals an ideological reaction against the work of the "Bells" that has all the force of political panic. Bearing in mind that, for Rigby, the writings of all three Bells incarnated the same subversive spirit, it is worth citing at length her diatribe against *Jane Eyre:*

> There is throughout it a murmuring against the comforts of the rich and against the privations of the poor, which, as far as each individual is concerned, is a murmuring against God's appointment. . . . [T]here is that pervading tone of ungodly discontent which is at once the most prominent and the most subtle evil which the law and the pulpit, which all civilized society in fact has at the present to contend with. We do not hesitate to say that the tone of the mind and thought which has overthrown authority and violated every code human and divine abroad, and fostered Chartism and rebellion at home, is the same which has also written Jane Eyre. (quoted in Allott 1974, 2:109–10)

We might add for Rigby, it is the same which has also written *Wuthering Heights*.

Significantly, Rigby was under the impression (given her by the *Quarterly*'s editor, J. G. Lockhart) that the Bells were "brothers of the weaving order in some Lancashire town" (Shorter, 349). This would in part explain her willingness to see insurrection everywhere in the work of the "brothers." That said, it is not hard to see Rigby bristling at the transgressive or "pagan" drama of limitless desire enacted between Cathy and Heathcliff in the novel, or at the violently vengeful story of the vagabond Heathcliff unscrupulously seizing the property, privileges, and position that had been denied to him. Rigby might indeed see subversion here, might indeed blanch at the insurrectionary force embedded in such motifs; for if her fury at the Bells was, as she put it, at a spirit "overthrow[ing] authority and violat[ing] every code human and divine abroad" and "foster[ing] Chartism and rebellion at home," this revolutionary spirit was very materially convulsing or wuthering the world of Britain and Europe during the 1840s. In Britain, the 1840s (as Rigby indicates) saw the years of Chartist unrest and demonstrations, in which working-class men petitioned for political reform: they saw crippling misery and starvation among workers in the north of England, notably weavers dislodged by the mechanization of labor; and they saw mass working-class actions in the form of strikes, marches, and riots. In 1842, for example, the "Plug" strikers passed through Lancashire into Yorkshire and traversed Haworth on their way, while, during that summer and autumn, "[m]obs would assemble suddenly and descend upon the larger country houses and levy a toll of food and drink before the military could be summoned. That harvest time saw many a field unreaped on the Pennine slopes."[4] Abroad (the other focus of Rigby's fears), Europe was shaken by violent insurrection as the revolutions of 1848 broke out in rapid succession in France, Italy, Hungary, and southern Germany, prompted by economic depression, crop failures, and a veritable cauldron of frustrated political ambitions. Moreover, 1848 saw the publication of Karl Marx's and Friedrich Engels's *Communist Manifesto*—which famously began by announcing, "A spectre is haunting Europe—the spectre of Communism."[5] If Elizabeth Rigby trembled at the chill of that specter, it was a chill that she felt blowing through *Wuthering Heights,* too.

In this context, David Musselwhite rightly insists on the "revolutionary provenance" of Heathcliff in *Wuthering Heights:* for it is Heathcliff who (as we will see) is the key agent of wuthering in the structures of the novel's social world (1987, 105).[6] Heathcliff's origins, nonetheless, remain obscure. All we are told of his beginnings is that he is discovered "starving, and houseless, and as good as dumb in the streets of Liverpool" (*WH*, 37) by old Mr. Earnshaw and brought back to the Heights as a nameless foundling. But the mixture of specificity and obscurity with which Brontë surrounds Heathcliff's beginnings is, as Nancy Armstrong points out, crucial in determining his symbolic effectivity in the text. She writes:

> We should recall that *Wuthering Heights* was written against the background of swelling industrial centers and Chartist uprisings that had reached alarming proportions by the forties, as had the hoards of migrant workers who were newly arrived on the English social scene. . . . Simply by giving [Heathcliff's] character a particular point of origin in the slums of a major industrial city rather than leaving the matter open to more romantic possibilities, Brontë made her protagonist capable of acquiring whatever negative meaning adhered to such a potentially hostile social element.[7]

As a center of "potential" social and political disturbance, then, Heathcliff becomes a metaphor for the wuthering of the world of the 1840s.

However, as a revolutionary metaphor, Heathcliff's significance does not reside solely in his class beginnings; he is also of indeterminate racial origins. Winifred Gérin's account of Branwell Brontë's visit (like Mr. Earnshaw) to Liverpool in August 1845 is now famous. She writes:

> It was the time when the first shiploads of Irish immigrants were landing at Liverpool and dying in the cellars of the warehouses on the quays. Their images, and especially those of the children, were unforgettably depicted in the *Illustrated London News*—starving scarecrows with a few rags on them and an animal growth of black hair almost obscuring their features. The relevance of such features . . . cannot be overlooked in explaining Emily's choice of Liverpool for the scene of Mr Earnshaw's encounter with "the gipsy brat" Heathcliff, "dirty, ragged, black-haired," "as dark almost as though it came from the devil." It spoke "some gibberish that nobody could understand," as did the children of the famine who knew nothing but Erse. . . . [W]ho can say that [Heathcliff] was not first given a being and a body by Branwell's report of starving immigrant children in the Liverpool streets? (Gérin, 226)

Branwell's visit to Liverpool was on the eve of the great Irish potato famine of 1845 (the crop failed catastrophically in 1845 and again in

1846). But if, as Gérin contends, Branwell encountered impoverished Irish immigrants during that summer of 1845, it was during 1845 and 1846 (the time *Wuthering Heights* was being written) that Irishness was to become the very signifier of destitution and hunger for the Victorian reading public, since by 1847 some 300,000 victims of the famine had landed in Liverpool, and the newspapers of the day were filled with accounts of starving immigrants crowding the Liverpool docks, dying and leaving an orphaned population destitute of food and protection.[8]

For Terry Eagleton, indeed, Heathcliff should be read as "a fragment of the Famine." Eagleton argues that the "hunger in *Wuthering Heights* is *called* Heathcliff" (emphasis added), since Heathcliff's destitution, insurgency, and ferocious desire (or "hunger") may be understood as a buried political or revolutionary metaphor for a subjugated nation starving and aspiring on the doorstep of its colonial master (1996, 11). On this allegorical level, then, Heathcliff becomes the signifier of a political and colonial repressed and, insofar as *Wuthering Heights* is the tale of his implacable vengeance, of the revolutionary *return* of that repressed. Like an unappeased and unquiet specter, Heathcliff haunts *Wuthering Heights* with a famished and potentially insurrectionary desire, wuthering the world into which he enters. Yet it is crucial to remember, as noted previously, that Brontë's text maintains a scrupulous silence on the exact nature of Heathcliff's origins. Heathcliff's darkness of complexion is mentioned throughout the novel—as when he is introduced to the Heights (*WH*, 36–39)—and there is a sense in which, on top of his shadowy Irish lineage, his "gipsy" (*WH*, 94) swarthiness renders him exotic and demonizes him at the Heights and Grange on a broader colonial level, too. Old Mr. Linton, for example, refers to Heathcliff as "that strange acquisition my late neighbour made in his journey to Liverpool—a little Lascar, or an American or Spanish castaway" (*WH*, 50). But if Heathcliff's dusky face makes him racially ambiguous, so that— in Eagleton's words—he "may be a gypsy, or (like Bertha Mason in *Jane Eyre*) a Creole, or any kind of alien" (1996, 3), his phylogenetic indeterminacy renders him all the more powerful as a figure of *otherness* in general: of that which is excluded from the constituted structures of civility, ideology, and nationality in the novel, but which enters in irresistibly to disrupt the equanimity and self-identity of these categories. In this context, it is worth remembering that, aside from its significance as the gateway from Ireland into England, Liverpool was throughout the seventeenth and eighteenth centuries a major center of colonial trade, specifically of the British slave trade with Africa and North America.

Thus, when Nelly Dean asks, "Where did he come from, the little dark thing, harboured by a good man to his bane?" (*WH,* 327), we might wonder whether or not Heathcliff's prehistory or lineage (mediated by some unknown miscegenation) encrypts a history more brutal than even his subsequent treatment at the Heights: a history of enslavement unconsciously silenced by the text as its *own* colonial repressed, its own ideological condition of utterance.

If contemporary historical and ideological structures are wuthered in *Wuthering Heights,* the same can be said of the literary idioms invoked by the text. Generically, *Wuthering Heights* is a formal hybrid that refuses to settle into any single mode. For example, at the level of structural form, the text incorporates diary entries (Lockwood's), spoken narrative (Nelly's), and letters (such as Isabella's to Nelly after her marriage to Heathcliff). Within these forms, it invokes the generic accents of gothic romance, the folktale, the ghost story, and realistic fiction.[9] The formal hybridity of the text, however, is significant primarily for the way that it *relativizes* the various idioms on which it draws; in this sense no single genre or language in *Wuthering Heights* is capable of containing or symbolizing the turbulent energies that the text mobilizes. No "truth" of the text is attested to by any of the novel's speakers or styles—even though Nelly Dean's housekeeperly sobriety and Lockwood's penchant for romantic imaginings mean that the action is colored at times in certain ways. The fact that the novel marshals a plurality of perspectives, then, means that there is no single authoritative voice in the text that might command its meaning, truth, or significance: instead, the perilous work of interpretation is left to the reader. As author and storyteller, Emily Brontë eschews the role of omniscient narrator, declining to take up a position on the characters and events that she lays before the reader. If Brontë goes anywhere, in fact, she vanishes—as we saw earlier—into the figure of "Ellis Bell," himself a *fiction* who, like Lockwood and Nelly Dean in the novel, presents to the reader a speech that is to be judged rather than accepted as truth. "[T]here is no 'I' in *Wuthering Heights,*" wrote Virginia Woolf in 1916.[10] Although Woolf's primary meaning was that *Wuthering Heights* transcended particularity and individuality in its focus on the grandeur of the "human race" and the "eternal powers" (Woolf, 202), her general point was that there is an aesthetic of *impersonality* in Brontë's novel that divorces it from any creed of self-expression or self-revelation. *Wuthering Heights,* Woolf intimates, is a protomodernist work dissolving its author into a fiction that multiplies rather than unifies perspectives, and disperses rather than centralizes the

"I." Like the fictional personae of Gondal, then (see chapter 2), *Wuthering Heights* is a theater of Brontëan self-invention: a ventriloquy of voices calling up Lockwood, Nelly Dean, Catherine Earnshaw, Heathcliff, Isabella Linton, Catherine Linton, and Ellis Bell, but no "I."

For feminists, the formal dispersiveness of *Wuthering Heights* is—as if to confirm Woolf's "modernist" reading of the text—the novel's most significant strength. Patricia Yaeger, for example, argues that the novel as a genre is an emancipatory form for the nineteenth-century woman writer since it embraces discursive heterogeneity and polyphony in contrast to the single-voiced idiom of the lyric. Yaeger states:

> [T]he lyric poem, for all its gorgeous attentiveness to the painful desires and limits of a culturally constructed "I," also denies its female speaker . . . formal access to the shifting voices, the plural perspectives, the openness to dialogue among diverse points of view that are necessarily in debate with one another in the invention of a female tradition. . . . Thus in *Wuthering Heights,* Brontë's conversation with her culture is . . . projected into the voices of characters who are at war with one another. . . . As a place of dialogism, parody, and laughter, the novel admits a new intersection of body and text, provides another way to rupture the authoritative, the normative, the social. (195)

Allowing no position of dominance and no utterance of mastery, the multiple voices of the novel induce for Yaeger what, in Brontëan mode, we might call an emancipatory "wuthering" of social codes, symbolic positions, and literary styles. The novel thus becomes an arena of unstillable dissensions in which perspectives and meanings are continually interrogated and transformed, and in which a certain formal liberation or play becomes the very idiom of the text.

Margaret Homans, similarly, considers *Wuthering Heights* to be better fitted to feminist possibilities than is Brontë's poetry. What is significant, according to Homans, is the opportunity that the novel provides, in contrast to the poetry, for the wuthering, or dispersion, of gendered identities. For Homans, the "[l]oss of self" and "dispersal of identity" enacted in Cathy's and Heathcliff's relationship in the novel transforms the anxious self-divisions of the speakers in the poems into an effective celebration of self-loss. "[T]he diffuseness of *Wuthering Heights,*" she writes, "provides a successful answer to difficulties in the poems that arise from the poet's femininity. . . . There is no single self in the novel to compare with the poems' troubled selves. The only comparable figure is the surface of the entire text. If the novel's text is like a psyche, this psyche is so diffuse as to include, and therefore not be threatened by, its own potential destroyers" (1980, 129, 131). Like a plural and permeable psyche, then, the text becomes a site of multiple and mutable inscriptions of subjectivity, a scene of shifting positions that plunges identity into alterity and makes the self a dance of diffusion rather than a center of anxious utterance.

Brontë does "novelize" her Gondalian verse as well as her lyric poetry, as shown in chapter 3;[11] and to this extent Brontë's writing mounts a general dispersion of the self. But in *Wuthering Heights* the wuthering of identity becomes a key trope by means of which gendered subjectivity and ideology are interrogated, as we will see; yet this wuthering of being involves terror as well as emancipation. Significantly, in a later discussion of *Wuthering Heights,* Homans is less sanguine about the liberatory "diffuseness" of the novel than she is in the remarks quoted above— locating the text's emancipatory force only in the fugitive maternal identifications staged in Cathy's delirium, in which Cathy frees herself from patriarchal symbolic structures by precipitating herself into the "maternal" defiles of fantasy. For Homans, Cathy refuses to move "from the maternal and nature to the world of adulthood governed by paternal authority." The result is that "at the end of her life, this refusal of the symbolic order becomes something positive. Temporarily, she names the mother, and names her outside the symbolic order. . . . Cathy yearns deliriously to return to her childhood and to an unmediated merging with actual nature."[12] Yet if Cathy thus pulverizes patriarchal norms and structures in a fever of delirious aberration, this delirium is nevertheless a prelude to her dissolution, her wuthering into the grave. Emancipation, then—in a patterning seen repeatedly in Brontë's poetry— becomes the intimation of death.

In *Wuthering Heights* instability or wuthering is constantly introduced into seemingly solid structures in order to disclose their perilousness, their provisionality, their changeability. This, indeed, is a major source of the novel's *radical* force, for Brontë's text relentlessly affirms the wuthering of the world that it enters by embracing change and disclosing the precariousness of the structures it mobilizes. Remorselessly, *Wuthering Heights* wuthers fixity into unfixity and stability into disturbance. Lockwood's first entrance into the scene of the Heights, for example, is an entry into a scene of general disturbance. Meeting the second Catherine, whom he genteelly dubs "the lady of the house," Lockwood misunderstands her question when she surlily asks, "Were you asked to tea?"—thinking it an invitation rather than a literal inquiry. And when, irritated, she repeats the question, Lockwood, "half smiling" in bemusement, replies: "No . . . You are the proper person to ask me" (*WH,* 11, 12). What Lockwood thus encounters at the Heights is a disruption of the "proper," a derangement of the familiar—specifically of the "properly" feminine, for Catherine, instead of being an "amiable lady" and "presiding genius" of the house (*WH,* 13), turns out to be a petulant and powerless prisoner of the older Heathcliff's grim patriarchal power. In a dark comedy, Lockwood on his first visit to the Heights is in fact hard put to sort out exactly what "relation[s]" pertain between Heathcliff, Catherine, and the churlish Hareton: he first takes Catherine to be Heathcliff's wife, then Hareton's, and then he takes Hareton to be Heathcliff's son (*WH,* 13–14, 17). The reader, too, is placed in much the same position as Lockwood in relation to the Heights, for Lockwood is the reader's bumbling surrogate in the text. But the familial complexities of *Wuthering Heights* serve as much to disorient as to organize the reader's sense of its genealogical structures. "I began to feel unmistakably out of place in that pleasant family circle," Lockwood comments ironically (*WH,* 14). Indeed, *everything* is "out of place" in *Wuthering Heights,* for not only does the text derange familial structures, but it generalizes that wuthering to social structures and to the very interior of the self, as we will see.

The sense of placelessness and disturbance that is endemic to the Heights—and that is typified in the figure of Heathcliff, the waif with no origin or place—is the modus operandi of the whole text. Frank Kermode has memorably described this feature of the novel, seeing the narrative as characterized by "transformations and displacements," with Heathcliff as the main operator of those displacements—since, without a place, Heathcliff is "neither inside nor out, neither wholly master nor wholly servant, the husband who is no husband, the brother who is no brother, the father who abuses his changeling child, the cousin without kin" (McNees, 2:348). When Heathcliff returns from his three years away, Edgar Linton spits exasperatedly at Cathy, "Catherine, try to be glad, without being absurd! The whole household need not witness the sight of your welcoming a runaway servant as a brother" (*WH,* 95). To welcome a "runaway servant *as* a brother" is to refuse to accept relations or familial places as given; instead, it is to constitute them in an act of invention or fabrication—for while Heathcliff "is" not Cathy's brother, he is figured into that place (and others) by the relentlessly transformational energies of the text. "Cathy and Heathcliff are reborn on the occasion of their becoming friends as children," notes Homans, "and their identification with each other forms a new origin that replaces parental origins" (Homans 1980, 156). In fact, characters are continually being reborn into different roles throughout *Wuthering Heights,* and identities are continually being displaced and remade. Thus, Hindley comes to take up a paternal position after Mr. Earnshaw's death, Cathy is transmuted from wayward girl at the Heights to bourgeois lady at the Grange, Hareton in effect loses his position as Hindley's child and becomes the brutalized son of Heathcliff, Heathcliff moves from gypsy to gentleman and from rebel to master, and so on. As subjects of invention and reinvention, the novel's characters are constantly convulsed or wuthered into new forms, so that self-identity surrenders to the discipline of difference, and characters repeatedly find themselves "out of place."

In a war against stability, *Wuthering Heights* installs contradiction at the heart of seeming coherence. For example, as if to write large the strategy of her Brussels *devoir,* "The Palace of Death"—in which "Civilization" is exposed as a malign destroyer in opposition to its ideological self-image (see chapter 3)—the text wuthers the institution of the law. Throughout his career of brutality (whether in his violence to Isabella or in the machinations by which he secures both the Heights and the Grange as his own), Heathcliff takes scrupulous care to stay within the bounds of the marriage and property laws; yet the text's radical point is not that such laws can be abused but that the law itself is abusive, since it enables Heathcliff as a monstrous patriarch to dispossess all around him—not least the second Catherine, who is robbed of Thrushcross Grange by Heathcliff's canny manipulation of the laws of inheritance. (In Brontë's time, a married woman's property passed automatically to her husband; thus, forced by Heathcliff to marry his son, Linton, Catherine cedes her property rights first of all to Linton and then, after his death, to Heathcliff.) Heathcliff's grim gothic villainies in the latter part of the text—in which he acts first as a tyrannical jailor and then as a dispossessing patriarch—thus carry a critical force. Brontë's text inscribes Heathcliff's gothic tyranny as social reality insofar as his actions reveal that the "law" is an instrument of patriarchal power—and so, wuthered into its opposite by Heathcliffian extremism, the law is shown to be an agent of crime.

Describing the difference between Heathcliff and Edgar Linton, Nelly Dean remarks, "The contrast resembled what you see in exchanging a bleak, hilly, coal country for a beautiful fertile valley" (*WH,* 69). This contrast names a key structural opposition in *Wuthering Heights:* the

opposition between excess and constraint, storm and calm, boundlessness and containment. But if the "Romantic" Heathcliff typifies the ter-
rors and exhilarations of the sublime, and the "Victorian" Edgar the
comforts and securities of the beautiful, what is crucial about *Wuthering
Heights* is that it inscribes these seemingly opposed categories within one
another—revealing their mutual contest and their mutual "proximity"
(*WH*, 202). Indeed, as we will see, the borders of constraint in *Wuthering
Heights* are continually wuthered by what they exclude, while turbulence is shown to condition what appears secure and tranquil.

Wuthering the Self

"Heathcliff, indeed, stands unredeemed," writes Charlotte Brontë in her
preface to the 1850 edition of *Wuthering Heights* (*WH*, xxxvi); and it is
Heathcliff who, as we have seen, most insistently shakes, or wuthers, the
fixed structures of the novel's world. Disrupting Lockwood's language
of civility—his invitation to Lockwood to "walk in" to the Heights in
the opening chapter is uttered in a tone that inverts its civil sense: "[it]
expressed the sentiment, 'Go to the Deuce!' " (*WH*, 3)—Heathcliff restlessly invades and overturns the generic and narrative protocols of the
novel. As an unquiet and contradictory presence, Heathcliff can be seen
as a trope of radical displacement: to the extent that he lacks a knowable origin (he appears, as if magically, from beneath the cloak of old
Mr. Earnshaw's benefaction in a kind of mock nativity [*WH*, 36]),
Heathcliff comes from the outside, from the *other*, yet he activates an
instability already implicit in the world that precariously incorporates
him. Never stably lodged in any of the social or symbolic places that he
assumes, Heathcliff remains an unappeasable exile, an irreducible
stranger within the social body.

     While acknowledging that Heathcliff is "proletarian in appearance,"
Terry Eagleton recognizes that the novel insists on the indeterminacy of
his social origins, for Heathcliff is an agent of disruption rather than a
character with a fully fledged social history.[13] But this does not, in Eagleton's reading, strip him of historical or ideological significance; rather,
Heathcliff's uneasy relation to the culture of the Heights (his simultaneous presence in it and otherness to it) serves to expose or intensify the
contradictions on which the Heights is itself built. Thus, confronted by
Heathcliff, the Heights is split between Catherine's rebellious identification with the alien energies that he represents, and Hindley's vicious
reduction of him to the status of farm-laborer—once the ideology of

humanitarian benevolence has died with old Mr. Earnshaw. For Eagleton, in fact, Heathcliff is a divided figure within whose history the novel's contradictory ideological meanings are played out. Describing him as "contradiction incarnate," Eagleton traces the ways in which Heathcliff figures both a form of protest against the bourgeois capitalist forces of Thrushcross Grange and also the purest embodiment of those forces (1975, 112). Likewise, Heathcliff is split, Eagleton shows, between the Romantic sublimities of the Heights—particularly in his relation to Cathy—and the commercial or Victorian accommodations of the Grange (thus, in the second half of the novel, Heathcliff darkly parodies the Grange's bourgeois capitalist prerogatives). Eagleton, then, sees Heathcliff as a figure of ideological conflict in whose contradictory history the irresolutions of Emily Brontë's own historical moment—together with the irresolutions of her novel—are unflinchingly acted out.

As with his divided ideological role, Heathcliff's narrative function is to open up fixed meanings and identities to otherness, or wuthering— invading the seemingly self-identical and turning it inside out. Strikingly, his entire history in the novel is framed in terms of *taking the place* of others; his history, as Nelly Dean puts it, is "a cuckoo's" (*WH,* 35). A foundling, he is christened "Heathcliff" because it is the name of a son who died in childhood in the Earnshaw household; installed at the Heights, he takes the place of Hindley in old Earnshaw's affections; later, he takes Hindley's place as the master of the Heights; and, finally, he takes Edgar Linton's place (and Isabella's and Cathy Linton's) as the master of Thrushcross Grange. Certainly, Heathcliff usurps not only literal places but social and symbolic places, as well. In fact, in a critical metaphorical activity—in which the novel represents Heathcliff as a grim parody of those whom he supplants—Heathcliff gives back to his victims an ironic image of their own repressed significance: grotesquely repeating or exaggerating the characteristics of those he ousts, Heathcliff's deeds reveal the lines of force that invisibly constitute these characteristics in the first place. Thus, returning from his three-year absence, Heathcliff wields economic power explicitly where Edgar Linton disguises it with civility—and then rules the Heights with an autarky that defeats (and yet mirrors) the violence of Hindley Earnshaw's patrilineal regimen.

Throughout the novel Heathcliff's unquiet presence articulates and exacerbates the internal instabilities of the world that he invades. In this sense he is the mode of the novel's deconstruction of its own world, for his indeterminate social and symbolic position introduces a wuthering into the structures that compose the text's frames of reference. This is strikingly evident in the way that Heathcliff's presence divides the familial and domestic economy of the Heights, since his arrival exposes the ways in which the world of the Heights is contradictorily coherent. Describing Heathcliff's first night at the Heights—in which he is spat upon by Cathy and expelled from the children's bedchamber by Cathy, Hindley, and Nelly herself—Nelly Dean comments ironically: "This was Heathcliff's first introduction to the family." (WH, 37). Heathcliff's "introduction" to the family, here, is in fact an expulsion from it: when he is in he is out, and when he is incorporated he is also excluded. Heathcliff's unstable or wuthering position in the family structure, then, dramatizes the forces that constitute that structure: forces of incorporation and expulsion gather round him in such a way as to make him both marginal to the family and exemplary of its instabilities. Heathcliff's history metaphorizes the indeterminacies of the boundary that divides the family's inside from its outside. Benevolently incorporated into the family by old Mr. Earnshaw, Heathcliff is viciously excluded from it by the others: indeed, his contradictory position at the Heights (as favorite and pariah) exposes Earnshaw's benefactory ideology to the contradiction that structures it—since the waif's inclusion is haunted throughout by his banishment.

If Heathcliff's presence at the Heights troubles the family's borders, his arrival also disturbs the system of Earnshaw patriarchy—as Sandra M. Gilbert and Susan Gubar have shown—by mobilizing Catherine's rebel desire (see Gilbert and Gubar, 248–308). Whether one sees *Wuthering Heights,* as do Gilbert and Gubar, as a feminist mythos of Catherine's and Heathcliff's androgynous oneness or not, it is certainly the case that the text explores and transgresses gender identities in the same way that it anatomizes class structures and ideological ambiguities. In this light, one of the effects of Heathcliff's arrival at the Heights is to divide Catherine from her father's governance, reconstituting her as a "wild, wicked slip" (WH, 42) who transgresses Earnshaw's will and repudiates her own role as the quiescent daughter of patriarchy. Thus, she returns her father's words to him in a mocking mimicry, refusing his language of authority from her position of daughterly disempowerment:

> "Why canst thou not always be a good lass, Cathy?"
> And she turned her face up to his, and laughed, and answered, "Why can you not always be a good man, father?" (WH, 43)

As old Earnshaw slides toward death and Cathy's relationship to Heathcliff shifts from fierce hostility to mutuality, a rivalry develops between herself and her father for power over Heathcliff. Earnshaw idealizes Heathcliff ("He took to him strangely, believing all he said"), since Heathcliff figures the "son who died in childhood" whose name he bears (*WH*, 38). The fact that Earnshaw takes to the child "strangely" demonstrates Heathcliff's liminal position at the Heights as both other to and part of its affective structures; "strangely," Heathcliff is an Earnshaw son and not an Earnshaw son, belongs to the Heights and does not belong to the Heights, is the fulfillment of Earnshaw's patriarchal desire and exceeds that desire as an unincorporated other. Indeed, if Heathcliff figures Earnshaw's desire, he also disfigures that desire through his relation to Cathy, since Cathy's power reverses and defeats Earnshaw's paternalism. Cathy delights in doing "just what her father hated most, showing how her pretended insolence, which he thought real, had more power over Heathcliff than his kindness. How the boy would do *her* bidding in anything, and *his* only when it suited his own inclination" (*WH*, 43).

Scorning Earnshaw's benefaction, Heathcliff embraces Cathy's insubordination: and from a figure of Earnshaw's paternity Heathcliff shifts to a figure of Cathy's perversity. As both Eagleton and Gilbert and Gubar have indicated, Cathy's identification with Heathcliff in her famous self-naming—"Nelly, I *am* Heathcliff" (*WH*, 82)—can be understood as an act of self-reinvention: for in a crucial sense Heathcliff's alterity to the Heights tropes her own disempowered relation to the Earnshaw world (see Eagleton 1975, 130; Gilbert and Gubar, 265). As a legally and economically disinherited daughter, Cathy finds in the powerless Heathcliff a figure of her own dispossession. As an outsider, Heathcliff metaphorizes Cathy's otherness to the patriarchal world of the Heights—and Cathy "is" Heathcliff insofar as he images her own eccentricity to that world. But if Heathcliff and Cathy identify with each other in their mutual otherness, their subsequent histories in the novel seem to reverse that situation entirely. Cathy, assimilated to the politely bourgeois patriarchal world of the Lintons, becomes the "lady of Thrushcross Grange" (*WH*, 124), while Heathcliff goes from being the nascent insurrectionist (under Hindley's rule) to a narcissistic capitalist—brutally subjecting the Heights, the Grange, and their inhabitants to his will. In their differing trajectories, both Cathy and Heathcliff move from socially deviant to socially dominant positions, from sites of social marginality to those of centrality. But just as Brontë uses Heathcliff and Cathy to wuther the ideological worlds that constitute them early in the novel, so she disturbs and displaces the identities of bourgeois "lady" and capitalist "master" that they assume later in the text.

When Cathy returns to Wuthering Heights after her five weeks' stay at Thrushcross Grange—a time she spends recovering from the wound the Lintons' guard-dog inflicted on her when she and Heathcliff peeked in mischievously through the Grange windows in chapter 6, like Milton's Satan surveying Eden in *Paradise Lost* book 4—she is no longer a "wild, hatless little savage" but a "very dignified person." "You look like a lady now," says Hindley (*WH*, 52). For Gilbert and Gubar, this *rite de passage* in Cathy's history signifies her "fall" from female autonomy into conformist femininity, and from protest into patriarchy. Indeed, Gilbert and Gubar see Cathy's experience as an oblique rewriting of Miltonic Fall—with Cathy playing the role of a female Satan who, in a Blakean reversal of orthodox hierarchies, falls into the "decorous 'heaven' of femaleness." As they note, too, this moment also marks a turning point in the treatment of Heathcliff, Cathy's "alter ego"—who is banished from the Grange while Cathy is taken in and is persecuted and separated from her once she returns to the Heights (Gilbert and Gubar, 273, 274). In this sense *Wuthering Heights* offers a critical allegory of Cathy's insertion into a socially sanctioned femininity, while her loss of Heathcliff figures her violent separation from her earlier, rebellious self.

The repercussions of this moment for the novel as a whole are huge. Instead of a "rough-headed counterpart to himself" returning to the Heights, Heathcliff witnesses a "bright, graceful damsel" enter the house, who is alien and other to him. The division of Cathy's self between "savage" and "damsel" in this moment is repeated in her division from Heathcliff, for Heathcliff is reduced to a "forbidding young blackguard" who, in contrast to Cathy's ladylike grace, is "black and cross" and "funny and grim" (*WH*, 53). Heathcliff's savagery remains, while Cathy's is transformed into gentility. However, to suggest that the separation of Cathy from Heathcliff is a "fall" from unity into self-division, as Gilbert and Gubar do, is to pass over the *wuthering* energies that constitute the agon of Cathy's self in the novel. For, while Gilbert and Gubar argue that Cathy's "union" with Heathcliff offers her a "wholeness" of being in which she becomes "a perfect androgyne" called "Catherine-Heathcliff" (Gilbert and Gubar, 265), it can also be argued that the Catherine-Heathcliff relation is constituted as *division* from the start. Indeed, as Carol Jacobs argues, although the passion between Cathy and Heathcliff in the novel appears to be the "last refuge of identity," their relationship is in fact structured in terms of the "disjunction it would seem to transcend." Cathy's act of self-naming—"I *am* Heathcliff"—is, as Jacobs points out, a "self-imposed usurpation, [a] willed dispossession of self-unity" as well as a declaration of identity. Consequently, Catherine and Heathcliff's passion becomes "a mode of self-naming, a self-reflection which is necessarily self-sundering"—with the result that Cathy's self emerges only in a splitting, and her unity is produced in a drama of division.[14] Thus, Cathy's separation from Heathcliff is less a fall into division than a reconfiguration of the split that already constitutes her. Cathy's self, in fact, is generated in a *wuthering* in which she is eccentric both to the patriarchal structures of Wuthering Heights and to the conjugal gentility of Thrushcross Grange. Her history in the novel—as rebellious daughter at the Heights and delirious wife at the Grange—is a history of instability in which she is both constrained by and in excess of the filial and marital identities that are assigned to her.

"My great miseries in this world have been Heathcliff's miseries . . . my great thought in living is himself" (*WH*, 81), Cathy says to Nelly in the celebrated passage in which she asserts her identity with Heathcliff. In identifying herself with Heathcliff, Cathy fictionalizes her own being; rhetorically, she produces herself as tenor to Heathcliff's vehicle and incarnates her identity as the gendered meaning of Heathcliff's history. Since her identity is produced in a movement of wuthering, however, Cathy doubles Heathcliff's troubled relationship to his own selfhood; for, as a marginal figure, Heathcliff also lacks a stable sense of identity and is forced to figure or frame himself into being. "Who knows," says Nelly to Heathcliff, "but your father was Emperor of China, and your mother an Indian queen, each of them able to buy up, with one week's income, Wuthering Heights and Thrushcross Grange together? . . . Were I in your place, I would frame high notions of my birth; and the thoughts of what I was should give me courage and dignity to support the oppression of a little farmer!" (*WH*, 57). Thus, Nelly advises Heathcliff to "frame" his own origin in an act of self-invention, for an origin is exactly what Heathcliff lacks; indeed, Heathcliff later literalizes Nelly's narrative by "buying up" (with legal as well as literal capital) the Heights and the Grange and by inventing himself as a propertied patriarch in the process. At the same time, however, Heathcliff's being is produced only in relation to Cathy's—"I *cannot* live without my life! I *cannot* live without my soul!" he says after Cathy's death (*WH*, 167)—and this mutual othering means that Cathy and Heathcliff are brought into being at the same time as they are dispossessed of being. The identity of each is inseparable from the nonidentity of each, for Cathy and Heathcliff are born in a turn toward otherness. In this sense each of them is a "framed" or invented self; produced in terms of one another, they trope each other into existence in a precarious, impossible conflation of identity and alterity.

In chapter 9, Cathy explains to Nelly the dreams and phantasms that make up her desire: "I've dreamt in my life dreams that have stayed with me ever after, and changed my ideas; they've gone through and through me, like wine through water, and altered the colour of my mind." In this oneiric autobiography, Cathy says that she has been "altered" in dream and vision, but the fantasies that figure her desire are not just "ghosts and visions," as Nelly describes them (*WH,* 79). Rather, Cathy's dreams inhabit and radically reshape her relation to the real. In other words, Cathy is "altered," othered, refigured, and reinvented by the visions that course through her. Moreover, it seems that these visions are both poured in from without and excited from within; Cathy's visions go "through and through" her in a conditioning of her being rather than a simple disturbance of it. Cathy, in fact, is *defined* in terms of these disturbing and disruptive alterations that puncture and punctuate her selfhood. As a subject of desire, Cathy is a subject of alteration; she figures her identity in terms of nonidentity, and her belonging in terms of her homelessness. When she insists on recounting the dream that Nelly does not wish to hear, Cathy says: "If I were in heaven, Nelly, I should be extremely miserable . . . I dreamt, once, that I was there . . . heaven did not seem to be my home; and I broke my heart with weeping to come back to earth; and the angels were so angry that they flung me out, into the middle of the heath on the top of Wuthering Heights; where I woke sobbing for joy" (*WH,* 80). In this passage the Heights is figured less as Cathy's home than as the place of her exile: an exile whose meaning, to be sure, is transformed for Cathy from lapsarian agony into transgressive ecstasy, but whose homelessness remains irreducible. "Heaven" fails to exhaust Cathy's desire, and her return to earth and the Heights can be read as a return to the scene of that desire—to the transgressive alterity that inhabits her, and that heaven delusively claims to annul in the name of its own absoluteness. Like Milton's Satan, Cathy rejects heaven's regimen, exceeding its perfection in a demonic return to the world that it excludes. Cathy's remark that she wakes "sobbing for joy" in her dream reveals the mingling of agony and ecstasy that her relation to exile involves, for the site of her desire is by the same token the site of her division. Indeed, her mock fall from the stability of heaven to the tumult of the Heights mythologizes her whole history in the novel: a story of exile that finds its most appropriate metaphor, as we have seen, in the troubled history of Heathcliff.

Insofar as Heathcliff is the figure of Cathy's alterity, her relationship to him is shot through with ambivalence; theirs is a precarious misce-genation that mixes agony and ecstasy, never settling into identity. "He's more myself than I am," says Cathy of Heathcliff (*WH*, 80). Becoming "more" herself than herself in the figure of Heathcliff, Cathy exceeds the bounds of her own being yet fails to coincide with this other in whom she is summed up, and who makes her what she is. Conse-quently, Cathy and Heathcliff enact a drama of desire and identification in which their separate selves wuther into the other, but also in which the "frame" of the self is shaken from within and its coherency is scripted and erased. In a striking discussion of *Wuthering Heights* to which mine is indebted, Leo Bersani shows how the novel contrives a "subversion of individuality" by dramatizing "a radical open-endedness of being" that suspends the idea of a "coherent, unified, describable self."[15] With this in mind, Cathy's declaration that her miseries have been Heathcliff's can be seen as both an identification with Heathcliff's story and a radical dissolution of her own, since for Cathy self-identity coincides with self-loss. If Cathy and Heathcliff, then, emerge in a play of mutual substitution and displacement in which each tropes the other into being—and, by the same token, dispossesses the other of being—we might ask, further, what the sexual and textual politics of that rela-tion is. Moreover, if *Wuthering Heights* allegorizes gendered identity as division rather than mythical androgyny, what form does that division take in the narrative, and how does the novel wuther into otherness the selves and histories it narrates?

Wuthering the Text

Recently, Anne K. Mellor has argued that *Wuthering Heights* counter-points a "masculine" Romantic ideology with a "feminine" one and dra-matizes but also departs from the ideologies of desire that characterize the work of the major male Romantic poets.[16] Against the "narcissistic" structures of desire or theogonies of the self that are readable in such high Romantic works as Shelley's *Epipsychidion* (1821) and Byron's *Man-fred* (1817)—in which the female other acts as the "mirror image" of the male poetic self, supporting a myth of transcendence and the egotistical sublime—Emily Brontë, says Mellor, propounds a feminized Romanticism that affirms the values of continuity, community, and generation. Mellor argues that the latter values are the explicit desiderata of the second phase of the novel, the narrative of the second Cathy's romance with and eventual marriage to Hareton Earnshaw; but, she argues, as a whole *Wuthering Heights* is split between applauding the narcissism or "Eros" of the Cathy-Heathcliff relation and the "agape" or "mutual esteem" of the Cathy-Hareton relation. For Mellor the love between the second Cathy and Hareton is founded on a "recognition of otherness" that the first Cathy and Heathcliff deny in their fierce attempts to incorporate the other into the self (195, 206). But Mellor's description of the Cathy-Heathcliff relation as narcissism ignores the divisive energies that, as we have seen, constitute that relation throughout, while her claim that in the first half of *Wuthering Heights* Brontë is in thrall to a "masculine" Romanticism of selfhood overlooks the way in which the Cathy-Heathcliff story reshapes the narcissistic plot of Romantic desire.[17] If, as Mellor shows, Byronic and Shelleyan desire is constructed narcissistically, Brontë's text can be said to critique this narcissism by literalizing and enacting its patriarchal priorities and their consequences in the story of Cathy Earnshaw. In asserting "I *am* Heathcliff," Cathy presents herself as the personification of Heathcliff's desiring self: the figural support, that is, of his precarious narcissism. Indeed, Cathy in effect elides her separation from Heathcliff in an attempt to become *herself* the fantasized completion of his identity, even imagining that her division from him (in her marriage to Edgar Linton) will "aid Heathcliff to rise" (*WH,* 81). Vis-à-vis Heathcliff, Cathy thus takes upon herself the burden of fulfilling the Shelleyan dream of desire that is scripted in *Alastor*—in which Shelley's male "Poet" (140) fantasizes into existence a female figure whose voice is "like the voice of his own soul" (153), and whom he then pursues relentlessly in a doomed quest for self-completion. But if Cathy figures or materializes Heathcliff's desire, she at the same time *exceeds* that desire.

Cathy's transgression of her earlier identification with Heathcliff in becoming the "lady of Thrushcross Grange"—which Heathcliff reads as a betrayal of *herself* as much as of him (*WH,* 160–61)—leads to the latter's departure and absence for three years, during which time he achieves bourgeois economic status and returns to destroy, in a systematic yet self-defeating scheme of vengeance, the barriers that earlier divided him from Cathy, as if symbolically to reappropriate her. The young Cathy's relative disempowerment is, as we saw, an image of Heathcliff's—indeed, Cathy reads it this way herself—but the destruction of Cathy-Heathcliff's mutual mirroring sends them in radically different narrative directions: Cathy toward agonized delirium and Heathcliff toward self-assertive capitalism. If Heathcliff's story after his return is one of rapacious self-advancement, Cathy's is one of delirious self-loss—and the gender politics of this difference is, as we will see, one which Brontë's text both dramatizes and anatomizes.

After his economic rise, Heathcliff rapidly embarks on revenge. But although his property schemes seem a perversely displaced attempt at recovering Cathy—since they were divided by class and money in the first place—Cathy herself insists that Heathcliff's revenge against Edgar will be a revenge against *her,* and his recovery of her will be a loss of her. "I begin to be secure and tranquil," she says, "quarrel with Edgar if you please, Heathcliff, and deceive his sister; you'll hit on exactly the most efficient method of revenging yourself on me" (*WH,* 112). Indeed, Heathcliff's symbolic struggle with Edgar over Cathy's desire reopens the precariousness of the latter's relationship to patriarchal-bourgeois society, dividing her from its genteel expression at the Grange and from herself, too, as lady of the Grange. For, this time, Cathy's estrangement from the social structures that constrain her propels her not toward insurrection but toward illness. Heathcliff's return to reclaim Cathy's being from Edgar thus succeeds only in sundering her from the provisional identity that she assumes as Linton's wife at the Grange, pulverizing the precarious construction of herself as "lady" at this point in the text ("I begin to be secure and tranquil . . . "). With Heathcliff's rearrival, then, the earlier phase of Cathy's story—namely, her childhood at the Heights—returns like the repressed in psychoanalysis, breaking into the bourgeois complacencies of the Grange with all the delayed and destructive significance of trauma. Like the patient in psychoanalysis, Cathy then plunges into a symptomatic reenactment of her own earlier history in an anguished delirium that only ends with her death: for the contradiction that is opened up in Cathy's self as a result of Edgar and Heathcliff's struggle divides and eventually destroys her.

In this light, Brontë's text politicizes Cathy's illness and death by showing how she is effectively sacrificed to the agon of Heathcliff's and Edgar's desire—and, ultimately, to the oppositions that structure the novel itself—for these two male figures wrestle over her with all the violence of narcissism and proprietorship. As Edgar himself puts it, in a language of conjugal power and ownership: "Will you give up Heathcliff hereafter, or will you give up me? It is impossible for you to be *my* friend, and *his* at the same time; and I absolutely *require* to know which

you choose" (*WH*, 116). And shortly before her death—after having
been precipitated into illness by the conflict over her—Cathy says: "You
and Edgar have broken my heart, Heathcliff. . . . You have killed me—
and thriven on it, I think" (*WH*, 158). Significantly, Heathcliff then
later describes his return to the Heights and his elaborate plan of
revenge as a failed attempt to "*hold* my right, my degradation, my pride,
my happiness, and my anguish" (*WH*, 321; emphasis added): to hold
Cathy, that is, as "his" over against her loss to him and her assimilation
to the world of the Lintons.

In the second half of the novel, Heathcliff's struggle to defeat the
Lintons and Earnshaws represents an inversion of his position of dispossession earlier in the text: he moves from marginality to centrality, even
if only in economic terms. If *Wuthering Heights*, in its opening phase, presents Heathcliff's and Cathy's subjectivity as a radical mutual inhabita-
tion—or as Raymond Williams sees it, as the image of a radical sociality
opposed to the alienated structures of Brontë's surrounding world[18]—in
its second phase the text dramatizes the violent energies of patriarchal,
narcissistic, and capitalist desire in the figure of Heathcliff himself. As
noted above, Heathcliff in fact becomes a grim parody of Edgar's proprietorial efficacy, restlessly appropriating to himself the powers and
resources that earlier divided him from Cathy in an impossible dream of
repossessing her, fruitlessly striving, by means of capitalist accumulation, to staunch the wound that her loss has opened up in him. What
Heathcliff is unable to endure, however, after Cathy's departure from
the Heights and her death (and what Brontë's text insists on), is her *otherness* to him: the fact that she eludes him in life and in death. "She
showed herself, as she often was in life, a devil to me!" he says to Nelly
late in the novel, referring to his ghostly intimations of Cathy's presence
(*WH*, 287)—for, this side of death and the other, Cathy's desire and her
body exceed his narcissistic grasp.

If Heathcliff, however, fights his dispossession through acquisition,
Cathy lives her disempowerment as delirium. While Cathy's and Heathcliff's relationship is affirmed early in the novel as a structure of mutual
othering, the structure later shifts into the story of Heathcliff's self-
consolidation and Cathy's self-dissolution. Bizarrely, Heathcliff substi-
tutes property gain for affective loss—that is, his relentless acquisitions
figure his attempts to "hold" Cathy—while Cathy fractures into a series
of delirious substitutions that discompose and destroy her identity. In
her delirium, Cathy's wuthering *breaks* her just as—in her early relation
to Heathcliff—it *makes* her. Before Cathy's final plunge into illness,

Edgar, as shown above, insists on the mutual exclusiveness of his and Heathcliff's claims upon her: but the "choice" between Heathcliff and himself that Edgar enjoins on Cathy cannot be resolved in the divided terms in which Cathy's subjectivity is constructed in *Wuthering Heights*. In fact, Cathy's famous description of the contrast between her love for Edgar and Heathcliff—"My love for Linton is like the foliage in the woods. Time will change it, I'm well aware, as winter changes the trees—my love for Heathcliff resembles the eternal rocks beneath—a source of little visible delight, but necessary"—is not a statement of the unity of her desire, but of its multiplicity, plurality, and discontinuity (*WH*, 82). Cathy's subjectivity, then, is wuthered from the start: troped by but not stably identified with either Heathcliff or Edgar, her desire effectively straddles the oppositions on which *Wuthering Heights* itself is built. These oppositions—to which Heathcliff and Edgar correspond—include the aesthetic categories of the sublime and the beautiful, the generic forms of the gothic and domestic, and the literary-historical forms of the Romantic and Victorian. Like *Wuthering Heights*, Cathy herself is a divided text—and her division into contrary idioms is writ large in the novel as a whole when the second Cathy and Hareton repeat the tensions of the earlier Cathy-Heathcliff relationship in a more socially accommodating form, as the novel moves from a Romantic-gothic to a Victorian-domestic plot (see Pykett). Like Cathy Earnshaw, *Wuthering Heights* itself wuthers between alternative lives, straddling generic forms just as Cathy wuthers between contradictory avatars of her desire.

In her delirium at the Grange Cathy, significantly, becomes incapable of recognizing her own face in the mirror: effectively, she loses her identity as Catherine Linton. "Don't *you* see that face?" she says to Nelly, as she gazes "earnestly at the mirror"—and Nelly comments, "[S]ay what I could, I was incapable of making her comprehend it to be her own." Cathy is convinced that her image in the mirror is a ghost and that the "room is haunted" (*WH*, 122): unable to recognize her image as her own, she is certain that it belongs to another. Failing to coincide with herself in reflection, she becomes other to herself and is fractured into an alterity that is not resolved in identity. Shortly afterward, she suddenly interprets her own error: "Oh dear! I thought I was at home . . . lying in my chamber at Wuthering Heights. Because I'm weak, my brain got confused, and I screamed unconsciously" (*WH*, 123). Cathy's delirium makes her incapable of resolving her history into a continuous narrative, a linear movement ending in her present consciousness; instead, the narrative of her past self breaks in upon her, erupting on the scene of the present and disorganizing it according to the aberrant logic of desire and fantasy. Deliriously, "Cathy Earnshaw" interrupts "Cathy Linton." Cathy goes on to explain to Nelly that she has a recurrent fantasy—indistinguishable from her knowledge of reality—that the "last seven years" of her life have grown a "blank," and that she is "enclosed in the oak-panelled bed at home," just after Hindley's order of "separation" between herself and Heathcliff. As she mourns their separation, her fantasy suddenly breaks and "memory burst[s] in," twisting her violently into a shape that she cannot recognize, conscripting her into an identity with which she cannot coincide, and which is experienced as trauma. She says to Nelly:

> But, supposing at twelve years old, I had been wrenched from the Heights, and every early association, and my all in all, as Heathcliff was at that time, and been converted, at a stroke, into Mrs Linton, the lady of Thrushcross Grange, and the wife of a stranger; an exile, and outcast, thenceforth, from what had been my world—You may fancy a glimpse of the abyss where I grovelled! Shake your head, as you will, Nelly, *you* have helped to unsettle me! (*WH,* 124)

The abyss into which Cathy falls here is the disjunction between the incommensurable moments of her own story, which interrupt each other and dissolve the coherence of her identity. Shuttling between discrete and unrelated temporal instances, Cathy haunts *herself* with the nightmare of her own alien incarnations. Her past returns to her as fantasy, but with all the force of truth, as if to confirm Freud's remark that those who experience delusions are "suffering from their own reminiscences"—the delusion itself owing its power to "the element of historical truth which it inserts in the place of the rejected reality."[19] Rather than mere falsity, then, Cathy is the subject of alternative and interruptive realities.

Commenting on Freud's account of delusion and interpretation, Julia Kristeva describes "delirium" as that discourse in which knowledge is disturbed by desire: a discourse in which a "presumed reality" is reconstituted less as truth than as wish and in which "the paths of desire ensnarl the paths of knowledge."[20] According to Kristeva, delirium is characterized by a mobile logic of "deformations and displacements" that echoes the "constitution of the dream or the phantasm" in psychoanalysis. Delirium is propelled forward, she says, by means of a constitutive "lack" in the subject according to which the subject's knowledge fails to coincide with reality, leaving its relation to the "Other" as the "minus 1" of desire: thus "even in perception-knowledge, the subject signifies himself as subject of the desire of the Other." Kristeva's argument implies, in fact, a generalized delirium that conditions human subjectivity insofar as the subject is a subject of lack, desire, and signification. In this context, she points out that the function of delirium is not to open up an abyss in the subject; rather, if the dynamic of delirium is that of the dream or phantasm, it becomes the function of delirium to "hold" the subject, albeit precariously, in the defiles of fantasy. (The Latin root of "delirium"—*delirare*—means "to go out of the furrow, to deviate from the straight" [Oxford English Dictionary], suggesting precisely the phantasmal displacements and deformations of desire of which Kristeva speaks.) Kristeva states, "Yet delirium holds; it asserts itself to the point of procuring for the subject both *jouissance* and stability" (1986, 307). Thus, one might say that Heathcliff "holds" himself in the second half of *Wuthering Heights* as the delirious subject of capitalist accumulation—even though his phantasmally acquisitive project is underscored by its own impossibility. Similarly, Cathy is "held" by the names or narrative identities that comprise her history in the text—even though she exceeds each of these identities in turn and, eventually, plunges into the abysmally delirious *jouissance* that undoes her stability in illness.

Likewise, Heathcliff is dissolved late in the text as he fails to "hold" the phantasm of his desire. With Cathy irremediably—and, in a sense, always already—lost (see chapter 5), Heathcliff strangely surrenders his proprietorial quest, his fantasy of appropriation, and *identifies* with rather than strives to surmount his deprivation. Merging with rather than seeking to overcome his loss, Heathcliff abandons all relation to an "object" that might be found in the world—whether Cathy, Wuthering Heights, or Thrushcross Grange—and instead plunges into alterity itself. In effect, he *fuses with the scene of otherness* in which Cathy is unattainably inscribed: the unlocatable place where, like "a devil," she eludes him. Heathcliff becomes a paramour of "unearthly vision" (*WH*, 328). When, in Kristeva's words, "no other exists, no object survives in its irreducible alterity . . . he who speaks . . . identifies himself with the very place of alterity, he merges with the Other, experiencing *jouissance* in and through the place of otherness" (1986, 308). Thus, Heathcliff disengages from all objects or scenes in the world and turns strangely toward absolute otherness; he communes with the absent, the dead, the nonexistent. In a radical volte-face, the capitalist becomes a delusionist,

the proprietor a hallucinator, the master a mystic: "I wish I could annihilate [my property] from the face of the earth," he says, abandoning
everything except the otherness where his desire is located (*WH*, 329).
Refusing to take food or nourishment, Heathcliff gluts himself on the
void and sates himself on vacancy. "I'm animated with hunger," he says
to Nelly; "and, seemingly, I must not eat" (*WH*, 325). Like the house
Wuthering Heights itself, which is always about to pass into atmospheric storm, Heathcliff's body begins to "vibrate" into alterity; it is as
though his physical frame was about to wuther into the unreachable
place of desire itself, the unlocatable place of the other where Cathy is
(not). Nelly speaks of his "frame shivering, not as one shivers with chill
or weakness, but as a tight-stretched cord vibrates—a strong thrilling,
rather than trembling" (*WH*, 325). "Thrilling" into otherness, Heathcliff becomes a subject of dispossession, a votive of the void; for, like
Brontë's desiring speakers in her poems, he is "swallowed in . . . anticipation" of some unnameable fulfillment (*WH*, 322). His "frame" shivers
on the threshold of the unframable. Abandoning the world in the name
of the other, his head turns "continually aside," as if he is commanded,
like Cathy in her delirium, by another scene, another place, another
location (*WH*, 327).

Sitting at his table, his gaze fixed on vacancy, Heathcliff asks Nelly,
"Tell me, are we by ourselves?"—and although Nelly insists, "Of course,
we are!" Heathcliff nonetheless scrutinizes nothingness:

> With a sweep of his hand, he cleared a vacant space in front among the
> breakfast things, and leant forward to gaze more at his ease.
>
> Now, I perceived he was not looking at the wall, for when I regarded
> him alone, it seemed, exactly, that he gazed at something within two
> yards distance. And, whatever it was, it communicated, apparently, both
> pleasure and pain, in exquisite extremes, at least, the anguished, yet rap-
> tured expression of his countenance suggested that idea.
>
> The fancied object was not fixed, either; his eyes pursued it with
> unwearied vigilance; and, even in speaking to me, were never weaned
> away. (*WH*, 328)

Heathcliff's gaze, "never weaned away," is, Brontë's language suggests,
glued to the maternal—glued to it, that is, insofar as the maternal,
according to Kristeva, disrupts the "paternal function" of the law and
prohibition by means of the shattering and delirious force of the "discourse of desire" and fantasy (1986, 308). But if, for Homans, Cathy

momentarily and deliriously "names" the mother by surrendering to the irruptions of desire and fantasy, Heathcliff himself is irrevocably engulfed by desire, too: for his patriarchal-narcissistic-capitalist mastery is deconstructed in the ghostly discipline of longing, as the world is emptied of everything except that unreachable object to which his desire is impossibly dedicated.

The object pursued by Heathcliff's gaze is "not fixed." Similarly, Cathy in her delirium wuthers between what Kristeva calls "*jouissance* and stability"—or unfixity and fixity. As distraction grips her, Cathy is unable to recognize her husband, Edgar Linton. "[H]e was invisible to her abstracted gaze," writes Brontë. "The delirium was not fixed, however; having weaned her eyes from contemplating the outer darkness, by degrees, she centred her attention on him, and discovered who it was that held her" (*WH*, 126). If Cathy's delirium, like Heathcliff's gaze, is "not fixed," we might gloss this by recalling that according to Kristeva delirium is the very discourse of the unfixed: the discourse of a subject plunged into dream-displacement. "Weaning" herself from delirium—again, as with Heathcliff, from the maternal, the phantasmal, the libidinal, from the unstable discourse of desire itself—Cathy "centres" her gaze on her husband, Edgar. Emblematically, then, she arrests her delirious unfixity in the novel's figure of masculine stability: Edgar Linton, the image of genteel patriarchy. Cathy moves from delirious woman to bourgeois wife.

Yet if Cathy veers between Kristevan *jouissance* and stability, between *wuthering* and centering, the delirious logic of her desire is writ large in the text of *Wuthering Heights*. Early in the novel, Cathy's writing on the window ledge—observed and then dreamed of by Lockwood on his first visit to the Heights—adumbrates the psychic delirium that overtakes her later:

> The ledge, where I placed my candle, had a few mildewed books piled up in one corner; and it was covered with writing scratched on the paint. This writing, however, was nothing but a name repeated in all kinds of characters, large and small—*Catherine Earnshaw*, here and there varied to *Catherine Heathcliff*, and then again to *Catherine Linton*.
> In vapid listlessness I leant my head against the window, and continued spelling over Catherine Earnshaw—Heathcliff—Linton, till my eyes closed; but they had not rested five minutes when a glare of white letters started from the dark, vivid as spectres—the air swarmed with Catherines . . . (*WH*, 19–20)

The air around Lockwood's half-dreaming consciousness becomes the very text of delirium as it "swarms" with substitutions, deformations, and displacements of the name "Catherine"—which jostle with each other and exchange places in an atmosphere of mutual encroachments and interruptions. Carol Jacobs, indeed, reads the textual and oneiric deformations of chapter 3 of the novel—which includes Lockwood's terrible dreams of Jabes Branderham's sermon and Cathy's ghostly invasion of his chamber (*WH*, 22–26)—as the text's "mode of elaborating on its own textuality." She sees the disturbances of the chapter—its dreamlike dramatizations of "naming, usurpation, homelessness, and passion"—as a "pre-figuration of the narrative to come" insofar as they foreshadow in an accelerated form the usurpations, displacements, and disjunctive repetitions of the narrative as a whole (65). In light of Jacobs' argument, the air that "swarm[s] with Catherines" could be said to figure *Wuthering Heights* itself as a text that contains two characters called Catherine—who are versions of each other—and in which the first Catherine passes through plural incarnations as "Earnshaw," "Heathcliff" (indeed, she "is" Heathcliff), and "Linton" before she herself, like Lockwood, finally closes her eyes. Even beyond death, however, Cathy returns as a waif to trouble Lockwood in his sleep, to torment Heathcliff with her image—"I cannot look down to this floor," he says, "but her features are shaped on the flags!" (*WH*, 320)—and to haunt local legend with her appearance, along with Heathcliff, "walking" abroad (*WH*, 333). Identity, then, is restlessly reinscribed in dreamlike displacements.

Cathy's delirium, then, enacts the delirium of *Wuthering Heights* as a text that uncannily displaces, deforms, and exhumes its own earlier incarnations (the second generation rehearsing and displacing the first, characters echoing and imaging each other: Hindley and Heathcliff, Edgar Linton and Linton Heathcliff, Heathcliff and Hareton) in a disconcerting movement of textual wuthering in which all the characters are in some sense versions of each other. This is not to suggest that *Wuthering Heights* is simply a "delirious" text but that it approximates the play between *jouissance* and stability that, for Kristeva, characterizes delirium; it is also to show how the text allegorizes and incorporates its own instability.[21]

Cathy's identification with Heathcliff is less about unity than sundering; and her turn toward identity is a turn toward the otherness of Heathcliff's unstable presence in the narrative. But if Cathy's relationship to Heathcliff literalizes the narcissistic object of Romantic quest (in that she tropes herself as the image of Heathcliff's selfhood), Cathy nevertheless exceeds that identification, and all others, in the theater of alterities that comprises her history—and, indeed, her delirium—in the novel. The wuthering of Cathy's identity at last materializes in the swarming deliria of her illness: and, fittingly, her final turn toward identity is a turn toward alterity—the absolute interruption of identity in death. Desiring to "come home," Cathy asserts that she will return to Heathcliff and Wuthering Heights by a "rough journey . . . and we must pass by Gimmerton Kirk, to go that journey!" (*WH*, 125). As in her first return from the Grange, then, Cathy finally comes back to the Heights only as the ghost of her former self—divided from herself, othered in relation to her own history—and, this time, literally as a phantom. Throughout *Wuthering Heights,* Cathy's subjectivity is scripted as a scene of otherness that transgresses or eludes the identifications that trope it; indeed, even though the second Cathy's romance is the domestic fulfillment of the first Cathy's story, Cathy Earnshaw continues to haunt the text with her unreconciled and unquiet desire. Like Brontë's mystical female prisoner in "The Prisoner (A Fragment)," Cathy's being is constituted in an excess in which "visions rise, and change, that kill me with desire!" (*CP,* 14–16; 40). Whether it is marked as ecstasy, illness, or death, this exorbitant desire rises and changes in *Wuthering Heights* in a visionary delirium that, like the text itself, broaches the unsymbolized.

Chapter Five
Gloomy Guests:
Mourning, Ghosts, and Crypts

The Crypt of Vision: The Poetry

In a lyric fragment that Brontë wrote in 1838, a bereaved speaker stands over a burial plot, mourning her beloved "Deep deep down in the silent grave":

> Here with my knee upon thy stone
> I bid adieu to feelings gone
> I leave with thee my tears and pain
> And rush into the world again.
>
> (*CP*, 63; 3 – 6)

The departure of the poem's speaker is a second act of burial; having been interred literally, the beloved is now dispatched symbolically by the lover into the earth, as the speaker turns away mournfully to rejoin the land of the living. The dead are left to the dead, while the "feelings gone" that were linked to the beloved are likewise buried in the grave. The worlds of the living and the dead are separated in an act of mourning.

But what one stanza of the poem inters, the next disinters; and the act of mourning embraced in one moment is fiercely refused the next. Rejecting the form of elegy, the poem is transformed in its third stanza into a visionary invocation to the departed, a calling up of the dead. The speaker demands that the loved one "come again," and leave "thy dwelling dark and cold / Once more to visit me" (7, 9–10). But the return of the beloved takes the form of a visionary manifestation that is only precariously sustained. Recalled from the grave, the beloved is wrested from a specific location and is ecstatically fused with the whole universe. Yet the omnipresence of this desired object is inseparable from its absolute disappearance:

> Was it with the fields of green
> Blowing flower and budding tree
> With the summer heaven serene
> That thou didst visit me?
>   (11–14)

The speaker's questions veer perilously between affirmation and anxiety, between rhetorical and literal questioning; for the beloved here is simultaneously everywhere—or sublimely unlocatable—and nowhere, a presence utterly effaced. The final stanza of the text, indeed, insists on the anxiety rather than the ecstasy of the speaker's longings, lamenting that "not the flowery plain" nor "the fragrant air" bears the beloved's presence: for "Summer skies will come again / But *thou* wilt not be there" (15, 16, 17–18). If, earlier, the poem fleetingly fused the beloved with the world, the last stanza disjoins the two absolutely; and the poem's visionary refusal of mourning collapses into a perception of nature as the very scene of mourning, the very panorama of loss. The speaker's return to mourning is thus characterized by an awareness of nature as containing a gap within itself and as enshrining the place where the beloved is absent: "But *thou* wilt not be there." Nature itself becomes a tomb, while visionary experience becomes an invocation to a lost presence in the grave.

If "Deep deep down in the silent grave" commemorates and mourns a loss in nature, "A Day Dream" envisions nature less as a scene of mourning than a scene of *haunting* (*CP,* 17–19). Both poems, however, elegize the absence that inhabits nature's presence. "A Day Dream" is spoken by a sullen guest at the marriage feast of "May / With her young lover, June" (3–4), the topos of the poem mournfully recalling the bitter exile dramatized in Coleridge's "The Rime of the Ancient Mariner" (1798), in which a Wedding-Guest is stunned and saddened by the Ancient Mariner's dark tale of Romantic isolation. Beginning with its speaker musing on a "sunny brae," Brontë's lyric similarly depicts a scene of exile:

> The trees did wave their plumy crests,
> The glad birds carolled clear;
> And I, of all the wedding guests,
> Was only sullen there!
>   (9–12)

In contrast to the fullness of nature's song, the poem's speaker hears the rhythms of loss and silence in the caroling of the birds and darkens the "general glow" (20) of the scene with intimations of spectrality:

> The birds that now so blithely sing,
> Through deserts, frozen dry,
> Poor spectres of the perished spring,
> In famished troops, will fly.
>   (29–32)

The speaker grimly converts the vernal plenitude of the scene—dubbed a "vision vain, / An unreal mockery" (27–28)—into a spectacle of haunting: nature's singing presences are envisioned as nothing more than famished specters of themselves, as gaunt ghosts who are gripped by the inevitability of their own disembodiment. The brightness of their presence is blighted by the token of what they will ineluctably become, since the "leaf is hardly green / Before a token of its fall / Is on the surface seen!" (34–36). In the speaker's darkly privative logic, absence inhabits nature's presence to the extent that nature itself becomes a kind of ghost, the figure of its own demise. Nature itself becomes a specter, a phantom of loss.[1]

It is out of this loss in nature, however, that the vision of the poem is generated. For, unexpectedly, the peevish speaker witnesses a vision that transfigures the blighted scene before him into one of celestial joy, in which "A thousand thousand gleaming fires / Seemed kindling in the air" and "A thousand thousand silvery lyres / Resounded far and near" (41–44). This blissful song is visionary, not natural, and the speaker overcomes spectral nature with spiritual power by affirming his inspiring vision against nature's phantom half-life: "Methought, the very breath I breathed / Was full of sparks divine . . . " (45–46). But if the speaker's vision is in this way self-affirming, it is also self-questioning; while he joys in the echoing of the earth with song, he also insists that the bright spirits "sung, / Or *seemed* to sing, to me" (51–52; emphasis added). Self-doubtingly suspending the vision he celebrates, the speaker seems in constant danger of disincarnating his own vision, as if the "glittering spirits" (51) of the vision were in danger of becoming themselves no more than "poor spectres" of the speaker's perishing and powerless "Fancy" (71). In this sense the poem bears the "token of its fall" within itself, and its transformation of the ghostly into the visionary—of moribund nature into transfigured spirit—is only tremulously affirmed. As in "Deep deep down in the silent grave," the poem's spiritual vision is called up with ghostly incertitude. Moreover, as again in the other poem, the vision is called up *from the grave*. The visionary spirits sing to the speaker:

> To thee the world is like a tomb,
>   A desert's naked shore;
> To us, in unimagined bloom,
>   It brightens more and more!
> And could we lift the veil, and give
>   One brief glimpse to thine eye,
> Thou wouldst rejoice for those that live,
>   *Because* they live to die.
>   (61–68)

The celestial spirits sing to the speaker from the other side of death; but, although the speaker considers nature to be a tomb, the spirits insist that life, not death, issues from nature's demise. If nature entombs, the spirits argue that it entombs or encloses a transcendent vision, an "everlasting day" (60) that is obscured by mortality. For them, the veil of death hides a visionary bliss that transcends mortal life and exists as the "unimagined," the splendor beyond earthliness. In the first part of the poem, the speaker mourns the loss that inhabits nature, but the latter part of the poem daringly discovers visionary plenitude in that very loss; for it is in nature's demise that the poem finds visionary bliss: "And could we lift the veil . . . / Thou wouldst rejoice for those that live, / *Because* they live to die." The poem conjures visionary bliss from the grave and summons glory from death; in this sense the vision of the poem resurrects the living contents of a crypt.

If nature encrypts visionary transcendence in "A Day Dream," in "I saw thee child one summer's day" (*CP*, 40–42) a specter balefully "banish[es] joy" (24) from a child's world and similarly entombs its hope:

> Cut off from hope in early day
> From power and glory cut away
> But it is doomed and morning's light

Must image forth the scowl of night
And childhood's flower must waste its bloom
Beneath the shadow of the tomb.
                                                    (48–53)

The tomb that buries the child's hope here is not just the literal grave
but a death-in-life that shadows "light" with "night" and installs death
in the bloom of the flower. The "spectre's call" (28) that resistlessly summons the child in the poem entombs his joy and "[c]ut[s] off" his hope,
sealing it up in a sepulchre. But, as in "A Day Dream," this ghostly
sepulchre entombs more than a body: it entombs a vision of "power and
glory," inurning the bright promise of the child's "early day."
   If "A Day Dream" engages in sullen dialogue with Coleridge's "The
Rime of the Ancient Mariner," "I saw thee child one summer's day" anatomizes the visionary creed of Wordsworth's "Intimations Ode" (1807).
The fate of the child in Brontë's poem echoes the plight of the speaker in
Wordsworth's ode, who demands "Whither is fled the visionary gleam? /
Where is it now, the glory and the dream?" (56–57); but Wordsworth's
poem, in contrast to Brontë's, is a hymn of imaginative reparation.
Although, for Wordsworth, "there hast past away a glory from the earth"
(9)—because of the loss of the "vision splendid" (74) that attends childhood—the ode insists that "in our embers / Is something that doth live, /
That nature yet remembers / What was so fugitive!" (130–33). For
Wordsworth, nature is a power whose forms recall the visionary grandeur
that, on another level, they threaten to efface. In Brontë's text, however,
the "power and glory" of visionary light is "cut away" and is entombed
inaccessibly in the lost life of the self. In this sense Brontë's poem,
mouthed by a specter, is a ghostly riposte to Wordsworth's song of immortality, burying beyond recall the vision that Wordsworth's poem strives
to recover. For Brontë, vision is not a sign of the "Soul's immensity"
(110) but of its ghostly half-life; and her poem is an anti-Wordsworthian
entombment of the self's "glory."
   In "O Dream, where art thou now?" (*CP,* 85), Brontë again commemorates the loss of what Margaret Homans calls "a Wordsworthian
gleam" (1980, 111). The poem elegizes a "Lost vision" (16) whose recol-
lection does not restore glory to the self in Wordsworthian mode but
inflicts a further deprivation. Indeed, memory in the poem sunders the
self from its desired object all over again, and the remembrance of pleasure becomes another loss:

> Alas, alas for me
> Thou wert so bright and fair,
> I could not think thy memory
> Would yield me nought but care!
> (5–8)

In this text "memory" harries the self rather than healing and harmonizing it; for if, in Wordsworth, remembrance is a force for organic continuity in the life of the self, in Brontë it is an agent of disruption, invading the self's present being with unappeased ghosts from the past. Addressing its lost visionary light, the poem concludes, "Thou canst not shine again" (16); and to the extent that this vanished vision is internal to the self, it is lodged commemoratively like a tomb inside the psyche. "It is too late to call thee now" (*CP*, 124–25) enacts this gesture of visionary entombment in the self still more explicitly. The poem again addresses a faded "dream," lamenting the loss of the "golden visions" that had once transfigured the "barren mountain-side" (2, 6, 8). It concludes:

> Yet ever in my grateful breast
> Thy darling shade shall cherished be
> For God alone doth know how blest
> My early years have been in thee!
> (9–12)

As Homans comments, the "internalization" of this vision "contracts [it] to a relic of [its] former power and makes the self a mortuary without any compensatory gain in power" (1980, 111). The self thus becomes the cemetary of its own hopes, the graveyard of its own ambitions, the sepulchre of its own desires. Housing its "darling shade" within itself, the self becomes the tomb of visionary power and encrypts its bliss within. Indeed, this visionary entombment is less an obliteration of the beatific vision than its ghostly preservation. Paradoxically, the vision is simultaneously lost and preserved inside the self; it is at once interior to the self and exterior to it (as the speaker laments: "It is too late to call thee now"). Visionary beatitude is both inside the self—a power that it owns—and outside it, a bliss that it has lost.

The demise of visionary power in Brontë's verse generates a poetics of mourning that compulsively elegizes loss and places her poetry in a

troubled relationship to the dominant literary tradition that she inherits
as a woman poet: that of male Romanticism. As a number of recent
feminist critics have shown, Brontë's poetry continually and conflictu-
ally negotiates the difficulties and contradictions of her position as a Victorian woman poet writing in the male-defined tradition of Romantic
lyric verse.[2] If male Romantic poetry involves—in however embattled a
style—the affirmation of visionary or imaginative power (as in
Wordsworth's "Immortality Ode"), that sublime affirmation effectively
disenfranchises woman of Romantic poethood. For, as Lyn Pykett
observes, male Romanticism's poetic imperatives of autonomous subjectivity and imaginative transcendence "sit . . . uneasily with dominant
nineteenth-century views of the feminine," insofar as the latter enshrine
what Sandra M. Gilbert and Susan Gubar call a "culturally conditioned
[female] timidity about self-dramatization" and an "anxiety about the
impropriety of female invention" (Pykett, 45). The perilous dream of
visionary power enacted in Brontë's poetry, then—along with the
trauma of its loss—registers both the spectral afterlife of visionary male
Romanticism in her work and her separation from it as a woman poet.
Mourning a divorce from Romantic vision, Brontë's poetry is nonetheless haunted by its ghostly beatitude.

Insofar as Brontë's poems elegeically encrypt the visions they commemorate, they entomb the glories of Romantic transcendence; yet it is
the *phantom* of Romantic power, not its visionary incarnation, that
inhabits Brontë's lyric songs. Indeed, Romantic vision shadows Brontë's
poetry like an elusive specter, harrying her with dreams of imaginative
sovereignty while at the same time dispossessing her of the power it
promises. The nimbus of Romantic vision is spectralized in Brontë, calling to her with a treacherously phantom voice from the grave in which
it is lost. In "To Imagination" (*CP,* 19–20), for example, imaginative
power is invoked as "call[ing] a lovelier Life from Death" (28), as if it
would recover life's trophies from the tomb; but it is also accused of pur-
veying a "phantom bliss" that betrays the self's desire (31). Imagination
is a ghost whose "hovering vision" haunts the self with longing (26), but
whose life is self-defeatingly born from the death that it is supposed to
overcome.

If visionary power eludes the Brontëan poetic self, this elusiveness is
nevertheless situated *within* that self, as in "O Dream, where art thou
now?"; as we have seen, vision in Brontë is not so much appropriated by
the self as incorporated within it as an alien bliss. Visionary light is thus
embraced by the self *in its alterity,* in its ghostly otherness; and the self is

turned inside out by a power that it enfolds but with which it cannot merge, and that possesses it rather than is possessed by it. The otherness of the "phantom bliss" inhabiting Brontëan poetic subjectivity is dramatized strikingly in a poem published in 1846, "My Comforter" (*CP,* 29–30). The poem addresses "my" Comforter in an audacious act of appropriation, for the title recalls the "Comforter, which is the Holy Ghost" (John 14:26) who is promised by Christ to his disciples as their spiritual guide after his death. Brontë's Comforter, however, disrupts both the language of Christian orthodoxy and the language of Romantic self-expression. Enclosed within the self, the Comforter is a spirit whose identity is encrypted in secrecy:

> Deep down, concealed within my soul,
> That light lies hid from men;
> Yet, glows unquenched—though shadows roll,
> Its gentle ray cannot control,
> About the sullen den.
>
> (6–10)

The "sullen den" in which the Comforter is housed images the self as a prison that paradoxically interns the "gentle ray" of spiritual liberty. At once uncontrollable and unrevealable, this spirit is an avatar of freedom that is sealed up unreachably in the fugitive sublime of the Brontëan poetic self. The immurement of vision—or of what the poem calls the "bliss before my eyes" (20)—is an act of elegeic preservation, for the poem lovingly inters its light so as to protect it from the grim world. But, although it preserves its bliss, the poem also reinvokes loss:

> Was I not vexed, in these gloomy ways
> To walk alone so long?
> Around me, wretches uttering praise,
> Or howling o'er their hopeless days,
> And each with Frenzy's tongue;—
>
> A brotherhood of misery,
> Their smiles as sad as sighs;
> Whose madness daily maddened me,

Distorting into agony
　　The bliss before my eyes!

So stood I, in Heaven's glorious sun,
　　And in the glare of Hell;
My spirit drank a mingled tone,
　　Of seraph's song, and demon's moan;
What my soul bore, my soul alone
　　Within itself may tell!
　　　　　　　　　　　　　(11–26)

The speaker's "soul" here bears within itself a simultaneous bliss and loss, a secret and unspeakable duplicity that holds the seraphic and the demonic together in the self and makes the self a "mingled tone" whose meaning is at once ecstatic and traumatic. This "mingled" life endured by the self is both inspiring and alienating, for the soul's bliss is harried by the loss that it attempts to deny, and its comfort is disturbed by the agony it strives to exclude. In this way, the division that the poem sets up between the heavenly inside and hellish outside of the "soul" breaks down, and the opposition between interior bliss and exterior loss reappears *within* the self. Ecstasy and trauma structure the interiority of the self in an unresolvable division, for the "bliss" of Heaven and "agony" of Hell are both "borne" by the soul in an unspeakable derangement of categories, a mingling of comfort and privation that preserves visionary rapture *and* entombs it in a secret place in the self, inaccessible to utterance:

Like a soft air, above a sea,
　　Tossed by the tempest's stir;
A thaw-wind, melting quietly
　　The snow-drift, on some wintry lea;
No: what sweet thing resembles thee,
　　My thoughtful Comforter?
　　　　　　　　　　　　　(27–32)

　　Here the poem refuses the language of likeness and resemblance and, in a way, refuses language itself; for while the poem hymns its visionary comfort, it also refrains from naming its bliss, sealing it off in the "sullen den" of the psyche. The "Comforter" is a secret that the poem and the psyche enclose. In this sense the Comforter, although housed in the self, retains its otherness to the self, disrupting the self's governance of its own house: it is silenced, unspeakable, encrypted. A foreigner housed in the soul, the Comforter takes up residence inside the self as an alien presence. Indeed, although—as an internal enshrinement of bliss—the Comforter overcomes agony and encloses glory in the soul, its secrecy is also the sign of its loss, for the poem both preserves and buries its vision, sealing it off from the world and sealing it up inexpressibly in the self.

In this sense the poem's blissful Comforter is the object of a silencing and, in a certain way, of a repression, but a repression that is best understood as "preservative" in the sense outlined by Nicolas Abraham and Maria Torok in their remarkable work on the psychical mechanisms of mourning and loss in psychoanalysis.[3] For Abraham and Torok, the mechanism of "preservative repression" is not a repression of libidinal forces in the strictly Freudian sense—which they call "dynamic repression" (159)—but of an illicit object that, "for some reason unspeakable," has been placed in a "sealed-off psychic space, a crypt in the ego" where it has become unavailable to language and symbolization. As the figure of the "crypt" suggests, this repression is, according to Abraham and Torok, an act of burial: the interment of a loved and lost object whose memory, in a preservative gesture, is "entombed in a fast and secure place [in the psyche], awaiting resurrection." The entombment of this loved and lost object is the repression in the self of an "illegitimate idyll *and* its loss" (Abraham and Torok, 141; emphasis added): for the idyll is preserved in the psyche in a cryptic repression, while its loss is repressed in cryptic preservation. Thus, the object of preservative repression is sealed up as a transgressive other in the psyche, both lodged and lost in the self: it is, as Jacques Derrida says, the ghostly "inhabitant of a crypt belonging in the Self."[4]

Brontë's "idyll" inhabits "My Comforter" like a ghost; it is, moreover, the object of a preservative interdiction that renders it silent, making it enclose a speech that it fails to utter. (Indeed, the spirit speaks to Brontë throughout the poem, but not to the reader: "And yet a little longer speak . . . " the last stanza begins [33].) The bearer of a prohibition on speech, the Comforter seals up the power of Brontëan utterance and encrypts its discourse. But what prohibition is at work in this strange withdrawal from speech, and what loss is encrypted in this silence? According to Emma Francis, the "prohibition nineteenth-century women poets were under was against the use of the language of the Sublime, which the male romantics used": the sublime, that is, as a language of "empowerment" in which the self affirms its potency and autonomy in the face of the threat to it.[5] Indeed, although, as Francis recognizes, Brontë's poetry broaches the language of sublime power, it more characteristically exhibits what Kathryn Burlinson calls "a post-romantic (and Victorian) preoccupation with the legacy of romanticism, where doubts about the self and its potentiality underpin poetic articulation."[6] Specifically, the entombments of visionary transcendence that we have traced in Brontë's texts show that it is the *ghost* of Romantic empowerment that is encrypted in her poetry: a ghost whose elegeic half-life rises up as the spectral trace of visionary power, the perilous sign of a lost or encrypted transcendence. The post-Romantic and gendered prohibition on sublime power leads, in this sense, to its preservative entombment in the crypt of the Brontëan self; and visionary bliss arises like an unquiet ghost from the grave of Romantic sublimity.

If vision is housed in the grave in Brontë, the logic of its inurnment—and its spectral return—is dramatized in one of the most remarkable of the Gondal poems, published in 1846 under the title "Remembrance" (*CP,* 8–9). This poem is an act of mourning by a female speaker for her lost beloved, who has been "Cold in the earth" for "fifteen wild Decembers" (9). The poem charts the speaker's struggle to replace the beloved with "other" desires and hopes and maps the mourner's attempt to substitute for the lost object:

> Sweet Love of youth, forgive, if I forget thee,
> While the world's tide is bearing me along;
> Other desires and other hopes beset me,
> Hopes which obscure, but cannot do thee wrong!
>
> (13–16)

According to Freud, the "work of mourning" consists in the painful withdrawal of the subject's attachment to a loved but lost object and its reluctant reinvestment in "a substitute [that is] already beckoning" to it.[7] In his striking discussion of mourning in *The English Elegy,* Peter Sacks shows that the work of mourning can be understood primarily as an act of substitution. Sacks draws a parallel between the resignatory processes of mourning in the psyche and the story of Oedipal renunciation in psychoanalysis, in which the mother's body is relinquished in the child's passage to the cultural and " 'symbolic order' of signs." Sacks writes: "At the core of each procedure is the renunciatory experience of loss and the acceptance, not just of a substitute, but of the very means and practice of substitution."[8] In this sense to mourn is to symbolize, whether it is to replace the body of the mother with signs or to denote the dead through signification. Mourning is the act whereby the lost object is substituted by the employment of signs and symbols that elegeically commemorate its departure. To mourn, then, is to embrace the order of symbolization as such: to enter the realm in which, in Maud Ellmann's words, the "symbol . . . bespeaks the absence rather than the presence of its referent."[9] To this extent, to mourn is also to forget, to dispatch the dead through the ritual of symbolization. And for Brontë's poem, indeed, mourning *is* a forgetting, a separation from the dead, a symbolic "weaning" of the soul from its love:

> But, when the days of golden dreams had perished,
> And even Despair was powerless to destroy;
> Then did I learn how existence could be cherished,
> Strengthened, and fed without the aid of joy.
>
> Then did I check the tears of useless passion—
> Weaned my young soul from yearning after thine;
> Sternly denied its burning wish to hasten
> Down to that tomb already more than mine.
>
> (21–28)

As Sacks notes, these lines enact the psychodrama of the Brontëan lyric subject: the self here becomes the mother and the father of its own soul, "weaning" itself in maternal style from its desire but also "[s]ternly den[ying]" in paternal mode its dangerously regressive identification with a maternal imaginary (15).[10] In a recapitulation of Oedipal renunciation, the self opts for the world rather than for the impossible—the lost, prohibited, or encrypted—object of its desire. Simultaneously and mournfully, the self renounces both a lost beloved and a prohibited maternal object, weaning itself from longing and repudiating its own self-destructive wish for extinction in the tomb—and the womb—of its love. But if the speaker of the poem in this way embraces mourning and substitution, obeying the law of renunciation, there is another level on which the poem fiercely *refuses* that surrender and repudiates the work of mourning. In this sense "Remembrance" undoes the work of mourning even as it performs it. Transgressively refusing the paternal protocols of renunciation, the speaker insists on the imaginary triumph of identification with its maternal and sepulchral beloved:

> No later light has lightened up my heaven,
> No second morn has ever shone for me;
> All my life's bliss from thy dear life was given,
> All my life's bliss is in the grave with thee.
>
> (17–20)

Here the self encrypts its own bliss, just as visionary beatitude is, as we have seen, preservatively entombed in Brontë's lyrics on poetic power. Already "in" the grave, the self hurries suicidally to the tomb even as, elsewhere in the poem, it "forgets" its lost beloved and turns recuperatively to the world. Suspended between the world and the grave, hovering between life and death, the speaker lives a divided existence in which it is simultaneously buried and alive; in which it is both encrypted in the earth and at large in the world. The subject of the poem lives a half-life in which, despite its "cherishing" of existence, the tomb where its love is lodged is "already more" than its own. In this sense the self of the poem is *already a ghost:* a phantom being whose life is in the grave but who continues, like a revenant, to stalk the earth. Although on one level, then, "Remembrance" sustains the symbolic distances of elegy, the fusion of its speaker with the entombed object of desire radically suspends the work of mourning and plunges the self toward death. The collapse of mourning resurrects the ghost of lost love. The last stanza of the poem, moreover, relocates the tomb of the beloved not in the world but in the *self.* Alluding to the denial of its own longings, the self of the poem can only tremulously sustain the labor of mourning and the vigilance of renunciation:

> And, even yet, I dare not let it languish,
> Dare not indulge in memory's rapturous pain;
> Once drinking deep of that divinest anguish,
> How could I seek the empty world again?
>
> (29–32)

The world is emptied of presence and signification here because of the absence of the beloved, while the speaker, as Robin Grove writes, "bear[s] in the memory what one might call a living absence—the gap in nature where her beloved used to be" (59). The speaker, that is, carries within herself the beloved's tomb and encrypts on the inside the lost object that is supposed to be buried in the world. The dead object is incorporated in the self; it is sealed up, enclosed, or entombed in the subject. It lives a phantom life in the interior of the speaker.

If the work of mourning in Brontë's poem is a process of forgetting, the power of "memory" comes to cancel that forgetfulness; but memory returns the loved object to the self in the mode of absence, in the strange and ghostly idiom of "rapturous pain" and "divinest anguish." In this light, the speaker of the poem entombs within herself the object *and* its loss; for, if the burial of the object inside the self is in one sense the refusal of loss, that loss is encrypted in the self, too, in the mode of preservative repression or buried trauma. In these terms, Brontë's speaker enacts poetically the process that Abraham and Torok call "incorporation": that is, the magical psychical fiat in which the subject "swallows" a lost object rather than mourns it, and in which the object is "incorporated" in the self as if it had never been lost, rather than "introjected" by the psyche in the gradual symbolic process of mourning, whereby the loss of the object - is accepted and the psyche is accordingly reorganized (126–27).[11] "Incorporation" for Abraham and Torok is, indeed, a radical refusal of mourning: a refusal of loss and of the psychical reordering that loss occasions. To this extent, incorporation denotes the phantom survival in the self of its past: a scene of psychical *revenance,* it marks the place where the lost or the dead return, like a ghostly room in the house of the self. As Abraham and Torok write: "Inexpressible mourning erects a secret tomb inside the subject. Reconstituted from the memories of words, scenes, and affects, the objectal correlative of the loss is buried alive in the crypt as a full-fledged person, complete with its own topography. . . . Sometimes in the dead of night, when libidinal fulfilments have their sway, the ghost of the crypt comes back to haunt the cemetary guard, giving him strange and incomprehensible signals, making him perform bizarre acts, or subjecting him to unexpected sensations" (130).

If the ghost of a crypt, then, returns to haunt the speaker of Brontë's "Remembrance," radically suspending the work of mourning, its phantom presence marks the subject herself as ghostly, enlisting her on the side of the dead. The speaker becomes a stranger to the "empty world" and is dissolved from what "The Philosopher" calls the self's "present entity" (*CP,* 7–8; 22). Haunted and harried by a power of "remembrance" that undoes her, the speaker remains in the world through the forgetfulness that underpins mourning; memory, however, summons her to the grave. As Nina Auerbach remarks, "Memory here is not the source of growth, but a dark call like suicide" (222). Insofar as memory encrypts the past life of the self, preservatively entombing its desires and deprivations, the self in Brontë becomes a kind of cemetary: the living sepulchre of its history, the gallery of its own ghosts. And it is the nature of these Brontëan phantoms to return to the self undiminished, as though they had the power to "cancel time" ("What winter floods what showers of spring" [*CP,* 192–93; 7]), like the specters who rise up in "The Death of A.G.A." (*CP,* 158–68) as the dead body of Gondal's Queen is watched by her friend, Lord Eldred:

> But he who watched, in thought had gone
> Retracing back her lifetime flown;
> Like sudden ghosts, to memory came
> Full many a face, and many a name,
> Full many a heart, that in the tomb
> He almost deemed might have throbbed again.
>
> (310–15)

If memory in Brontë is an agency of *revenance* rather than remembrance, of punctual haunting rather than temporal continuity, it also— to the extent that it cancels time and mourning—opens up the realm of the visionary. For memory in Brontë is the idiom that refuses to mourn and refuses to forget, and that enshrines its lost or remembered bliss in the visionary heaven of the mind. In "The Prisoner (A Fragment)" (*CP,* 14–16), for example, the subjectivity of the visionary female prisoner in the poem is governed by a remembrance that is indistinguishable from transcendence. The poem is set in the "dungeon-crypts" of an imperious lord and his grim warder (1). As shown in chapter 3, it can be read as presenting the image of an imprisoned—or entombed—femininity, inurned by the powers of patriarchy.[12] The "context of political oppression" (Francis, 30) in the poem, however, does not just involve the incarceration of female vision by patriarchal power. The longer version of the poem, entitled "Julian M. and A. G. Rochelle" belongs to the Gondal narrative and tells the tale of the bereaved A. G. Rochelle who is possessed by grief at her parents' deaths, presumably at the hands of Lord Julian's forces (*CP,* 177–81; 43). In this longer narrative version, Rochelle is eventually reconciled to the world and, indeed, to her jailor,

Lord Julian (with whom she had been childhood playmates), who abandons his pursuit of military glory and instead conquers Rochelle in love. In the sparer, more lyrically based "The Prisoner," however, this narrative of accommodation is suspended; and the poem is dominated by the stark lyric solitude of its nameless female prisoner, who defiantly hymns her alterity to the world and to her imprisoners. If, in "Julian M. and A. G. Rochelle," Rochelle arrives at accommodation with the world, replacing her marriage to loss with marriage to Lord Julian (152)—and thus embracing the substitutionary work of mourning—"The Prisoner" dramatizes the visionary refusal of that mourning, and rejects the labors of reconciliation. The grisly gothic warder in the poem tries to terrify the languishing woman—as if to solicit her supplication—but fails:

> About her lips there played a smile of almost scorn,
> "My friend," she gently said, "you have not heard me mourn;
> When you my kindred's lives, *my* lost life, can restore,
> Then may I weep and sue,—but never, friend, before!"
>
> (29–32)

The prisoner's obdurate refusal to mourn is less a repudiation of loss than a radical identification with it; the speaker weds herself to loss, merging with its vacancy in a melancholic turn away from the world toward absolute otherness. Her kindred's lost lives, she says, are "her" life; their entombment is her own. In this sense the prisoner of the poem—like the speaker in "Remembrance"—is already dead: she lives a phantom life that is constituted in a gesture of self-encryptment, in a visionary entombment of "life" within. As Stevie Davies writes, the prisoner in the poem is a "waif between the two worlds of the living and the dead" (1983, 91). In the Gondal version of the poem, indeed, Rochelle refers to herself as a "living grave" (60); her life and her love are enclosed within the tomb that the self has become. Incorporating a love—again as in "Remembrance"—that is at once maternal and sepulchral, the prisoner raises her face toward her captors like a "slumbering unwean'd child" (14). Buried in the self, the life that she has lost gives way to the phantom benedictions of vision, and her remembrance of death cedes to the visitations of "desire":

> Desire for nothing known in my maturer years,
> When Joy grew mad with awe, at counting future tears.

When, if my spirit's sky was full of flashes warm,
I knew not whence they came, from sun, or thunder storm.

But, first, a hush of peace—a soundless calm descends;
The struggle of distress, and fierce impatience ends.
Mute music soothes my breast, unuttered harmony,
That I could never dream, till Earth was lost to me.

                                                              (41–48)

Losing "Earth," the imprisoned speaker, in a sublime counter-investment, gains heaven. However, the vision that this loss of Earth opens up is predicated, as the dungeon setting of the poem insists, on the speaker's material and worldly disempowerment. Like a ghost or spirit disembodied of flesh, the speaker seems to intone her unappeased desire from some other scene, some other life, some other world—from a place of fleshly exile. To the extent that the life the speaker gains, then, is determined by a loss of material life, her vision is an index of her entombment; and her immortality is inseparable from her spectrality. Speaking from a site of death and loss, the prisoner's visionary dream is a ghost of material power; and its liberty is the measure of her disempowerment. Inhabiting the poem's "dungeon-crypts" like a specter, the prisoner's vision is the denizen of a crypt: for vision here is enclosed in the self as the prisoner is enclosed in the prison.

If visionary power is sealed within the self in "The Prisoner," its transcendent sublimity survives at the cost of being sepulchred: it is, in this sense, preserved and lost at the same time. Living on in a kind of posthumous Victorian afterlife, this Romantic sublimity is a specter of bliss that haunts Brontë's post-Romantic world and shadows her disenfranchised position as a Victorian woman poet like an elusive "Shade of mast'ry" ("Strong I stand though I have borne" [CP, 56; 5]). To this extent, Brontëan poetic power rises from the crypt of Romantic vision: a crypt whose unquiet shades harry her work—like the ghosts of Catherine Earnshaw and Heathcliff at the end of *Wuthering Heights* (*WH*, 333–34)—with an uncontainable promise.

The Crypt of Identity: *Wuthering Heights*

Brontë's poetry, as we have seen, enshrines bliss and loss together, immuring its "Lost vision" (*CP*, 85) in a language of elegy and rhapsody.

Unstably, Brontë's poetry mourns the loss of glory *and* affirms its preservation in a visionary brightness secreted in the self. Ratifying and refusing the work of mourning, Brontë's poetry perilously guards the glory of what it has lost. Like the poems, *Wuthering Heights,* too, can be read as a drama of mourning and the repudiation of mourning; as in the poems, the novel entwines deprivation and benediction in a hymn to loss and the refusal of loss.

In "Stanzas," Brontë muses, "Follow out the happiest story— / It closes with a tomb" (*CP,* 29; 7–8); but, famously, *Wuthering Heights* refuses the finality of that closure and insists on a logic of *revenance* rather than of resolution. In *Wuthering Heights,* indeed, tombs are never securely closed and the dead are never safely buried: they come back, disturbing the borders of life and death, and haunting the lives of those who are left. As David Cecil wrote in 1934, *Wuthering Heights* undoes "the most universally accepted of all antitheses—the antithesis between life and death"; more than that, it insists on "the immortality of the soul *in this world,*" rejecting orthodox Christian immortality in favor of the heretical creed that "the disembodied soul continues to be active in this life."[13] *Wuthering Heights,* then, allows its dead to walk—and to invade the lives of its living.

The sense of the novel as disrupting the boundaries of life and death is registered in the responses of the contemporary reviewers, as well— specifically in relation to the book's power to unsettle and disturb. One English reviewer, for example, responded to the novel as though it were itself a specter or wraith, commenting, "It should have been called *Withering* Heights, for any thing from which the mind and body would more instinctively shrink, than the mansion and its tenants, cannot be imagined" (quoted in Allott 1974, 2:229). Similarly, an American reviewer, having described the novel as a "coarse, original, powerful book," sought eagerly to consign its unquiet life to the grave and to lay its troubled ghosts to rest: "[*Wuthering Heights*] will live a short and brilliant life, and then die and be forgotten. . . . The public will not acknowledge its men and women to have the true immortal vitality. Poor Cathy's ghost will not walk the earth forever; and the insane Heathcliff will soon rest quietly in his coveted repose" (quoted in Allott 1974, 241). In her 1850 preface to the novel, moreover, Charlotte Brontë herself conspired with this textual laying of ghosts. Focusing her exorcising eye on the figure of Heathcliff, she described his passion for Catherine as a thing to "boil and glow in the bad essence of some evil genius; a fire that might form the tormented centre—the ever-suffering soul of a magnate of the infernal world. . . . [W]e should say he was child neither of Lascar nor gipsy, but a man's shape animated by demon life—a Ghoul—an Afreet" (*WH*, xxxvi). And, in a letter of 1848, Charlotte saw Heathcliff as the presiding spirit of the novel, haunting it with his malign half-life: "The worst of it is, some of his spirit seems breathed through the whole narrative in which he figures: it haunts every moor and glen, and beckons in every fir-tree of the Heights" (*BLFC*, 2:245). As a text harboring ghosts, then, *Wuthering Heights* becomes ghostly itself, as if it breathed forth the life of the dead from its pages.

As a haunted book, *Wuthering Heights,* like the house Wuthering Heights itself, as described by Lockwood, "swarm[s] with ghosts and goblins" (*WH*, 27). But if Wuthering Heights the house is haunted by the traces of what Lockwood ironically calls its "hospitable ancestors" (*WH*, 27), the novel, too, recycles its generations and replays its scenes spectrally: echoing itself, as J. Hillis Miller shows, in a play of uncanny repetitions, in a "repetition in difference of one part of the text by another."[14] It is as though the novel itself refused to let its dead die but, instead, preserved their existence in the posthumous life of its own later incarnations. The repetition-with-a-difference of the Cathy-Heathcliff relationship in the Cathy-Hareton romance is, as shown in chapter 4, the most obvious narrative example of the ways in which the novel rewrites its patterns and haunts itself with its own past life. The first Catherine herself is, indeed, ghosted by her former self in her delirium at Thrushcross Grange; but the novel as a whole compulsively commemorates its own earlier lives, as if it carried its ghosts within it like so many precious tombs, lost loves, or familiar spirits. Refusing to leave its dead simply behind or quietly in the grave, *Wuthering Heights* carries its dead inside it in a strange gesture of preservative textual encryptment; to this extent, the novel is—in an exemplary way—a house of ghosts. In Nicholas Royle's words, *Wuthering Heights* is "itself a crypt—[the crypt] of itself."[15]

Stevie Davies demonstrates the novel's cryptic effects by showing how, in the narrative's scant array of names, textual identities inhabit one another in a ghostly or uncanny verbal haunting. She writes:

> The Heights' characters share a cryptic ground of identity both with one another and with the earth from which they came and to which they are designed to return. The central names are clearly (but not obviously) anagrammatic. Both CATHERINE and HARETON contain HEART and Emily Brontë's favourite word EARTH, the last word in the novel. . . . CATHER-

INE contains most of HEATH, and EARNSHAW most of the words EARTH and HEART while HEATHCLIFF . . . compounds HEATH and CLIFF. His name contains CATHIE, whilst CATHERINE and EARNSHAW each contain most of HARETON. The complex mirror-tricks derive from the author's selection of a limited number of letters of the alphabet for permutations which cross-reference in a devious way, hinting at but never guaranteeing common identity. Games of deep concealment and displacement are played by the mind of the novel, miming the losses and suppressions which are both its subject-matter and narrative manner. (1994, 65)

Davies's insightful comments show how *Wuthering Heights* can be read as a novel of encryptment; the text's cryptic incorporations and inclusions compulsively enclose or contain one identity within another in an unsettling play of textual phantoms, with the result that the novel unfolds nothing less than a poetics of haunting. Furthermore, in its gestures of preservative enclosure and textual encryptment—in which names, identities, and stories inhabit one another in a mutual ghosting— *Wuthering Heights* seems elegeically to commemorate its *own* losses as a novel. More precisely, the novel *refuses to mourn* those losses. Instead, it insists on retrieving and recycling its elements in a preservative immurement of its own lost life. *Wuthering Heights,* in this sense, keeps its dead safe, encrypting them so they can live a second life from the tomb.

As a novel of impossible or unfulfillable mourning, in fact, *Wuthering Heights* vigilantly commemorates a founding loss to which it gestures but which it can never recover or name. Instead, as Davies remarks, the novel hallows some "cryptic ground of identity" between its elements that might, in some primordial time, have grounded oneness; but that oneness is now irremediably lost, fractured beyond recall in differentiation. It lives on only in the crypts commemoratively constructed by the novel's housing of the dead. Thus it is that the novel's cryptic effects—signaled in the repetition of plots and the enclosure of names within names—solemnize a radically inaccessible condition of unity whose disappearance is endlessly repeated even as it is endlessly lamented. As a novel of loss, *Wuthering Heights* thus grounds its stories and identities in a constitutive act of mourning, in a founding loss or privation. The novel generates itself out of what Davies calls an "unfulfillable want [poised] over an abyss of loss which cannot be filled in" (1994, 220); to this extent, *Wuthering Heights* memorializes an unquenchable deprivation.

The most striking example of lost or encrypted unity in the novel is, of course, the perilous relationship between the first Catherine and

Heathcliff. Cathy and Heathcliff's identification with one another is leg-
endary; but, as noted in chapter 4, this identification is itself predicated
on the agony of loss and division. As John T. Matthews eloquently puts
it, "Even the paradisiacal state of unity" is, in Catherine and Heathcliff's
case, "already a curative ghost called forth by what was an intolerable
present. The remembered wholeness of childhood is the memory of a
dream that was to have redeemed what was already lost. Nelly's account
of the earliest phases of Heathcliff's and Catherine's positions in the
family . . . invariably demonstrates that separation is the condition of
their attraction, displacement the location of their alliance, exile the origin of their union."[16] As a "ghost" of unity, then, Cathy and Heathcliff's
relationship becomes a crypt interring a vanished bliss; and, insofar as
their relation is defined by division, each commemorates the loss of the
other in a love that is inseparable from mourning.

Famously, though, Cathy and Heathcliff's union is a site of transgression. It is the mutual identification of a daughter of patriarchy with a
rootless boy "gipsy" that—by flouting the hierarchies of gender and
class governing the relationships both at Wuthering Heights and
Thrushcross Grange—threatens to dissolve the social and familial bonds
defining the novel's world. After old Mr. Earnshaw's death, the son of
the family—Hindley Earnshaw—viciously reestablishes the hierarchized
distinctions that had been disturbed by his father's introduction of the
waif Heathcliff to the family. Banishing Heathcliff from his place as
putative family son, Hindley's regime projects Cathy and Heathcliff's
relationship into the very register of transgression. Under Hindley's law,
Nelly reports, Cathy and Heathcliff are likely to "grow up as rude as
savages" (WH, 46); and their connection becomes one of wild illegality
within the domestic economy of the Heights—"one of their chief
amusements" being, says Nelly, "to run away to the moors in the morning and remain there all day . . . the after punishment [growing] a mere
thing to laugh at" (WH, 46). Exiled from the rigid structures of the
Heights, Cathy and Heathcliff's liaison fashions a utopian space on the
"moors" that Terry Eagleton calls a "revolutionary refusal of the given
language of social roles and values" (1975, 108). This refusal, however,
tragically maps Cathy and Heathcliff's exile as much as their emancipation; for the famous moors of the novel are a scene of simultaneous
transgression *and* of loss, the "liberty" (WH, 47) that is enacted on them
becoming the object of an insuperable prohibition away from them. The
moors, in this sense, are a site of freedom to the extent that they are a
site of loss.

What the moors embody is an *other* scene, a scene *of* otherness: a scene that subversively exceeds the protocols of the novel's world. Pre-eminently, it is a scene of desire in which social interdiction is swallowed up by the demands of pleasure. Remarkably, though, as Margaret Homans has pointed out, this scene of desire is the object of a strange interdiction in the narrative regime of the novel. For the celebrated moors remain a largely silent cipher within the representational eco-nomy of the text. Although Cathy and Heathcliff repeatedly repair to them, the moors—as Homans notes—are never presented directly in any scenes of the novel, and Cathy and Heathcliff are "never represented on the moors, together or apart, in either Lockwood's narrative or in any of the narratives that his encloses" (1986, 69).[17] The moors are thus the occasion of a strange figural silence in the text—as though they them-selves were the object of a symbolic prohibition. For Homans, this eli-sion or silencing of nature is designed to "preserve nature from the effects of symbolization"—symbolic effects that, insofar as they displace the "literal" object of nature with rhetorical signs of it, would lead to the "death of the object" and to the loss of nature's thinghood in language (1986, 73). For Homans, though, *Wuthering Heights* resists the occlusion of its beloved moors by paradoxically removing them from the scene of representation altogether.[18] Detaching nature from language, the novel locates it in a space beyond representation, and honors nature's primacy through the very rigor of its silence about it. In this sense the text shields nature and the moors—the excluded scenes of desire—by extracting them from language and sealing them up in silence. The scene of Cathy and Heathcliff's bliss is thus a repressed scene, but one that is at the same time *preserved* by this very repression.

In the drama of loss and mourning we have been tracing, the moors in the novel are thus the object of an encryptment: they are the place, that is to say, where the delirious Cathy Earnshaw finds her home—but a home that is also a grave or crypt, the sepulchre of her desiring self. In her delirium at the Grange, Cathy addresses her distraught husband, Edgar Linton, and hymns her unbridgeable separation from him, declar-ing her identification with the deadly site of her love:

> Ah! you are come, are you, Edgar Linton? . . . You are one of those things that are ever found when least wanted, and when you are wanted, never! I suppose we shall have plenty of lamentations, now. . . . I see we shall . . . but they can't keep me from my narrow home out yonder—My rest-ing place where I'm bound before Spring is over! There it is, not among

the Lintons, mind, under the chapel-roof; but in the open air with a head-stone, and you may please yourself, whether you go to them, or come to me! (*WH,* 126)

Cathy's "narrow home . . . in the open air" is the grave or crypt where her transgressive desire is buried. It is her "home" insofar as, separated from the object of her love, Heathcliff, she is already half dead to herself—and is already living the half-life of the tomb in which her illicit longing is interred. Cathy's prohibited love for Heathcliff finds its home beyond the borders of acceptability—beyond the orthodox "chapel-roof"—in a place where it is preserved stubbornly in its illegality. In a radical sense, moreover, Cathy's love is preserved insofar as it is *lost;* for her dream of death situates her fulfillment in dispossession and her home in dissolution. Cathy's life already belongs to the tomb; it is already a monument to privation.

According to Abraham and Torok, "preservative repression," as we have seen, involves the repression of an "illegitimate idyll and its loss"; it simultaneously walls up a transgression—the "illegitimate"—*and* a "loss." For *Wuthering Heights*—and Cathy's story—the moors are a similarly repressed scene in which a vision of illegitimate and lost bliss is commemorated, preserved, and encrypted: it is the place where liberty and insurgency are enshrined, as though in a living tomb. Indeed, Cathy identifies the fierce energies of her freedom with the blessing of the grave; raging in her illness, she insists to Nelly, "I'm burning! I wish I were out of doors—I wish I were a girl again, half savage and hardy, and free. . . . Why am I so changed? . . . I'm sure I should be myself were I once among the heather on those hills. . . . Open the window again wide, fasten it open! Quick, why don't you move?" And when Nelly replies, "Because I won't give you your death of cold," Cathy counters: "You won't give me a chance of life, you mean" (*WH,* 124–25). For Cathy, the moors are an immense, living crypt whose open spaces paradoxically sepulchre all she has lost, sealing it up in a tomb to which she longs to repair.

If the moors are mourned, then, in Cathy's story—and, in a sense, by the novel itself—it is because they are the place where emancipation is broached. They are the place where, in the exorbitant energies of the Cathy-Heathcliff relationship, boundaries are dissolved and differences overturned—even the boundary and difference between life and death. As Davies notes, Cathy and Heathcliff's identification "trespass[es] into the forbidden, subverting the power-hierarchy based on difference, refus[ing] the distinction between male and female, master and servant, sacred and profane" (1994, 212–13). Famously, Cathy and Heathcliff's relationship is also an aspiration to identity; but, in the world of the novel, this dream of fusion is in fact lethal, for it threatens to collapse back into radical undifferentiation the elaborate structures of difference—social, psychical, sexual—on which the novel's relationships are based. Cathy and Heathcliff's relationship aspires to unity and identity but discovers identity only in the liquefying work of death. To this extent, the moors—and the death and freedom they figure forth—are a parody of unity, collapsing distinction into undifferentiation, separation into dissolution. The moors enclose the ghost of unity, hosting a specter of lost love. As Homans notes, Cathy's "relation to Heathcliff . . . and her relation to nature [are] motivated by a desire to obliterate boundaries between self and other," but "within the terms of the literary work she inhabits any lack of differentiation . . . is fatal" (1986, 77–78).

At the level of the narrative, the drive toward undifferentiation is sustained by the figure of Heathcliff. In a radical sense Heathcliff's tragedy in the text is to be the *victim* of difference; he is excluded and exiled from any sanctioned place in the structure of familial, social, and symbolic distinctions governing the novel's universe. He is a subject of violent exclusion. Even before his death, he is the specter of *Wuthering Heights:* having no sanctioned place in its world, he is—as Charlotte Brontë divined—a wraith or spirit who cannot find a home in it, a malign demon haunting the novel's borders. Divided from Catherine by the violence of hierarchical difference, Heathcliff's revenge on the world that exiles him can be understood as the furious project of obliterating the divisions and hierarchies that brutally subjected him during his childhood at the Heights after old Mr. Earnshaw's death. Heathcliff's avenging ferocity after his return from the three-year absence that mysteriously brings him wealth and power threatens to annihilate the whole architecture of social and familial distinctions in place at the Heights and the Grange. Rapaciously, Heathcliff seeks to engulf the world that mastered him.

In his revenge, Heathcliff perversely and ruthlessly devours the whole symbolic and economic scene of the Heights and Grange, incorporating them within his power and subduing them to his narcissism. It is as though Heathcliff's project was to supplant every symbolic position in the novel with his own interloping life. Before his departure, Heathcliff supplants Hindley as favored son in old Earnshaw's eyes; later he usurps Hindley's role as father to Hareton (Hareton dubs him "Devil daddy"

[*WH,* 109]); and, still later, he becomes the second Catherine's "father" (*WH,* 268), usurping Edgar Linton's place both in relation to the daughter and the mother. Greedily and eagerly, Heathcliff ingests the symbolic roles debarred to him by the novel's forces of exclusion; he ventriloquizes the identities of son, father, and husband, playing the parts and miming the roles as if denying his severance from legitimized relationship, as though refusing to mourn the lack of origin that defines his history. Heathcliff's incorporation of the symbolic identities around him, in this sense, is a denial of his own loss of a story and identity.

But, if Heathcliff incorporates the roles and identities around him, he also annihilates their significance and stability, producing a demonic parody of the familial positions he supplants. Taking the places of others, he threatens the whole social world of *Wuthering Heights* with collapse; he is, indeed, a dark angel of destruction, swallowing the scene that disenfranchises him into his power, voraciously assimilating all its elements to himself. "[E]verything is ready, and in my power," he muses to Nelly late in the text, just before reporting the "strange change" that has finally robbed him of his will to destroy (*WH,* 320). Even his name suggests a force of engorgement and assimilation—a power of reduction back to archaic or primal elements, as though to enact Catherine's characterization of him as "an unreclaimed creature, without refinement—without cultivation; an arid wilderness of furze and whinstone" (*WH,* 101). As Nicholas Royle notes, "The desire inscribed in Heathcliff's name could be described as the desire for the appropriation of all that his name so commonly embraces: Penistone Crags, for instance, and the ubiquitous moors themselves" (39). "Heath-cliff," to this extent, denotes the fall into natural or primal undifferentiation of the social and cultural differences of the novel's world. If the name "Heathcliff," then, presides over the novel's narrative, it does so as a force of disintegration, plunging difference into dissolution.

To the extent that he impels differentiation into undifferentiation—into the maw of his own "power"—Heathcliff undoes distinction in the name of (his own) identity. He becomes lord and master of the novel's world. A victim of the novel's system of differences, he obliterates that system by engulfing it with his ego; his rapacious capitalism, in this sense, is a burlesque of the collapse of distinction, a mockery of the unity to which he aspires in his relation to Catherine. But if his manically acquisitive capitalism is a repression of the loss that defines him, Heathcliff's name nevertheless carries loss within itself: he is christened "Heathcliff" by the Earnshaw family as the "name of a son who died in childhood" (*WH*, 38). In this sense Heathcliff is the bearer of a crypt within himself—the crypt of the lost Earnshaw son—and "[d]eath is inscribed in [his] name" (Royle, 41). In terms of the novel's narration of generations, then, the living Heathcliff encloses a dead Heathcliff: a narrative corpse whose loss denotes deprivation in the Earnshaw clan. But, if Heathcliff is supposed to supply the place or make up the loss of this dead son, he ironically revisits upon the Earnshaws the deprivation silently marked in his name: for he plunges the Earnshaw inheritance into ruin and dispossesses Hareton Earnshaw of his hereditary rights. When Royle asks the question, "What is commemorated or concealed in the name of 'Heathcliff'[?]" (41), we might reply that it is *loss itself* that is enclosed or encrypted in his story. For Heathcliff lacks a knowable origin and history, and, when he returns like a "revenant" (Davies 1994, 89) from his three years away accoutred with wealth and power, his adult story remains as obscure as his infant origins. What Heathcliff encloses or carries within himself, then, is a condition and commission of loss: a dispossession or occlusion of known being. Nelly wonders of him, "Is he a ghoul, or a vampire?"—and, dismissing such thoughts, muses:

"But where did he come from, the little dark thing, harboured by a good man to his bane?" . . . And I began, half dreaming, to weary myself with imaging some fit parentage for him . . . I tracked his existence over again, with grim variations; at last, picturing his death and funeral; of which, all I can remember is, being exceedingly vexed at having the task of dictating an inscription for his monument, and consulting the sexton about it; and, as he had no surname, and we could not tell his age, we were obliged to content ourselves with the single word, "Heathcliff." That came true; we were. If you enter the kirkyard, you'll read on his headstone, only that, and the date of his death. (*WH*, 327)

Remarkably, Nelly's funereal cameo here erects the name "Heathcliff" itself as a crypt: the crypt, that is, of the "dark thing" that it names. For, lacking a knowable origin and end, Heathcliff's history is a conundrum and an aberration: without proper parentage, age, or name, he is a walking secret, an animate enigma whose being resists any attempt to know or master its meaning. Heathcliff himself is a crypt or secret, and his opaquely resistant name is the cryptic inscription over the unquiet tomb of his life. His obscure origin and mysterious three-year absence from the Heights effectively sepulchre the meaning of his being—removing it from the scene of the text and burying it within the novel's own inaccessible repressed. Whatever literary contexts or interpretive analogues are marshalled around him, "Heathcliff" escapes explanation and understanding; he resists the telling of his tale and encloses his truth in an unreachable place, in the living tomb of his story and psyche.

To the extent that he *is* a crypt, then, Heathcliff lives a spectral life. Enclosing loss and death inside himself, he carries the crypt of Heathcliff Earnshaw within and entombs the ghost of lost unity in his relation to Catherine. Heathcliff encrypts a lost life. But, as Abraham and Torok argue, the gesture of installing a "crypt" in the psyche—through the phantasmal act of "incorporation"—is not just a *response* to loss but also a *refusal* of loss. Specifically, it is a refusal of *mourning*—and is the preservative entombment of a loved and lost object within the self. They write:

> [I]n order not to have to "swallow" a loss, we fantasize swallowing (or having swallowed) that which has been lost, as if it were some kind of thing. . . . When . . . we ingest the love-object we miss, this means that *we refuse to mourn* and that we shun the consequences of mourning even though our psyche is fully bereaved. Incorporation is the refusal to reclaim as our own the part of ourselves that we placed in what we lost; incorporation is the refusal to acknowledge the full import of the loss, a loss that, if recognized as such, would effectively transform us. In fine, incorporation is the refusal to introject loss. The fantasy of incorporation reveals a gap within the psyche; it points to something that is missing just where introjection should have occurred. (126–27)

In this light, Heathcliff can be read as a veritable subject of "incorporation"; although he is defined by deprivation, he also *refuses the loss* that ravages him in the shape of his separation from Catherine. He refuses, that is, to "introject" Cathy's loss. Thus, famously, Heathcliff encrypts and incorporates the dead Catherine in his "soul" in an absolute refusal of her absence, a fierce repudiation of her death. He incorporates her and ingests her. Heathcliff is told of Catherine's death by Nelly, and, after Nelly has expressed the pious hope that Cathy should wake "kindly in the other world," Heathcliff delivers this astonishing reply:

> May she wake in torment! . . . Why, she's a liar to the end! Where is she? Not *there*—not in heaven—not perished—where? Oh! you said you cared nothing for my sufferings! And I pray one prayer—I repeat it till my tongue stiffens—Catherine Earnshaw, may you not rest, as long as I am living! You said I killed you—haunt me, then! The murdered *do* haunt their murderers. I believe—I know that ghosts *have* wandered on earth.

Be with me always—take any form—drive me mad! only *do* not leave me
in this abyss, where I cannot find you! Oh, God! it is unutterable! I *cannot*
live without my life! I *cannot* live without my soul! (*WH,* 167)

Heathcliff's fierce threnody rejects the orthodox idea that Cathy's
spirit is in heaven and her body destined for the earth. Repudiating the
spirit-matter dualism of conventional belief, Heathcliff commits Cathy's
soul to the errant life of the phantom: to a restless discontent rather
than repose, to being buried alive rather than buried. Refusing to locate
Cathy's presence either in heaven or the body, Heathcliff enjoins Cathy
to inhabit and "haunt" him rather than go to the next world or the
grave. He refuses to allow Cathy to depart either to beatitude or corruption; instead, he preserves her as the phantom of a crypt lodged inside
his self. In a radical sense, then, Heathcliff *refuses to mourn*. He refuses
Cathy's loss. He buries her in himself instead of in the grave: incorporating her like a phantom or a foreign body, *he himself becomes her tomb*. He
becomes the crypt where she is preserved; in this sense Cathy is the
phantom resident of an animate tomb. In this sense, too—and even
from beyond the grave—Cathy (to recall her famous formulation from
earlier in the novel) "is" Heathcliff. She becomes the ghostly life that
inhabits him.

During her illness, after insisting he has "killed" her because of his
conflict with Edgar, Cathy demands of Heathcliff, "How many years do
you mean to live after I am gone? . . . Will you forget me—will you be
happy when I am in the earth? Will you say twenty years hence, 'That's
the grave of Catherine Earnshaw. I loved her long ago, and was
wretched to lose her; but it is past. I've loved many others since.' . . .
Will you say so, Heathcliff?" (*WH,* 158). Effectively, Cathy's question
can be translated into the demand, "Will you mourn for me, Heathcliff?" The assumption built into her question is that *to mourn is to forget;*
and, as discussed in the reading of Brontë's poetry, according to Freud
mourning is that process through which the ego detaches its libidinal
investments from a lost (or dead) object and reinvests them elsewhere.
To mourn is to send the loved—and lost—object to the grave. Considered in this light, Cathy's demand is that Heathcliff refuse to mourn:
that he refuse to consign her to the destiny of the dead, to forgetfulness,
to replacement. Cathy's demand is to go unmourned, to live still, and to
be alive in Heathcliff.

Heathcliff responds to Cathy's accusation that he has killed her by
stating, "You have killed yourself" (*WH,* 160). Saying this, however,

Heathcliff insists that Cathy is in fact *already* dead: for the dead "Cathy" is Cathy Earnshaw, while the living Cathy is Cathy Linton, the mistress of Thrushcross Grange, wife of Edgar Linton. Loss, separation, and even death have, it seems, already occurred. Heathcliff anticipates Cathy's death as the interment of Cathy Earnshaw, but for him Cathy Earnshaw has already betrayed her "heart," has already murdered herself: "*Why* did you betray your own heart, Cathy? . . . What kind of living will it be when you—oh, God! would *you* like to live with your soul in the grave?" (*WH*, 161). Heathcliff encrypts the ghost of Cathy Earnshaw in his soul; but now, it seems, the grave threatens to purloin that lost phantom all over again.

The same is true for Catherine, however: insofar as Cathy and Heathcliff's relationship is defined by loss, it is a dramaturgy of mourning and of refused mourning *from the start*. Cathy and Heathcliff's is a wedding in disunion; it is a funereal nuptial. Characterized simultaneously by deprivation and refused deprivation, their relationship is the (mutually) preservative encryptment of a loved and lost other within the self *this* side of death. The antitheses between life and death, presence and absence, plenitude and loss are thus dissolved in the vicissitudes of a passion that unfolds as an agon of mourning and of refused mourning from the beginning. When Cathy speaks in her last stormy exchange with Heathcliff of "*my* Heathcliff"—as opposed to the one who torments her with reproaches now—she insists: "That is not *my* Heathcliff. I shall love mine yet; and take him with me—he's in my soul" (*WH*, 159). This demonstrates strikingly how, for her part, Cathy encrypts or enshrines a past or lost "Heathcliff" in her soul—and how she becomes the tomb or sarcophagus where that lost love is kept safe and preserved. Cathy is the crypt of Heathcliff, and Heathcliff the crypt of Cathy; and, just as each of their names uncannily encloses the letters of the other, so their identities strangely, privatively, and preservatively incorporate each other. Each "is" the other insofar as each cryptically ingests the other's life.

The crypt, however, is a monument to loss: it is, in Jacques Derrida's words, "the vault of a desire," the "tombstone of the illicit" (xvii, xxxiv). To the extent that Cathy's and Heathcliff's desire is transgressive and encrypted, then, it belongs to an unspeakable place in which it is an object both of prohibition and of preservation. Thus, Cathy, in her famous confession of her desire to Nelly, describes her illicit longing as a "secret" that cannot be voiced in the waking language of orthodoxy but only in the ghostly language of dream. Insisting, against herself, that she is "wrong" to marry Edgar Linton, she says: "It's my secret; but if you will not mock at me, I'll explain it; I can't do it distinctly—but I'll give you a feeling of how I feel" (*WH,* 79). When Nelly objects, "We're dismal enough without conjuring up ghosts and visions to perplex us" (*WH,* 79), Cathy insists on reporting to her the heretical dream in which, weeping and discontented in heaven, she is "flung" from beatitude by the angels back to the top of Wuthering Heights. Cathy thus defines her "secret" as her union with transgression and exile—that is to say, with Heathcliff: "That will do to explain my secret. . . . I've no more business to marry Edgar Linton than I have to be in heaven; and if [Hindley] had not brought Heathcliff so low, I shouldn't have thought of it. . . . I love him; and that, not because he's handsome, Nelly, but because he's more myself than I am. Whatever our souls are made of, his and mine are the same" (*WH,* 80).

Confessing her identity with Heathcliff, Cathy also discloses her strangeness to herself. She reveals that her identity resides in alterity, that she is enfolded and embraced by otherness. Famously claiming, "Nelly, I *am* Heathcliff," she says that the "secret" of her being is that she is not her own: that she exists not only "beyond" (*WH,* 81) her own self, but that her self is in fact the home of another, that she is inhabited—or haunted—by another. She "is" Heathcliff insofar as, this side of death, she is the living crypt that encloses him, while he is the "hidden ghost" (*CP,* 14) that has its home in her.

Clearly, this mutual identification of Cathy and Heathcliff—or, rather, mutual encryptment of Cathy and Heathcliff within one another—dismantles the notion of separate identity and autonomous selfhood. Instead, it makes the self the very house of the other, and identity the strange and uncanny host of difference. To this extent, the lost, prohibited, or excluded other—and, as we have seen, Cathy and Heathcliff's relationship is *defined* by such privation—appears within the self. The lost other takes up residence inside the self. As an ingestion of the lost object, incorporation lodges the other within the self as a foreigner, stranger, or uncanny guest: the object is at once interior and exterior to the subject. As Derrida remarks, it is an "outcast outside [installed] inside the inside" (xiv). In this strange structure of incorporation or encryptment—in which something is simultaneously lost to and kept inside the self—the autonomous subject is deconstructed, as the self becomes a house of phantoms, a room of ghosts, a lodging of strangers. Furthermore, this agon of spectral incorporation suggests that individual being is itself fashioned in and as a process of mourning: that is to say, in a process of mourning-as-separation that both Cathy and

Heathcliff, in different ways, refuse. The refusal of mourning in *Wuthering Heights* is, indeed, the refusal of separation and differentiation; Cathy and Heathcliff, scorning separation, inhabit each other in a mutual entombment and mutual encryptment. In this way we are returned to the fierce (and even impossible) repudiation of mourning—or separate subjectivity—figured in Cathy's and Heathcliff's celebrated and in a sense unreadable statements: "I *am* Heathcliff," "I *cannot* live without my life! I *cannot* live without my soul!"

What is preserved in the crypt is *what is lost;* but what is preserved is also what comes back—in the form of a phantom from the crypt. The ghost comes back, for example, in Cathy's fevered delirium at the Grange—in which, as discussed in chapter 4, her childhood past returns to her with all the delayed, destructive, and phantomatic force of trauma. Plunging hallucinatorily toward illness and death at the Grange, Cathy imagines herself (as she reports to Nelly) "enclosed in the oak-panelled bed at home," and she relates how her "heart ached with some great grief which, just waking, I could not recollect." In her derangement, she says, she became "a child; my father was just buried, and my misery arose from the separation that Hindley had ordered between me and Heathcliff—I was laid alone, for the first time" (*WH,* 124). Cathy's phantasmal return to the Heights is a return to a scene of both bliss *and* loss. "Enclosed in the oak-panelled bed," she revisits a loved idyll; but it is an idyll that has now become a crypt, the "enclosure" of her phantom desire. Envisioning herself immured in the childhood bed where she lay with Heathcliff, she returns to an encrypted scene and encrypted self; yet it is her *present* identity that is now the ghost that she does not recognize. The site that she revisits is one of both loss and pleasure, for it is the temporal and topographical commemoration of union and of "separation." The oak-paneled bed is, in this sense, a crypt that solemnizes deprivation and satisfaction. Insofar as Cathy's "recurring" fantasy (*WH,* 124), then, signifies her incorporation of her own lost childhood at the Heights, it stands, in Abraham's and Torok's terms, "[l]ike a commemorative monument . . . [and] betokens the place, the date, and the circumstances in which desires were banished from introjection": desires that are preserved for Cathy "like tombs in the life of the ego" (114). Cathy sepulchres her past at the Heights within her.

If Cathy carries the past at Wuthering Heights inside her like a crypt—a past that is at once lost and preserved—then the *return* of this crypt and its denizens to the world of Thrushcross Grange (and to

Cathy's later selfhood) deconstitutes her identity and plunges her into dissolution. The irruption of the crypt of the Heights into the comforts of the Grange resembles nothing so much as the return of a ghostly or gothic repressed into the house of Victorian fiction and identity: specifically, into Cathy's genteel identity as "the lady of Thrushcross Grange" (*WH,* 124). And this spectral return—revisiting Cathy's past self upon her present being—occurs at the price of her disintegration as a subject.

Heathcliff, too, bears a crypt inside himself, as we have seen. On the day of Cathy's funeral, Isabella notes that Heathcliff's face is "sealed in an expression of unspeakable sadness" (*WH,* 178); this "sealing" of Heathcliff denotes the sealing up of his grief, too—the burial of his mourning in an inexpressible or "unspeakable" interior where it is unavailable for symbolization and is interred in the crypt of his being. Heathcliff's subsequent history in the novel, indeed, can be read as a relentless and ferocious enclosure of his "sadness" within—the burial of his inconsolable grief—for Heathcliff ingests Cathy in an interminable commemoration. At the end of the novel, however, Cathy's ghost—and his own buried and preserved past—returns on Heathcliff with radically dissolving power in the story of the second Cathy and Hareton. What Heathcliff sees in the physical aspect of Hareton is, as he puts it, "the ghost of my immortal love, of my wild endeavours to hold my right, my degradation, my pride, my happiness, and my anguish—" (*WH,* 321). To "hold" bliss and loss together in this way is, for Heathcliff, to construct a commemorative crypt to a vanished love: but, at the end of the novel, Heathcliff is unable precisely to "hold" that happiness and anguish in the crypt where he has lodged them. Instead of Cathy being within Heathcliff in an inner tomb or sarcophagus, she comes back to haunt him *from without* in the shape of the young lovers, Cathy and Hareton. As Cathy and Hareton, in Nelly's words, "lift . . . their eyes together, to encounter Mr Heathcliff," they turn on him the phantom eyes of "Catherine Earnshaw" (*WH,* 319). Thus, strikingly, Cathy revisits Heathcliff from the *outside*—with the result that Heathcliff's narcissistic, incorporative, and proprietorial "hold" on her dissolves, and Cathy is reinscribed unredeemably in otherness. With this, Heathcliff's identity dissolves, too, for he wanes into detachment and death and is "swallowed in . . . anticipation" (*WH,* 322) of the unattained tomb. Instead of keeping her within him, then, Heathcliff forfeits Cathy to otherness all over again; and instead of Cathy being enclosed in the grave that *is* Heathcliff, the entire world becomes a crypt that encloses her. As Heathcliff famously intones:

. . . what is not connected with her to me? and what does not recall her? I cannot look down to this floor, but her features are shaped on the flags! In every cloud, in every tree—filling the air at night, and caught by glimpses in every object by day, I am surrounded with her image!—The most ordinary faces of men and women—my own features—mock me with a resemblance. The entire world is a dreadful collection of memoranda that she did exist, and that I have lost her! (*WH*, 320–21)

If the world thus memorializes Cathy's existence, nothing can contain or hold her phantom any longer: she is everywhere and, by the same token, nowhere. Mourning, then, dissolves in an uncontainable return of the dead, in an absolute *revenance*. The crypt engulfs the world. But, if mourning in Heathcliff's story therefore collapses in a play of *revenance* and haunting—if the dead come back uncontainably and shape themselves in clouds, trees, faces, and flags—the novel itself seems to end with a strange return of the dead, with a cryptic incorporation, and with an uncanny refusal of mourning. It ends with the eerie stories of the country folk about the "phantoms" (*WH*, 333) of Catherine and Heathcliff walking abroad. More crucially, the last two paragraphs of the novel—themselves Lockwood's own final act of mourning, his own attempt at laying the ghosts of the narrative to rest—are disturbed by a curious effect of textual *revenance*, by a ghostly return of the dead in the letters and figures that memorialize them. The novel ends:

> I sought, and soon discovered, the three head-stones on the slope next the moor—the middle one grey, and half buried in *heath*—Edgar Linton's only harmonised by the turf, and moss creeping up its foot— *Heath*[/]*cliff*'s still *bare*.
> I lingered round them, under that benign sky; watched the moths fluttering among the *heath,* and *hare-bells;* listened to the soft wind breathing through the grass; and wondered how anyone could ever imagine unquiet slumbers for the sleepers in that quiet earth. (*WH*, 334; emphases added)

As it closes, the narrative lays to rest *and* resurrects its own ghosts. For, of the three head-stones observed by Lockwood, Catherine's is "*half* buried in heath," Linton's is the "*only* [one] harmonised by the turf," and Heathcliff's is "*still bare*": these graves seem, strangely and unsettlingly, to be sites of only half-burial. In the verbal play of "buried in heath . . . Heathcliff . . . bare . . . fluttering among the heath, and hare-bells," moreover, the text seems to encrypt and decrypt its own names—*heath*/

Heathcliff . . . Heath-*cliff/bare* . . . bare/*Hare*-ton . . . Hareton/*hare*-bells . . . bells/Isa*bell*a . . . and perhaps, even, bells/Ellis *Bell*—in such a way that the novel's (and the author's) names survive as graphic ghosts to haunt the reading mind, marking the language of the text as itself ghostly: a linguistic crypt, one might say, that simultaneously lays to rest and raises its own phantoms, mourning and preserving its sleepless dead.

Chapter Six

An Interpreter between Her and the World: Emily Brontë's Critics

An interpreter ought always to have stood between her and the world.
(*WH*, xxxii)

So Charlotte Brontë wrote of her sister Emily in her "Biographical Notice of Ellis and Acton Bell," written to accompany the reprint of *Wuthering Heights* and of Anne Brontë's *Agnes Grey* in 1850. In this "Notice"—and, indeed, in her "Editor's Preface" to the 1850 edition—Charlotte appointed herself Emily's "interpreter" to the world; in these two texts, Charlotte aims to mediate between Emily's recusant writings and the metropolitan literary culture or "world" to which she desired that her own work, together with that of her sisters, should gain access. In this context, Charlotte's account of Emily amounts to both a defense and an apology, for she seeks to mollify the fierce energies of *Wuthering Heights* for the consumption of the polite Victorian audience that had—in the first reviews of the novel upon its 1847 publication—deprecated it as a work of "power," but a power that was at once "grotesque" and "purposeless" (Allott 1974, 224, 228).[1] In response to this judgment, Charlotte's strategy was to concur but to insist that the novel's strangeness and wildness sprang from the "inefficiently cultured" mind of her sister and the "alien and unfamiliar" world of the novel itself—bristling as it did with "the rough, strong utterance, the harshly manifested passions, the unbridled aversions, and headlong partialities of unlettered moorland hinds and rugged moorland squires" (*WH*, xxx, xxxiii). In this way, Charlotte naturalized both her sister and the novel she had produced: she represented Emily and her text, that is, as proceeding from "the impulse of nature" and as being rooted in an uncultivated rusticity that was recognizable, in fact, as a scene of Romantic literary inspiration, in which the artist who "possesses the creative gift owns something of which he is not always master—something that at times strangely wills and works for itself" (*WH*, xxxii, xxxvi). Herself a child of nature, and her novel a foster-child of nature, Emily Brontë and *Wuthering Heights* were thus constructed by Charlotte as literary ingenues, hardly knowing what they did but working their effects in a rude hybrid of human art and unconscious nature: "The statuary found a granite block on a solitary moor," Charlotte muses, "[and w]ith time and labour, the crag took human shape; and there it stands colossal, dark, and frowning, half statue, half rock: in the former sense, terrible and goblin-like; in the latter, almost beautiful, for its colouring is of mellow grey, and moorland moss clothes it; and heath, with its blooming bells and balmy fragrance, grows faithfully close to the giant's foot" (*WH*, xxxvii). Charlotte's terms here—"half statue, half rock"—seem always about to collapse Emily's artistry back into the uncultivated nature from which it is supposed to issue, as though *Wuthering Heights* itself were a work or product of nature's power.

This naturalization of Brontë's art is a persistent motif in criticism of her work up until the early twentieth century. Sydney Dobell, for example, writing in 1850 like Charlotte, speaks of the "native power" and "instinctive art" with which *Wuthering Heights* is imbued; moreover, he describes the novel's effect in terms of the more-than-human force of nature: "One looks back at the whole story as to a world of brilliant figures in an atmosphere of mist; shapes that come out upon the eye, and burn their colours into the brain, and depart into the enveloping fog." Dobell's other emphasis, however, completes the picture of Brontë that held sway up until the advent of a more formalistically based criticism in the 1920s and 1930s: describing Brontë's art as the "unformed writing of a giant's hand[,] the 'large utterance' of a baby god," Dobell melds the inartistry of the instinctual with the expansiveness of the metaphysical—and hints that, if Brontë's work issued from nature, it also passed irresistibly into supernature (Allott 1974, 279, 280). This heady mixture of natural and metaphysical terminologies has frequently characterized descriptions of Brontë, and it is exhibited at perhaps its most extraordinary in a remark of G. K. Chesterton's about *Wuthering Heights* in 1913, when he mused that Brontë's "imagination was sometimes superhuman—always inhuman. *Wuthering Heights* might have been written by an eagle."[2] Written by an eagle, *Wuthering Heights* would then, presumably, fly too high for mere human natural power to reach it, and in this way it could broach the glories of the transcendent.

Chesterton's remark may be risible, but it is not untypical: other (admittedly more sophisticated) versions of this point have also marked

Brontë criticism. For example, in many ways modern criticism of *Wuthering Heights* begins with David Cecil's chapter on Emily Brontë in his *Early Victorian Novelists* (1934)—Cecil's reading combines an interest in the naturalizing and metaphysical dimensions of *Wuthering Heights* with a newer emphasis on the formal or structural features of the text. Famously—and, as it proved for much later criticism, paradigmatically—Cecil's essay stages the novel as a myth of cosmic conflict and resolution that has little to do with the generic forms of nineteenth-century narrative realism but instead offers a drama of "natural forces" doing battle in the arena of the "eternal verities" (Cecil, 131, 133). Cecil writes:

> The setting is a microcosm of the universal scheme as Emily Brontë conceived it. On the one hand, we have Wuthering Heights, the land of storm; high on the barren moorland, naked to the shock of the elements, the natural home of the Earnshaw family, fiery, untamed children of the storm. On the other, sheltered in the leafy valley below, stands Thrushcross Grange, the appropriate home of the children of calm, the gentle, passive, timid Lintons. Together each group, following its own nature in its own sphere, combines to compose a cosmic harmony. It is the destruction and re-establishment of this harmony which is the theme of the story. (130)

Cecil's universe is a reassuring place of "natural" or "cosmic order" whose temporary disturbance is inevitably overcome by the forces of metaphysical harmony (Cecil, 131, 133). Furthermore, the harmonious pattern that for Cecil is the ideological desideratum of Brontë's novel is, he hints, mirrored by the formal and structural patterns of the text itself; he suggests that the text's "artistic structure" replicates and incarnates the "coherent order" that it espouses on the metaphysical level (Cecil, 130). In this sense Cecil's position is as formalist as it is metaphysical. Buried in Cecil's cosmology, however, is an ideological repression: the repression of the historical scene of Brontë's text itself. This elision is revealed most starkly not in Cecil's text but in a later reading by Dorothy Van Ghent—a reading that broadly follows Cecil's naturalizing and mythologizing emphasis. Van Ghent intones:

> Concerned with eternal principles of life, death, love and immortality, [*Wuthering Heights*] has a timeless quality that puts it far nearer to such a work as *The Faerie Queene* than to any contemporary Victorian novel. It has no concern for social questions, but is an expression of primitive pas-

sions, of the elemental forces in Man and Nature that the author shows as connecting all Creation. [Brontë's] is a cosmic vision that has little to do with nineteenth-century materialism.[3]

Van Ghent's metaphysical rhapsody abstracts Brontë's text from time, history, and politics and lodges it securely in the untouchable realm of universal myth. For Van Ghent, myth is a place where critical understanding gives way to the celebration of cosmic mystery. "No one questions the action of *Wuthering Heights*," she writes, "it is far too compelling to be explained and is invested throughout with the unequivocal nature of supernatural vision" (quoted in Kavanagh, 4).

Unsurprisingly, this anti-intellectual and ideologically conservative excision of Brontë's text from history has been furiously repudiated by Marxist critics; for such a position "block[s]," in Terry Eagleton's words, "any attempt to think through [the novel] in relation to the real historical world in which [it is] rooted" and fosters instead the view of the novel as some "unaccountable natural phenomenon which, like a storm or a sunset, is to be admired rather than analysed" (Kavanagh, ix). One could, for example, hardly imagine any critical distance greater than that between Cecil's and Van Ghent's cosmic mythologizing and the Marxist critic Arnold Kettle's baldly demystifying historicization of Brontë's text. Kettle writes, for example, that "*Wuthering Heights* is about England in 1847 and the years before"; he contends that the novel "is concerned not with love in the abstract but with the passions of living people, with property-ownership, the attraction of social comforts, the arrangement of marriages, the importance of education, the validity of religion, the relations of rich and poor."[4] Kettle's political reading thus debunks the antihistoricism of the mythological Brontë; as a result, a radically different *Wuthering Heights* emerges—one that stages not the conflict and resolution of abstract metaphysical forces but the violent antagonism of conflicting socioeconomic groups. Heathcliff, then, is not a principle of passion but a "waif from the Liverpool slums" (Kettle, 1:133); and his revenge against Hindley Earnshaw and Edgar Linton critically turns back upon the ruling class the unacceptable brutality of their own methods. Heathcliff's vengeance thus has a "moral force" and lays bare the weapons of the ruling class—namely, "money and arranged marriages, . . . expropriation and property deals"—with the result that a "veil [is] drawn from the conventional face of bourgeois man; he [is] revealed, through Heathcliff, without his mask." Consequently, Brontë's text both articulates and critiques the forms of sociopolitical power in "nineteenth-century capitalist society" (Kettle, 1:140, 143, 144).

Terry Eagleton's reading of Brontë in *Myths of Power* (1975)—discussed in chapter 4—remains, as Kavanagh notes, "the most complete recent Marxist analysis of *Wuthering Heights*" (Kavanagh, 10). But Eagleton's perspective is quite different from Kettle's. While Kettle tends to transpose social and economic class positions from the "outside" on to the novel—seeing the text as representing or reflecting an external class-political reality—Eagleton focuses on the ideological form of the text itself. Thus, *Wuthering Heights* for Eagleton does not so much reflect an ideology as produce one—and this ideology is read in the internal "fissuring" of the text between incompatible aesthetic and representational idioms. Eagleton argues, for example, that while Charlotte Brontë's fiction tends toward the "pragmatic integration" of "contending forces" in psyche and society, Emily's work presents the "exhausting confrontation" between such forces (1975, 98); consequently, it refuses any easy or premature accommodation of incompatible energies in some comforting ideology of social and individual harmony.[5] Instead, the value of Brontë's text for Eagleton is that it hurls social and aesthetic contradictions against one another and refuses to eradicate conflict in the name of mythical and ideological resolution. *Wuthering Heights,* says Eagleton, stages the "ineradicable contradiction" between the "passion and society it presents," a contradiction that synchronizes, at the formal level, "the most shattering passion with the most rigorous realist control." Thus, Heathcliff, in one respect, figures "an 'outdated' . . . increasingly mythical realm of personal value which capitalist social relations cancel"; but in another respect he is the purest embodiment of those venal social relations (1975, 100–101, 113). By presenting rather than smoothing over contradictions, then, *Wuthering Heights* makes possible for Eagleton a critical awareness of the conflictual shape of nineteenth-century social reality. In this way the novel exposes rather than conceals the fissures in the ideological forms in which it is enmeshed.

When *Wuthering Heights* first appeared, its reviewers charged it with inartistry (see chapter 4); and, as we saw, Charlotte Brontë herself colluded with this view in 1850 when she represented her sister's novel as an outpouring of passion rather than a work of art. David Cecil's mythological reading in the 1930s wedded an emphasis on the novel's passions with an appreciation of its structural form; but in the 1940s and 1950s critics increasingly stressed the "poetic" qualities of Brontë's text. It was in this period that the literary formalism of the New Criticism was dominant, and critics tended to import to the reading of Brontë's text the methods of verbal analysis previously reserved for the study of poetry. Thus, G. D. Klingopulos in 1947 published an essay in *Scrutiny* in which he hailed *Wuthering Heights* as displaying the linguistic and formal qualities characteristic of poetry and Elizabethan drama. Arguing that Brontë's text forged the intensities of passion into a triumphant literary form that symbolized rather than simplified the "vitality of the feelings" it invoked, Klingopulos contended that *Wuthering Heights* possessed the formal virtuosity of poetic drama, marrying content (passion) with form (the novel) in an aesthetic unity—the kind of unity beloved of English and American New Critics in the 1940s and 1950s.[6] And, again, Mark Schorer in an essay of 1949 celebrated the wedding of form (for him, linguistic and rhetorical form) and matter in *Wuthering Heights* by documenting in detail the ways in which the novel's metaphorical texture determined the meanings that it produced. "Emily Brontë's metaphors colour all her diction," says Schorer; and he shows how these metaphors "signify" or construct the novel's world by habitually linking "[h]uman conditions" to landscape, to the elements and to animals.[7] But perhaps the clearest statement of the critical formalism that dominated readings of Brontë until the 1960s is found in Dorothy Van Ghent's *The English Novel: Form and Function* (1953), when she writes: "The form of [*Wuthering Heights*] . . .—a form that may be expressed as a tension between the impulse to excess and the impulse to limitation or economy—*is* the content. The form, in short, is the book itself. Only in the fully wrought, fully realized, work of art does form so exhaust the possibilities of the material that it identifies itself with these possibilities."[8]

Van Ghent's formalist approach is part of a creed that celebrates the "fully wrought" and "fully realized" work of art but that in doing so effaces other crucially determining factors in the production of the text—for example, history and gender. Thus, just as the "metaphysical" reading of Brontë erased the historical scene of *Wuthering Heights,* so "formalist" perspectives effaced the dimension of gender. As Lyn Pykett observes: "The emphasis on the novel's metaphysics more or less entirely displaced questions of gender. [And t]he author's gender was also a matter of no interest to the New Critics of the 1950s, who eschewed biographical and historical specificities in favour of an exclusive interest in the novel as verbal structure" (127). It was, in fact, only with the rise of feminist criticism in the 1970s that the question of gender—and of Emily Brontë as a female writer working within (and against) a male literary tradition—was posed. Indeed, in richly diverse ways, feminist criticism has brought about a veritable revolution in the understanding both of Emily Brontë's work and that of her sisters.

Nevertheless, the issue of gender determined the very form in which *Wuthering Heights*—and *Poems by Currer, Ellis, and Acton Bell*—appeared first to the public. As Charlotte Brontë explained in "Biographical Notice of Ellis and Acton Bell," the Brontës' literary pseudonyms were chosen with an anxious eye on the sexual politics of the Victorian reading public. Charlotte wrote:

> [T]he ambiguous choice [of names was] dictated by a sort of conscientious scruple at assuming Christian names positively masculine, while we did not like to declare ourselves women, because—without at that time suspecting that our mode of writing and thinking was not what is called "feminine"—we had a vague impression that authoresses are liable to be looked on with prejudice; we had noticed how critics sometimes use for their chastisement the weapon of personality, and for their reward, a flattery, which is not true praise. (*WH*, xxvii)

Carol Ohmann notes that an ideological shift occurred in the critical responses of reviewers between the 1847 and 1850 editions of *Wuthering Heights*. In 1847, most reviewers—despite the fact that the name "Ellis" was, as Charlotte said, "ambiguous" in gender terms—simply "assumed without comment that the writer's sex was masculine."[9] Furthermore, some reviewers saw in *Wuthering Heights* a positive display of masculine daring and praised the novel for it—although they also struck a note of reservation in their praise (presumably, because of the effects that they feared such a "coarse" and tempestuous book might have upon the largely female reading public). An unsigned review in the *Examiner,* for example, declared: "We detest the affectation and effeminate frippery which is but too frequent in the modern novel, and willingly trust ourselves with an author who goes at once fearlessly into the moors and desolate places, for his heroes; but we must at the same time stipulate that he shall not drag into light all that he discovers, of coarse and loathsome, in his wanderings" (quoted in Allott 1974, 222). Another critic—G. W. Peck in the *American Review*—made the sexual-political agenda of the *Examiner*'s worries explicit: "We shall take for granted that a novel which has excited so unusual an attention, has been or will soon be in the hands of most of our readers of light literature. . . . If we did not know that this book has been read by thousands of young ladies in the country, we should esteem it our first duty to caution them against it simply on account of the coarseness of the style" (quoted in Allott 1974, 236).

But if the novel was judged to be powerfully—and even excessively—"masculine" on its first publication, a "gender-determined double standard" (Kavanagh, 2) took hold of the reviewers on its 1850 reprinting; for in 1850 the novel was prefaced by Charlotte's revelation that the powerful figure of "Ellis Bell" was in fact "[m]y sister Emily" (*WH*, xxvii). As a consequence, what was admired by the reviewers as manly and daring (if rude and rough) in 1847 was judged to be culpably and extravagantly feminine in 1850. Thus, in Sydney Dobell's 1850 review in the *Palladium, Wuthering Heights* was dubbed "the flight of an impatient fancy fluttering in the very exultation of young wings," while its "authoress" was castigated for having "too often disgusted, where she should have terrified . . . [allowing] us a familiarity with her fiend [Heathcliff] which has ended in unequivocal contempt" (quoted in Allott 1974, 278). The 1850 *Wuthering Heights,* then, was deprecated as "dangerously 'excessive' " (Kavanagh, 2) instead of daringly adventurous—the product of an immature feminine fancy rather than of mature masculine boldness.

The tendency to see *Wuthering Heights* in terms of an aberrant feminine fancy is, as Ohmann demonstrates, a pervasive feature of the patriarchal critical tradition surrounding Emily Brontë. Ohmann analyzes, for example, Thomas Moser's 1962 Freudian approach to the novel, in which he reads the text patronizingly as the dramatization of the repressed sexual longings of the "intense, inhibited spinster of Haworth" (Ohmann, 911)—asking in his title, "What Is the Matter with Emily Jane?"[10] Ohmann concludes: "Moser [approaches] *Wuthering Heights* with the idea that what is masculine is natural, unrestrained, energetically or vibrantly sexual, fearless, and forceful to the point of violence . . . [while w]hat is feminine is inhibited, inhibiting, timid, conventional, and censorious. The novel is a masterpiece when it appears to celebrate this idea of masculinity; it is trash when it does not." For Moser, Ohmann shows, Heathcliff in *Wuthering Heights* is a figure of uninhibited male sexual energy—which Brontë timorously affirms, but from which she ultimately retreats as a "sexually deprived and frustrated old maid" (Ohmann, 911).

If Brontë's early critics (and, as we have seen, her later male commentators, as well) tended to gender the novel as "masculine" to the extent that it was judged to be bold and adventurous, and "feminine" to the extent that it was fancifully uncertain, feminist critics have radically transvalued that judgment in recent years. Indeed, for feminist scholars, Brontë's literary daring is an index of her sexual-political protest against the patriarchy of the literary tradition that she inherits and the gendered categories of nineteenth-century culture; and her turbulent energies denote feminist rebellion rather than masculinist identification. The first fully developed account of Brontë as a feminist writer, in fact, comes in Sandra M. Gilbert and Susan Gubar's monumental *The Madwoman in the Attic: The Woman Writer and the Nineteenth-Century Literary Imagination* (1979). Their study is a groundbreaking analysis of the troubled place of the nineteenth-century woman writer in the male literary tradition; it exhaustively explores the strategies by which various female writers negotiated and subverted the oppressive forms of patriarchal culture. At the literary level, Gilbert and Gubar delineate a textual drama in which the woman writer struggles beneath the influence of what Virginia Woolf, in *A Room of One's Own* (1929), calls "Milton's bogey"[11]—that is, the cultural force of John Milton's masculinist myth of the Creation and Fall in his definitive Christian epic, *Paradise Lost* (1667). If Milton's patriarchal myth is the culturally dominant version of the origin and fall of "Man," the story that his epic in fact tells, according to Gilbert and Gubar, is that of "woman's secondness . . . [of] her demonic anger, her sin, her fall, and her exclusion" (191); Milton's Eve, they argue, becomes the paradigm of fallen femininity for the nineteenth-century woman writer. Concerning Brontë, Gilbert and Gubar chart the way in which *Wuthering Heights* dramatizes a woman's story—that of Catherine Earnshaw—as the simultaneous reception of and rebellion against Miltonic female fallenness. Thus, Gilbert and Gubar describe Brontë's revisionary feminist response to Milton in the following way: "Emily Brontë's *Wuthering Heights* . . . is a radically corrective 'misreading' of Milton, a kind of Blakeian Bible of Hell, with the fall from heaven to hell transformed into a fall from a realm that conventional theology would associate with 'hell' (the Heights) to a place that parodies 'heaven' (the Grange)" (189). Resisting and refiguring Milton, then—and presenting Cathy's movement from Wuthering Heights to Thrushcross Grange as an inverted "fall" into conventional goodness (see chapter 4)—Brontë's text transvalues the categories of orthodoxy, offering a "demonic" version of Milton's epic in which a rebellious woman preserves her fierce desires in contravention of conformity and piety.

    Stevie Davies, however, argues that Gilbert's and Gubar's assumption that Brontë's relationship to Milton is anxious is misplaced—and she seeks to "imagine a model . . . of the creative psyche less replete with anxiety and representing less an *agon* of oppression" than Gilbert's and Gubar's reading allows.[12] Thus, she sees Milton's influence as enabling rather than disabling to Brontë: "We can hypothesise an enabling Milton, whose punitive 'fatherhood' was a good excuse for the excitement of rebellion and whose own revolutionary Puritanism furnished the vindication for such heretical dissidence" (1988, 7). This means that Brontë is less "weakened and impaired" by patriarchal tradition than some feminist critics have implied; instead, the patriarchal Milton becomes an empowering figure who energizes Brontë's heresies. Brontë is thus an artist who rejects Milton's "creed of the Father-God" and, in a "joyous literary feud," celebrates the energies of earthly desire rather than heavenly bliss as, in a feminist rebellion, she displaces "the supernatural to the natural, the Father's transcendence to the mother's immanence" (1988, 15, 25, 118–19).

Another significant work on Brontë's relationship to patriarchal tradition, closer to Gilbert and Gubar's than Davies's, is Margaret Homans's *Women Writers and Poetic Identity: Dorothy Wordsworth, Emily Brontë, Emily Dickinson* (1980). Homans's book offers a sustained—to date the most sustained—feminist critique of Emily Brontë's poetry. According to Homans, nineteenth-century lyric poetry by women—including that of Emily Brontë—is in a necessarily agonistic relationship to the dominant idioms of lyric writing embodied in the forms of male Romantic poetry. Homans's argument is that, writing within the genre of the lyric, Brontë finds herself subjected to a formal "[s]elf-alienation" since the Romantic lyric posits a "central poetic self" that identifies itself as the origin of poetic power—yet such centered subjectivity is precisely what is denied to the woman writer by patriarchal culture. Homans argues, in fact (as noted in chapter 4), that the generic form of the novel allows for a greater "dispersiveness" of utterance than does the internalizing form of the lyric—and, consequently, that *Wuthering Heights* is more successful in evading or overcoming the anxieties of speech divisively displayed in the poems (1980, 129). As shown in chapter 3, however, Homans's argument, while suggestive, tends to underestimate the dialogic play of utterance—the *drama* of pluralized voices—that unfolds in Brontë's poetry: for Brontë's poetry is as dramatic as it is lyric. Homans's argument is valuable, nonetheless, for situating Brontë's writing within a gendered topography of generic forms.

The feminist reading of Brontë's work in terms of the gendering of generic and historical types is also pursued in work by Carol Senf, Nancy Armstrong, and Lyn Pykett. Senf argues that the temporal progression from the first to second generations in *Wuthering Heights* is a structural metaphor for Brontë's "feminist history" in her novel. She argues that Brontë's narrative is profoundly occupied with the forces of historical transformation, and that—despite appearances and the emphases of critics—"[t]he story of *Wuthering Heights* is not the story of Hareton, the patriarch, or even of Heathcliff. It is the almost buried story of Catherine, mother and daughter."[13] For Senf, this story is not just "buried" in the novel but in history, as well; it is the story of nothing other than woman's entrance into the "mainstream of history" (202). Senf quotes Gilbert and Gubar's remark that Isabella Linton in *Wuthering Heights* has been "taught to believe in coercive literary conventions" and is "victimized by the genre of romance"—for romance "reinforce[s] the traditional sexual roles that give power to men" (210)—yet she argues that the final relationship in the novel, Cathy and Hareton's, reshapes patriarchal dominance into a more "feminine" and "egalitarian" mode. The novel's earlier marriages, indeed—Catherine and Edgar's, Isabella and Heathcliff's—are based on the institutionalization of patriarchal power, yet Senf contends that the novel moves toward a situation in which "women are no longer the victims of patriarchal history" but escape the oppressive and archaic typologies of romance by breaking into a more progressive feminist history (209). Thus, Cathy teaches Hareton to read, interpellating him in a culture of which he is no longer the master; Cathy's and Hareton's relationship in this sense represents for Senf "a softening—a feminizing—of patriarchal history" (212).

Nancy Armstrong in *Desire and Domestic Fiction* (1987) offers a complex "political history of the novel" (the subtitle of her study) in which Emily Brontë's work is seen as colluding with but also subverting dominant nineteenth-century constructions of gendered subjectivity. On one level Armstrong reads *Wuthering Heights* (and the feminized genre of "domestic fiction") as colluding with the relegation of women's experience to the margins of history—that is, to a "domestic" space separate from politics and the institutions of power, where "subjectivity, . . . desire, pleasure, . . . the body, . . . gender differences, and family relations" are in the ascendant.[14] This marginalization means that the "production of the sexual subject" is necessarily accompanied by the "production of the political unconscious," as politics is occluded by family history (1987, 191). On another level, however, a "political history" *is* inscribed in Brontë's text, Armstrong insists: a political history of female desire. Thus, in the "disjunction of their social identities," the two Catherines in the novel chart a "shifting trajectory of female desire": a trajectory whose disruptive effects both disturb polite conjugality (in the first Cathy's marriage to Linton) and grimly ironize "monogamous desire" (in the second Cathy's grotesque betrothal to the dying Linton Heathcliff) (1987, 196). What *Wuthering Heights* narrates, according to Armstrong, is "a tale told by a woman . . . a history of sexuality" that, in Foucauldian mode, requires "another order of history that is no longer considered history at all" (1987, 197): for it is a "female" history of disjunctions, discontinuities and incoherences.[15]

Lyn Pykett in *Emily Brontë* (1989) makes a similar point but mounts her argument in explicitly generic rather than historical-cultural terms—and hints that the final outcome of *Wuthering Heights* is ambiguous in feminist terms. Pykett reads Brontë's text as effectively recapitulating the generic history of the novel itself as a form; for it moves from the mode of the "gothic plot" (an eighteenth- and early nineteenth-century Romantic form) in its first part to the mode of "domestic fiction" (a mid-nineteenth-century Victorian or realist form) in its second. For Pykett, Cathy and Heathcliff's story broadly belongs to the former idiom—while the second Cathy and Hareton's relationship belongs to the latter. The Cathy-Heathcliff plot is characterized by the generic priorities of Romantic-gothic form to the extent that it emphasizes the "passions," the importance of "childhood," and dramatizes a "romantic quest for selfhood" and "aspiring individualism" (73). Furthermore, the novel displays its gothic heritage by presenting—in the stories of the first and second Catherines, and of Isabella Linton—the "domestic space as [a] prison," and "the family as [a] site of primitive passions, violence, struggle and control" (85). The second half of the novel, however, moves "progressively in the direction of Victorian Domestic Realism," where a "conventional closure" is secured by which "the hero (Hareton) and heroine (Catherine) overcome the obstacles of an obstructive society and withdraw into a private realm of domesticity" (76). It is here, Pykett hints, that the novel's feminist ambivalence opens up. For while the first Catherine "is an image of female power [that is] doomed to find no channel in the social world of the novel" (91), the second Catherine accommodates herself to domesticity in a way that her mother never could—acquiring in the process, nevertheless, a power of self-definition that belies the seeming conventionality of the novel's ending. The second Catherine's story thus presents a feminist advance over the frustrated desires of the first generation, even though the second generation continues to be haunted by the fierce and uncompromising aspirations of the first; the two Catherines therefore together present a divided image of nineteenth-century womanhood, one half of which dramatizes the tragic contradictions of a female desire split between rebellion and conventionality (Catherine Earnshaw), and the other half of which charts the construction of a female subjectivity that negotiates its own limitations as it forges a new identity for itself (Catherine Linton).

Pykett's analysis is valuable for the way in which its discussion of formal and generic issues—such as the conflict between "gothic" and "domestic" modes—illuminates Brontë's dramatization of the politics of gendered identity. Formal, linguistic, or rhetorical issues are also the focus of a number of poststructuralist and deconstructive treatments of *Wuthering Heights*. While no politics of reading is explicitly broached by such readings, poststructuralist discussions valuably disclose the ways in which the structural and figural instabilities of *Wuthering Heights* mean that *all* readings of the text are hazarded in a theater of critical contestation—with the result that no interpretation is ever fully determinate or stable but is instead part of an ongoing process of dissension in which no position can claim mastery. This means that all readings are irreducibly political; that is to say, that criticism is inevitably a perilous negotiation of conflicts between meanings rather than the arrival at any final truth. For Frank Kermode, for example, in a famous essay on Brontë's novel, it is the very plurality or indeterminacy of meaning in *Wuthering Heights* that renders it a "classic"—classic being defined here as the quality of being disarmingly open to critical reconfiguration, rather than amenable to interpretive closure. Thus, Kermode insists that "it is not a question of deciding which is the single right reading [of Brontë's text], but of dealing, as reader, with a series of indeterminacies which the text will not resolve."[16] The position of the reader is, in this sense, necessarily precarious; repeating the instabilities inscribed in the form of the novel, the critic remains subject to the "intrinsic plurality of the text" (McNees, 2:348).

J. Hillis Miller, in a much anthologized discussion in *Fiction and Repetition: Seven English Novels* (1982), similarly focuses on the generation of indeterminacy in Brontë's text. Miller's aim in his reading is, in self-consciously paradoxical style, to present a "reasonable formulation of [the novel's] unreason" (1982, 51). Miller, in other words, is concerned not with the novel's meaning but with the ways in which the text allegorizes its own indeterminacy, luring the reader into interpretation while at the same time scrupulously resisting his or her grasp of the text's truth. Miller argues that the structures of repetition in *Wuthering Heights* eerily intimate "an original state of unity"—yet this unity is "generated by the state of division as a haunting insight, always at the corner or at the blind center of vision, where sight fails" (1982, 68). Miller adds that there is a "sense of 'something missing' " in *Wuthering Heights* (the sense, that is, of an absent ground or cause of the text's turbulence) and that the "form of 'undecidability' in *Wuthering Heights* . . . lies in the impossibility, in principle, of determining whether there is some extralinguistic explanatory cause or whether the sense that there is one is generated by the linguistic structure itself" (1982, 68, 69). The novel's insistent repetitions of its own motifs, Miller states, generate the expectation of a resolution of the text's differences into unity, yet forbid the realization of that unity even as the reader is haunted by the continual anticipation of its imminence. In a flaunting and flouting of interpretive desire, *Wuthering Heights* instructs its readers that "there is no secret truth that criticism might formulate" (1982, 51) about it. Instead, the text is haunted by the "uncanny" force of a principle that it cannot articulate and that the reader is likewise debarred from formulating.

Miller's argument that the novel marshals the "haunting insight" of an absent ground emphasizes the ghostliness of *Wuthering Heights*—and the novel's spectral effects are taken up by other poststructuralist critics of the text. John T. Matthews, for example, argues that the novel evokes the "spectral satisfactions and transgressions that haunt the repressive order of society"; for "Catherine's and Heathcliff's love is the ghost of the prohibitions that structure society: it has the air of unspeakably natural passion, even incest, the spaciousness of escape from tyrannous convention, the heedlessness of self-abandon, the dark allure of disease and deathliness" (65). For Matthews, the ghosts of *Wuthering Heights* are the phantom traces of what is repressed, excluded, and unspeakable in the novel's world. Furthermore, the text is predicated on the irreducibility of the "spacing and separation which constitute desire" (64)—on the ghostliness of desire's fulfillment as such. Similarly, Patricia Parker writes that, "once expelled" (or, we might add, once "lost"), the " 'outside' functions as a ghost: the identical is haunted . . . by what it excludes."[17] For poststructuralist critics, then, *Wuthering Heights* becomes an extended elegy to absence and loss: to desire's absent object and, generally, to all that is proscribed and prohibited by the dominant orders of cultural and symbolic meaning.

In a similar vein, *Wuthering Heights* is an "unacceptable text" for David Musselwhite because—through the blandness and conventionality of its telling at the hands of its respectable narrators, Lockwood and Nelly Dean—it dramatizes the fearful force of the very things that those anodyne narrators exclude: namely, ghostliness, violence, unread-ability, terror, illiteracy.[18] In this way, Brontë's text exposes the fissures in Lockwood's and Nelly's ideological worlds—and, by the same token, Musselwhite argues, disrupts the ideological complacencies of its mod-ern-day readers. *Wuthering Heights* is a text that broaches the insistent and disruptive force of "the Other" (1977, 156, 157). In this sense it is a text that—like the specters of Cathy and Heathcliff at the end of the novel—refuses to stay in any place to which we assign it.

Notes and References

Chapter One

1. Georges Bataille, *Literature and Evil* (London and New York: Marion Boyars, 1985), 15; hereafter cited in text.

2. Clement Shorter, *Charlotte Brontë and Her Circle* (Westport, Conn.: Greenwood Press, 1970), 144; hereafter cited in text.

3. T. J. Wise and J. A. Symington, eds, *The Brontës: Their Lives, Friendships and Correspondence* (Oxford: Basil Blackwell, 1933), 4:268, 269; hereafter cited in text as *BLFC* with volume and page number.

4. The letters are reproduced in *BLFC*, 1:298; and 2:41, 78.

5. The diary papers, both written with Anne, are dated 1834 (*BLFC*, 1:124–25) and 1837 (reprinted in *Brontë Society Transactions* 12, no. 1 (1951): 15; hereafter cited as *BST* with volume and page number); the birthday papers, written by Emily alone, are dated 1841 (*BLFC*, 1:238) and 1845 (*BLFC*, 2:49–51).

6. Katherine Frank, *Emily Brontë: A Chainless Soul* (Harmondsworth: Penguin, 1992), 3; hereafter cited in text.

7. Winifred Gérin, *Emily Brontë* (Oxford: Oxford University Press, 1971), vii; hereafter cited in text.

8. Ellen Nussey, "Reminiscences of Charlotte Brontë," *BST* 2 (1899): 75.

9. Ellis H. Chadwick, *In the Footsteps of the Brontës* (London: Pitman & Sons, 1914), 225.

10. Emily Brontë, "My Comforter," in *Emily Jane Brontë: The Complete Poems,* ed. Janet Gezari (Harmondsworth: Penguin, 1992), 30; hereafter cited in text as *CP*.

11. Juliet Barker, *The Brontës* (London: Phoenix, 1994), 153; hereafter cited in text.

12. Edward Chitham, *A Life of Emily Brontë* (Oxford: Blackwell, 1987), 184; hereafter cited in text.

13. Charlotte Brontë, "Biographical Notice of Ellis and Acton Bell," in *Wuthering Heights,* by Emily Brontë, ed. Pauline Nestor (Harmondsworth: Penguin, 1995), xxvii; hereafter cited in text as *WH*.

14. Nina Auerbach, *Romantic Imprisonment: Women and Other Glorified Outcasts* (New York: Columbia University Press, 1985), 212; hereafter cited in text.

15. Stevie Davies, *Emily Brontë: Heretic* (London: Women's Press, 1994), 31; hereafter cited in text.

16. Lyn Pykett, *Emily Brontë* (London: Macmillan, 1989), 17; hereafter cited in text.

162NOTES AND REFERENCES

17. Charlotte Brontë, "Prefatory Note to Selections from Poems by Ellis Bell," in *Wuthering Heights,* by Emily Brontë, ed. Ian Jack (Oxford: Oxford University Press, 1981), 370; hereafter cited in text as Jack.

18. Deirdre Lashagari, "What Some Women Can't Swallow: Hunger as Protest in Charlotte Brontë's *Shirley,*" in *Disorderly Eaters: Texts in Self-Empowerment,* ed. Lilian R. Furst and Peter W. Graham (University Park: Pennsylvania State University Press, 1992), 141; hereafter cited in text.

19. Hélène Cixous and Catherine Clément, *The Newly Born Woman* (Minneapolis: University of Minnesota Press, 1986), 92.

20. These observations are made by Fannie Ratchford in "The Significance of the Diary Paper," *BST* 12, no. 1 (1951): 16.

21. Elizabeth Gaskell, *The Life of Charlotte Brontë* (1857; Harmondsworth: Penguin, 1975), 231; hereafter cited in text.

22. C. Day Lewis, "The Poetry of Emily Brontë," *BST* 13, no. 2 (1957): 95. Stories of Emily's life that have encouraged the view of her as a "man" shut in a "woman's body" include her swift self-cauterizing of a wound she received from a dog bite (Gérin, 155); her physical beating of her dog, Keeper, to discipline him (ibid., 109–10); her separation of Keeper from another powerful dog during a fight (ibid., 146–47); and her proficiency at pistol shooting (ibid., 147–48). Needless to say, the interpretation of such details in terms of "masculine" or "feminine" qualities says more about the sexual politics of the interpreter than about Emily Brontë.

23. Teddi Lynn Chichester, "Evading 'Earth's Dungeon Tomb': Emily Brontë, A.G.A., and the Fatally Feminine," *Victorian Poetry* 29 (1991): 2; hereafter cited in text.

24. In February Thomas Newby, Emily's publisher, wrote to her concerning the "completion" of her "next novel"; it seems from this, therefore, that the writing of Brontë's second novel was already well advanced (Barker, 533–34).

25. As Catherine hurries toward delirium and death in *Wuthering Heights,* Nelly Dean warns her against "trying starving again" (*WH,* 123); later, she reports that Catherine has "locked herself up" and has "refused to eat" (*WH,* 128). Near the end of the novel, Nelly says to the dying Heathcliff, "Do take some food, and some repose. You need only look at yourself, in a glass, to see how you require both. Your cheeks are hollow, and your eyes blood-shot, like a person starving with hunger" (*WH,* 330). For a discussion of femininity and self-starvation in *Wuthering Heights,* see Sandra M. Gilbert and Susan Gubar, *The Madwoman in the Attic: The Woman Writer and the Nineteenth-Century Literary Imagination* (New Haven, Conn.: Yale University Press, 1979), 278–87; hereafter cited in text. For a discussion of the metaphorics of self-starvation in literature and political protest, see Maud Ellmann, *The Hunger Artists: Starving, Writing and Imprisonment* (London: Virago Press, 1993).

Chapter Two

1. Anne penciled this description, along with other Gondalian names, in her copy of *A Grammar of General Geography, for the Use of Schools and Young Persons* (1823) by J. Goldsmith.

2. At this time Anne was governess to the children of the Robinson family, residing temporarily in Scarborough; her own diary paper of 30 July 1841 (the same date as Emily's) attests to her unhappiness in her situation (see *BLFC,* 1:239).

3. J. Hillis Miller, *The Disappearance of God: Five Nineteenth-Century Writers* (London: Oxford University Press, 1963), 158; hereafter cited in text.

4. Stevie Davies, *Emily Brontë: The Artist as a Free Woman* (Manchester: Carcanet, 1983), 33, 34; hereafter cited in text.

5. Fannie Ratchford, *Gondal's Queen: A Novel in Verse by Emily Jane Brontë* (Austin: University of Texas Press, 1955), 20; hereafter cited in text.

6. Fannie Ratchford, "The Gondal Story," in *The Complete Poems of Emily Jane Brontë,* ed. C. W. Hatfield (New York: Columbia University Press, 1941), 14; hereafter cited in text.

7. David Musselwhite, *Partings Welded Together: Politics and Desire in the Nineteenth-Century English Novel* (London and New York: Methuen, 1987), 83–84; hereafter cited in text.

8. References to Brontë's poems throughout this work are to line numbers.

9. See Margaret Homans, *Women Writers and Poetic Identity: Dorothy Wordsworth, Emily Brontë, Emily Dickinson* (Princeton, N.J.: Princeton University Press, 1980); hereafter cited in text. Homans discusses Brontë in chapter 3, 104–61.

10. This is Ratchford's deduction: see Ratchford 1955, 122.

11. Christine Gallant, "The Archetypal Feminine in Emily Brontë's Poetry," *Women's Studies* 7 (1980): 83, 81.

12. Robin Grove, " 'It Would Not Do': Emily Brontë as Poet," in *The Art of Emily Brontë,* ed. Anne Smith (London: Vision Press, 1976), 41; hereafter cited in text.

Chapter Three

1. C. Day Lewis, "The Poetry of Emily Brontë," *Brontë Society Transactions* 13, no. 2 (1957): 94–95.

2. Pykett cites C. Day Lewis on p. 54.

3. John Keats, letter to Richard Woodhouse, 27 October 1818, in *Letters of John Keats,* ed. Robert Gittings (Oxford: Oxford University Press, 1975), 157.

4. Homans illuminatingly observes of Brontë's poem: "The first line of the last verse, 'Then let my winds caress thee,' recalls Wordsworth's address to

Dorothy at the end of 'Tintern Abbey': ' . . . let the misty mountain-winds be free / To blow against thee.' The speaker of 'Tintern Abbey' is for Brontë the type of the poet of the imagination, who dominates the woman he addresses by his privileged discourse with nature, by the maturity of his imagination, and also by his masculinity. By having the earth speak with his words, Brontë identifies the earth's powers with both imaginative power and with sexual dominance" (1980, 128).

5. For a discussion of Charlotte's 1850 revisions to Emily's poems, see Emily Tresselt Schmidt, "From Highland to Lowland: Charlotte Brontë's Editorial Changes in Emily's Poems," *Brontë Society Transactions* 15, no. 1 (1966): 221–26.

6. Lawrence J. Starzyk, "The Faith of Emily Brontë's Immortality Creed," *Victorian Poetry* 11 (1973): 298. Starzyk argues that the "coward" soul of Brontë's poem desires "the comforts of traditional religion's heaven" but that the soul that is "armed from fear" embraces a creed of annihilation in which the self dissolves beyond death into the "one" of the "Absolute" (302–3).

7. Irene Tayler, *Holy Ghosts: The Male Muses of Emily and Charlotte Brontë* (New York: Columbia University Press, 1990), 43, 44; hereafter cited in text.

8. Kathryn Burlinson, " 'What Language Can Utter the Feeling': Identity in the Poetry of Emily Brontë," in *Subjectivity and Literature from the Romantics to the Present Day,* ed. Philip Shaw and Peter Stockwell (London and New York: Pinter, 1991), 41–42; hereafter cited in text.

9. For an argument exploring this self-defeating logic of Romantic desire, see Catherine Belsey, "The Romantic Construction of the Unconscious," in *1789: Reading, Writing, Revolution,* ed. Francis Barker et al (Colchester: University of Essex, 1982), 67–80.

10. Isobel Armstrong, *Victorian Poetry: Poetry, Poetics and Politics* (London: Routledge, 1993), 335; hereafter cited in text.

11. Joseph Bristow, ed., *Victorian Women Poets* (London: Macmillan, 1995), 19.

12. Patricia Yaeger discusses "The Philosopher" as a poem that is divided between a "cacophonous mixture of voices"—a heterogeneity that she associates with women's writing—and a "unifying obsession" that she associates with the "masculine muse" of high Romantic poetry. In this context, she reads the poem's "spirit" as a masculine figure who, in Coleridgean mode, bleaches female multiplicity (and bodiliness) into spiritual unity. See Yaeger, *Honey-Mad Women: Emancipatory Strategies in Women's Writing* (New York: Columbia University Press, 1988) 192, 193; hereafter cited in text.

13. The longer version of the poem in Brontë's Gondal notebook, entitled "Julian M. and A. G. Rochelle" (*CP,* 177–81), incorporates a shadowy Gondalian narrative, with the woman, Rochelle, apparently the political prisoner of Lord Julian's forces. The version published in the 1846 volume as "The Prisoner (A Fragment)" strips this narrative frame away and allows the female

prisoner and her male jailors to stand forth as players in a sexual-political drama. See chapter 5 for further discussion of this poem.

14. Such a gothic plot appears, of course, in the second half of *Wuthering Heights* when Heathcliff pitilessly incarcerates the second Catherine at the Heights (*WH*, 268). For an analysis of the gender and generic aspects of this gothic motif, see Pykett, 71–85.

15. Denis Donoghue, "The Other Emily," in *The Brontës: A Collection of Critical Essays*, ed. Ian Gregor (Englewood Cliffs, N.J.: Prentice-Hall, 1970), 159.

16. Emily Jane Brontë, "Theme: The Palace of Death," in *The Belgian Essays*, by Charlotte Brontë and Emily Brontë, ed. and trans. Sue Lonoff (New Haven, Conn., and London: Yale University Press, 1996), 224–30; hereafter cited in text as *BE*.

17. For an authoritative account of Emily's and Charlotte's stay in Brussels and of the writing of their French *devoirs*, see Barker, 382–95.

18. The instability of tone in Brontë's essay is evidenced by the fact that antithetical readings are given of its concluding section by two recent commentators: Stevie Davies considers the passage to be largely ironic (1994, 107), while Juliet Barker regards it as an "eloquent statement of Christian belief" (389). Brontë's text, however, thrives on this ambiguity, unsettling orthodoxy even as it upholds it.

19. Fannie Ratchford, introduction to *Five Essays Written in French by Emily Jane Brontë*, trans. Lorine White Nagel (Austin: University of Texas Press, 1948), 6.

20. Julia Kristeva, *Black Sun: Depression and Melancholia* (New York: Columbia University Press, 1989), 44.

21. Emily Brontë's graphic work is reproduced and discussed in full (alongside that of Anne, Charlotte, and Branwell Brontë) in Christine Alexander and Jane Sellars, *The Art of the Brontës* (Cambridge: Cambridge University Press, 1995), 100–33, 369–93; hereafter cited in text. My discussion of Brontë's art work is heavily indebted to this fine volume.

22. In chapter 3 of *Wuthering Heights*, Lockwood comes across Catherine Earnshaw's personal library and finds many of its pages minutely scrawled with writing; on one page is a caricature of the pious servant Joseph, "rudely yet powerfully sketched" (*WH*, 20).

23. There is disagreement among commentators about the composition and provenance of this sketch. Mary Butterfield believes it is by Branwell and sees two hands, rather than one, struggling with each other in the central pane; she suggests the picture is an illustration by Branwell to Emily's novel ("*Wuthering Heights*: A Brontë Illustration?," *Brontë Society Transactions* 19, no. 5 [1988]: 220–21). Christine Alexander disagrees; she sees only one hand and reproduces the drawing the other way up so as to place the shadowed window sill at the top (Alexander and Sellars, 370). In either case, the ghostliness of the picture remains.

24. Charlotte Brontë, *Villette* (1853; Harmondsworth: Penguin, 1979), 240.

Chapter Four

1. Unsigned review from *Douglas Jerrold's Weekly Newspaper,* January 1848. It is reprinted in *The Brontës: The Critical Heritage,* ed. Miriam Allott (London: Routledge & Kegan Paul, 1974), 228; hereafter cited in text.

2. Unsigned review from *Paterson's Magazine,* March 1848; cited here from *Emily Brontë: Wuthering Heights: A Casebook,* ed. Miriam Allott (London: Macmillan, 1992), 48.

3. See chapter 6 for a discussion of the gender dimensions of Dobell's description.

4. David Wilson, "Emily Brontë: First of the Moderns," *Modern Language Quarterly Miscellany* 1 (1947): 98.

5. Karl Marx and Friedrich Engels, "The Communist Manifesto," in *Karl Marx: Selected Writings,* ed. David McLellan (Oxford: Oxford University Press, 1977), 221.

6. Musselwhite's argument is that Heathcliff's revolutionary origins are to be found specifically in the figures of Mirabeau and Cromwell—portraits of whom (by Hugo, Guizot, and Bossuet) Brontë read under the tutelage of Heger at Brussels (Musselwhite 1987, 97–106).

7. Nancy Armstrong, "Emily Brontë in and out of Her Time," in *The Brontë Sisters: Critical Assessments,* ed. Eleanor McNees (Sussex: Helm Information, 1996), 2:386; hereafter cited in text. Armstrong's essay was originally published in *Genre* 15 (1982): 243–64.

8. See Terry Eagleton, *Heathcliff and the Great Hunger: Studies in Irish Culture* (London: Verso, 1996), 3; hereafter cited in text. Chapter 1 of Eagleton's study is a brilliant meditation on the history of British-Irish relations in the nineteenth century insofar as, he argues, it can be seen to be allegorized in Heathcliff's story in *Wuthering Heights.*

9. See chapter 6 for a further discussion of the generic form of the novel.

10. Virginia Woolf, *"Jane Eyre* and *Wuthering Heights"* (1916), in *The Common Reader* (1925; London: Hogarth Press, 1945), 202; hereafter cited in text.

11. The term is used by Mikhail Bakhtin, who refers to the "romantic" poem as a "novelized poem" insofar as it is characterized by "indeterminacy, a certain semantic openendedness, a living contact with unfinished, still-evolving contemporary reality (the openended present)." See *The Dialogic Imagination: Four Essays* (Austin: University of Texas Press, 1981), 7.

12. Margaret Homans, *Bearing the Word: Language and Female Experience in Nineteenth-Century Women's Writing* (Chicago and London: University of Chicago Press, 1986), 75, 76; hereafter cited in text.

13. Terry Eagleton, *Myths of Power: A Marxist Study of the Brontës* (London: Macmillan, 1975), 102; hereafter cited in text.

14. Carol Jacobs, *Uncontainable Romanticism: Shelley, Brontë, Kleist* (Baltimore and London: John Hopkins University Press, 1989), 73–74.

15. Leo Bersani, *A Future for Astyanax: Character and Desire in Literature* (Boston: Little, Brown, 1976), 198, 212, 214.

16. Anne K. Mellor, *Romanticism and Gender* (New York: Routledge, 1993), 186–208; hereafter cited in text.

17. For an excellent discussion of the way *Wuthering Heights* recalls yet revises in a feminist direction Shelley's construction of desire, see Patsy Stoneman, "Catherine Earnshaw's Journey to Her Home Among the Dead: Fresh Thoughts on *Wuthering Heights* and 'Epipsychidion,' " *Review of English Studies* 47 (1996): 521–33.

18. Raymond Williams, *The English Novel from Dickens to Lawrence* (London: Chatto and Windus, 1970), 60–69.

19. Sigmund Freud, "Constructions in Analysis," in *The Standard Edition of the Complete Psychological Works of Sigmund Freud,* ed. James Strachey (London: Hogarth Press, 1953–1974), 23:268.

20. Julia Kristeva, "Psychoanalysis and the Polis," in *The Kristeva Reader,* ed. Toril Moi (Oxford: Blackwell, 1986), 307; hereafter cited in text.

21. In this connection—and recalling the Latin root of "delirium" as "to go out of the furrow"—it is interesting to note that Charlotte Brontë came close to identifying *Wuthering Heights* as "delirious" in her 1850 preface, when she wrote of the "creative gift" in general (and of Emily's gift in particular): "There comes a time when it will no longer consent to 'harrow the vallies, or be bound with a band in the furrow'—when it 'laughs at the multitude of the city, and regards not the crying of the driver' " (*WH,* xxxvi–xxxvii).

Chapter Five

1. Margaret Homans reads the depiction of nature in "A Day Dream" as a critique of the "marriage between mind and nature" that is projected in Coleridge's "The Rime of the Ancient Mariner." She argues that Brontë's poem insists instead on the "separation . . . between spirit and nature," and she usefully relates the poem's representation of nature to the desolate vision of natural cycle in Brontë's "The Butterfly" (see Homans 1980, 144–45; see chapter three of this study for a discussion of "The Butterfly").

2. For readings that variously situate Brontë's poetry in relation to the male Romantic literary tradition that she challenges, see Homans 1980, 104–61; Pykett, 36–70; Auerbach, 212–29; and Chichester, 1–11.

3. Nicolas Abraham and Maria Torok, *The Shell and the Kernel* (Chicago and London: University of Chicago Press,1994), 1:141; hereafter cited in text.

4. Jacques Derrida, " 'Fors': The Anglish Words of Nicolas Abraham and Maria Torok," in Nicolas Abraham and Maria Torok, *The Wolf Man's Magic Word: A Cryptonymy* (Minneapolis: University of Minnesota Press, 1986), 119 n. 24; hereafter cited in text.

5. Emma Francis, "Is Emily Brontë a Woman?: Femininity, Feminism and the Paranoid Critical Subject," in *Subjectivity and Literature from the Romantics to the Present Day*, ed. Philip Shaw and Peter Stockwell (London and New York: Pinter Publishers, 1991), 31; hereafter cited in text.

6. Burlinson, " 'What Language Can Utter the Feeling,' " 41.

7. Sigmund Freud, "Mourning and Melancholia," in *On Metapsychology: The Theory of Psychoanalysis*, Pelican Freud Library 11 (Harmondsworth: Penguin, 1984), 253.

8. Peter Sacks, *The English Elegy: Studies in the Genre from Spenser to Yeats* (Baltimore and London: John Hopkins University Press, 1985), 8.

9. Maud Ellmann, "The Ghosts of *Ulysses*," in *The Languages of Joyce*, ed. R. M. Bollettieri, C. Marengo Vaglio, and Chr. Van Boheemen (Philadelphia, Amsterdam, 1992), 106.

10. See Irene Tayler, *Holy Ghosts: The Male Muses of Emily and Charlotte Brontë* (New York: Columbia University Press, 1990), 18–71, for a broadly psychoanalytic reading of Brontë that considers the conflicts in her poetry in terms of the opposition between "father- and mother-worlds" (40).

11. For Abraham and Torok, introjection, as part of the gradual work of mourning, involves the transformation of the "absence of objects" into the "words" that symbolize them (128). By contrast, the act of incorporation is "instantaneous and magical. The object of pleasure being absent, incorporation obeys the pleasure principle and functions by way of processes similar to hallucinatory fulfillments" (113).

12. For readings that argue that Brontë's poetry dramatizes and critiques a patriarchal confinement of woman to the body, see Chichester and Auerbach.

13. David Cecil, *Early Victorian Novelists: Essays in Revaluation* (London: Constable, 1934), 125–26; hereafter cited in text.

14. J. Hillis Miller, *Fiction and Repetition: Seven English Novels* (Cambridge, Mass.: Harvard University Press, 1982), 69; hereafter cited in text. See chapter 6 of this study for a discussion of Miller's reading.

15. Nicholas Royle, *Telepathy and Literature: Essays on the Reading Mind* (London: Blackwell, 1991), 62; hereafter cited in text. Royle's chapter "Cryptaesthesia: the Case of *Wuthering Heights*" (28–62) is a dazzling reading of the "crypt-effect[s]" of language in *Wuthering Heights* (45). Royle's reading is different in emphasis from my own, but his reflections draw, as do mine, on Abraham's and Torok's work on the "cryptic" logic of "refused or impossible mourning" (29) in psychoanalysis.

16. John T. Matthews, "Framing in *Wuthering Heights*," in *Wuthering Heights*, ed. Patsy Stoneman (London: Macmillan, 1993), 60; hereafter cited in text.

17. An earlier version of Homans's argument appeared in "Repression and Sublimation of Nature in *Wuthering Heights*," *PMLA* 93 (1978): 9–19.

18. Homans's argument is that the omission of representations of nature from the novel is a strategy designed to protect and preserve what she calls the "literal" or "unnamed mother" from a language that would inevitably efface her (1986, 72, 73). She contends that the moors in *Wuthering Heights* recall a pre-linguistic, maternal, "unmediated merging" of the self with nature that obstinately avoids the "symbolic" or patriarchal agencies of language and law (1986, 76).

Chapter Six

1. The term "power" is invoked, for instance, in the unsigned reviews in *Britannia* and in *Douglas Jerrold's Weekly Newspaper*, both of 15 January 1848 (Allott 1974, 224, 228).

2. G. K. Chesterton, *The Victorian Age in Literature* (New York, 1913), 113.

3. Van Gent's remarks are cited in James H. Kavanagh, *Emily Brontë* (Oxford: Blackwell, 1985), 3; hereafter cited in text.

4. Arnold Kettle, *An Introduction to the English Novel* (London: Hutchinson, 1951), 1:130; hereafter cited in text.

5. Eagleton's argument utilizes the description of ideology given in Louis Althusser's celebrated essay "Ideology and Ideological State Apparatuses," in which ideology is seen as a form of discourse that works to efface material contradictions in the name of imaginary coherence. See *Lenin and Philosophy and Other Essays* (London: New Left Books, 1977), 123–73.

6. G. D. Klingopulos, "The Novel as Dramatic Poem: *Wuthering Heights*," in McNees, 2:142. The essay was originally published in *Scrutiny* 14 (1947): 269–86.

7. Mark Schorer, "Fiction and the Matrix of Analogy," in McNees, 2:186, 184. The essay was originally published in *The Kenyon Review* 11 (1949): 544–50.

8. Dorothy Van Ghent, *The English Novel: Form and Function* (New York: Holt Rinehart & Winston, 1953). The citation is from a reprint of Van Ghent's chapter in McNees, 2:205.

9. Carol Ohmann, "Emily Brontë in the Hands of Male Critics," *College English* 32 (1971): 907; hereafter cited in text.

10. Thomas Moser, "What Is the Matter with Emily Jane? Conflicting Impulses in *Wuthering Heights*," *Nineteenth-Century Fiction* 17 (1962): 1–19.

11. For Gilbert's and Gubar's use of Woolf's term, see Gilbert and Gubar, 187–88.

12. Stevie Davies, *Emily Brontë* (London: Harvester Wheatsheaf, 1988), 7; hereafter cited in text.

13. Carol A. Senf, "Emily Brontë's Version of Feminist History: *Wuthering Heights,*" *Essays in Literature* 12 (1985): 206; hereafter cited in text.

14. Nancy Armstrong, *Desire and Domestic Fiction: A Political History of the Novel* (Oxford: Oxford University Press, 1987), 191; hereafter cited in text.

15. For a powerful account of the "essentially disjunctive" (McNees, 2:391) character of *Wuthering Heights* at the level of genre and the ideology of genre, see Nancy Armstrong, "Emily Brontë in and out of Her Time," in McNees, 2:382–400.

16. Frank Kermode, "A Modern Way with the Classic," in McNees, 2:347–48. The essay was originally published in *New Literary History* 5 (1974): 415–34.

17. Patricia Parker, "The (Self-)Identity of the Literary Text: Property, Proper Place, and Proper Name in *Wuthering Heights,*" in *Wuthering Heights,* ed. Patsy Stoneman (London: Macmillan, 1993), 181.

18. David Musselwhite, "*Wuthering Heights:* The Unacceptable Text," in *Literature, Society and the Sociology of Literature,* ed. Francis Barker (Colchester: University of Essex, 1977), 154–60; hereafter cited in text.

Selected Bibliography

PRIMARY WORKS

Brontë, Emily. *Emily Jane Brontë: The Complete Poems,* ed. Janet Gezari. Harmondsworth: Penguin, 1992. Includes helpful annotations and a clear presentation of the different states in which Brontë's poems appeared.

———. *Wuthering Heights* (1847), ed. Pauline Nestor. Harmondsworth: Penguin, 1995.

Brontë, Charlotte, and Emily Brontë. *The Belgian Essays,* ed. and trans. Sue Lonoff. New Haven, Conn., and London: Yale University Press, 1996. Includes all of Emily's nine extant *devoirs* along with annotation and commentary.

Wise, T. J., and J. A. Symington, eds. *The Brontës: Their Lives, Friendships and Correspondence,* 4 vols. Oxford: Basil Blackwell, 1933.

SECONDARY WORKS

Alexander, Christine, and Jane Sellars. *The Art of the Brontës.* Cambridge: Cambridge University Press, 1995. A fine volume that reproduces all of the Brontës' graphic work and discusses the work of each artist informatively.

Allott, Miriam, ed. *The Brontës: The Critical Heritage.* London: Routledge & Kegan Paul, 1974. An invaluable resource for contemporary responses to the Brontës' works.

———, ed. *Wuthering Heights: A Casebook.* London: Macmillan, 1992. A wide-ranging selection of nineteenth- and twentieth-century critical views that includes excerpts from Eagleton 1975; Homans 1980; and Miller 1982.

Armstrong, Nancy. "Emily Brontë in and out of Her Time." *Genre* 15, no. 3 (1982): 243–64. A brilliant reflection on the historical and ideological implications of the disjunctive generic form of *Wuthering Heights.*

Auerbach, Nina. *Romantic Imprisonment: Women and Other Glorified Outcasts.* New York: Columbia University Press, 1985. Auerbach's chapter on Emily Brontë's Gondal verse presents a powerful feminist case for reading Brontë as a poet of mutability.

Barker, Juliet. *The Brontës.* London: Phoenix, 1994. A magisterial account of Brontëan history. The indispensable biography of the family.

Bersani, Leo. *A Future for Astynax: Character and Desire in Literature.* Boston: Little, Brown, 1976. Includes an elegant and searching account of the "deconstruction" of individual identity in *Wuthering Heights.*

Chichester, Teddi Lynn. "Evading 'Earth's Dungeon Tomb': Emily Brontë,
    A.G.A., and the Fatally Feminine." *Victorian Poetry* 29 (1991): 1–15.
    Suggestive consideration of the relationship between femininity and
    mortality in Brontë's poetry.
Davies, Stevie. *Emily Brontë: Heretic*. London: Women's Press, 1994. A stylish
    and searching reading that presents Brontë as a cultural dissident.
Eagleton, Terry. *Myths of Power: A Marxist Study of the Brontës*. London: Macmil-
    lan, 1975. Eagleton's hugely influential chapter on *Wuthering Heights*
    remains the most powerful account of the ideological contradictions of
    Brontë's text.
Frank, Katherine. *Emily Brontë: A Chainless Soul*. Harmondsworth: Penguin,
    1990. Oscillates between an account of the Brontës in general and of
    Emily in particular, but is notable for its provocative emphasis on Emily
    Brontë as a nineteenth-century anorectic.
Gérin, Winifred. *Emily Brontë*. Oxford: Oxford University Press, 1971. Still the
    standard biography, it offers a compelling account of the last weeks of
    Brontë's life.
Gilbert, Sandra M., and Susan Gubar. *The Madwoman in the Attic: The Woman
    Writer and the Nineteenth-Century Literary Imagination*. New Haven, Conn.:
    Yale University Press, 1979. The most influential feminist account of
    Wuthering Heights, showing how Brontë is in struggle with Miltonic tradi-
    tion.
Homans, Margaret. *Women Writers and Poetic Identity: Dorothy Wordsworth, Emily
    Brontë, Emily Dickinson*. Princeton, N.J.: Princeton University Press,
    1980. Homans's chapter on Brontë's poetry is a persuasive reading of her
    struggle with the weight of the masculine poetic tradition.
———. *Bearing the Word: Language and Female Experience in Nineteenth-Century
    Women's Writing*. Chicago and London: University of Chicago Press, 1986.
    Homans' chapter on *Wuthering Heights* analyzes the occlusion and preser-
    vation of the figure of the "mother" in the novel.
Jacobs, Carol. *Uncontainable Romanticism: Shelley, Brontë, Kleist*. Baltimore and
    London: John Hopkins University Press, 1989. Jacobs's chapter on
    Wuthering Heights is a sophisticated deconstructive analysis of the way in
    which Brontë's text allegorizes and suspends its own intelligibility.
Kavanagh, James. *Emily Brontë*. Oxford: Blackwell, 1985. Kavanagh's intro-
    duction is an excellent critique of the ideology of Brontë criticism. The
    body of his reading is bold and provocative, but the book's use of theo-
    retical material lacks textual subtlety.
Kermode, Frank. "A Modern Way with the Classic." *New Literary History* 5, no.
    3 (1974): 415–34. Kermode presents a clear account of the textual
    open-endedness of *Wuthering Heights* and emphasizes the transforma-
    tional dynamic of the narrative.
Matthews, John T. "Framing in *Wuthering Heights,*" *Texas Studies in Language and
    Literature* 27 (1985): 26–61. Matthews's reading is a strong poststruc-

turalist account of the "framing" effects of *Wuthering Heights*; it demonstrates how the text's frames simultaneously enclose and evacuate the meaning of the novel's core story.

McNees, Eleanor, ed. *The Brontë Sisters: Critical Assessments*, vol. 2. Sussex: Helm Information, 1996. A comprehensive selection of critical essays on *Wuthering Heights* from the 1840s to the 1980s. Includes chapters from Cecil 1935; Klingopulos 1947; Schorer 1949; Kettle 1951; Van Ghent 1953; Kermode 1974; Miller 1982; and Armstrong 1982.

Miller, J. Hillis. *Fiction and Repetition: Seven English Novels*. Cambridge, Mass.: Harvard University Press, 1982. The most well known poststructuralist account, Miller focuses on the "uncanny" effects of the textuality of *Wuthering Heights*.

Musselwhite, David. *"Wuthering Heights:* The Unacceptable Text." In *Literature, Society and the Sociology of Literature,* ed. Francis Barker. Colchester: University of Essex, 1977. A brief but searching consideration of the reproduction and disruption of ideology in *Wuthering Heights*.

———. *Partings Welded Together: Politics and Desire in the Nineteenth-Century English Novel.* London and New York: Methuen, 1987. Musselwhite's chapter on *Wuthering Heights* is a fascinating and speculative account of the relationship between the novel and Brontë's reading in Brussels in 1842, arguing for the "revolutionary" origins of the figure of Heathcliff.

Pykett, Lyn. *Emily Brontë*. London: Macmillan, 1989. Excellent feminist-historical reading of Brontë's poetry and novel, emphasizing throughout the interactions between gender and genre.

Stoneman, Patsy, ed. *Wuthering Heights*. London: Macmillan, 1993. Supplementing Allott 1992, this New Casebook is a selection of contemporary critical essays on Brontë's novel, including helpful editorial annotations on contrasting critical positions. It prints excerpts from Kermode 1974; Matthews 1985; Pykett 1989; Gilbert and Gubar 1979; and Davies 1988.

Yaeger, Patricia. *Honey-Mad Women: Emancipatory Strategies in Women's Writing*. New York: Columbia University Press. Yaeger's chapter on Brontë is a fascinating reading of Brontë's "sampler" text (produced when she was 11), her poem "The Philosopher," and *Wuthering Heights*. It uses the Bakhtinian theory of the novel to argue for the liberatory possibilities of the novel form for the woman writer.

Index

The Author

Steve Vine is a lecturer in English at the University of Wales, Swansea, where he specializes in teaching Romantic literature and literary theory, in particular psychoanalysis and postmodernism. He is the author of *Blake's Poetry: Spectral Visions* (Macmillan, St. Martin's Press, 1993) and is the editor of D. H. Lawrence's *Aaron's Rod* (Penguin, 1995). He has published articles on Coleridge, Mary Shelley, and Emily Brontë; on Blake and Wollstonecraft; and on Blake, Kant, and Derrida. His current research interests are in the Romantic and postmodern sublimes.

The Editor

Herbert Sussman is professor of English at Northeastern University. His publications in Victorian literature include *Victorian Masculinities: Manhood and Masculine Poetics in Early Victorian Literature and Art; Fact into Figure: Typology in Carlyle, Ruskin, and the Pre-Raphaelite Brotherhood;* and *Victorians and the Machine: The Literary Response to Technology.*

PR 4173 .V48 1998
Vine, Steven, 1961-
Emily Bront e
   93370

		DATE DUE		

VILLA JULIE COLLEGE LIBRARY
STEVENSON, MD 21153